Holloway Prison

An Inside Story

Hilary Beauchamp

With a Foreword by

Maggi Hambling

≋ WATERSIDE PRESS

Fifty Year Stretch

Prisons and Imprisonment 1980–2030
by **Stephen Shaw** Foreword **Martin Narey**

This innovative work—by one of the UK's leading experts—charts developments across a fifty year time frame. It begins in 1980 at the start of a growth in the prison population of England and Wales (and elsewhere) and travels across time to 2030, dealing with key events, issues and developments. It will be an invaluable aid to anyone wishing to cut through the mass of fine detail and data in other works in favour of a direct, authoritative and highly knowledgeable explanation. Novel, original, highly readable and thoroughly interesting, this book makes it altogether easier to understand penal affairs.

134 pages | April 2010 | Hardback ISBN 9781904380573

In Reading gaol
by Reading town
There is a pit of shame'
Oscar Wilde

Pit of Shame

The Real Ballad of Reading Gaol
by **Anthony Stokes** Foreword **Theodore Dalrymple**

A unique history of a most famous prison—a fame that flows directly from an account of the execution of Trooper Charles Thomas Wooldridge as written by Reading Gaol's best-known prisoner, Oscar Wilde. Based on close research over ten years, and written by a serving Reading prison officer with access to official records, hitherto unseen documents and the Execution Log. 'You won't put it down' Henry Kelly, *Irish Times*. 'Contains fascinating details about Wilde's isolation in prison': *Studies in English Literature*. 'Packed with little gems of fact': *Inside Time*.

192 pages | May 2007 | Paperback ISBN 9781904380214

Contents

About the author

Hilary Beauchamp was awarded an MBE in 1992 for her teaching work at Holloway Prison and in September 2008 won the ITV London Teacher of the Year Award. An artist in her own right, this is her story of a life spent at the sharp end working with some of the most troubled, recalcitrant and sometimes dangerous women students in Britain. The illustrations within the book are all the work of the author (with the exception of 'The Rain Forest' which was the joint work of Hilary Beauchamp and unnamed prisoners and no longer exists: see *Chapter 4*).

The author of the Foreword

Maggi Hambling's paintings and sculptures can be seen in the British Museum, National Gallery, National Portrait Gallery, Tate Gallery and other key venues in the UK and abroad. A household name in British art, she was the first person to be appointed Artist in Residence at the National Gallery (1980-81). Famously among her artistic achievements, Maggi Hambling was commissioned by the National Portrait Gallery to create a statue of the poet, writer, wit and sometime prisoner Oscar Wilde. The result, 'A Conversation with Oscar Wilde', was unveiled by Chris Smith, UK Minister for the Arts just off Trafalgar Square, London in 1998.

Foreword

With my friend the late, great Stephen Tumim, champion of prisoners and the Koestler Trust, I helped judge the annual Koestler Awards for painting and so entered prison buildings for the first time.

Confinement encourages freedom of the imagination. Artists are lucky – poets, composers or painters – because rather than commit murder they can produce a work of art on the subject instead. The urge to destroy is translated into the urge to create. Looking at the other side of the coin, T. S. Eliot said

> Artists don't borrow from other artists, they steal.

Again, criminals and artists have much in common. Henry Moore said his work was his therapy. How true for all of us. Art can help to heal the wounds of those who practise it and those who respond to it. It is generous food for the spirit which needs sustenance as much as the body.

In the hothouse of a prison, art must be encouraged to flourish. Hope might be the outcome.

Maggie Hambling
April 2010

Acknowledgements

I would like to thank Lord and Lady Casson, the late Sir Stephen Tumim and Ben Whitaker.

My appreciation is also due to the many people and organizations I have worked with or who have helped me from time-to-time. They include (in no particular order):

The Calouste Gulbenkian Foundation, Gavron Trust, Mercers' Company, Worshipful Company of Weavers, Paul Getty Trust, Lord David and Lady Puttnam, Lord David Ramsbotham, Maggi Hambling, Dorothy Salmon, Polly Toynbee, the Burnbake Trust, Olga Heaven and Hibiscus, Clean Break Theatre Company, Tim Robertson and the Koestler Trust, Jane Heartwell and the Morley Gallery, Hugh Stoddart and Not Shut Up, Jo Fisher, Eddie Toman, John Dawson, Kate Simpson, Jane England, Geraldine Toman, Richard Brown, Erlend Lee, Jenny Cole, Ulrica Thynne, Irena and Chris Andrews, Patrick Caulfield and Peter Blake.

I must also acknowledge the part played throughout my career by every one of the students who attended my classes and but who must remain nameless.

The drawings in the book were photographed for me by Robin Don to whom special thanks are also due.

Finally, I should like to thank the institution itself, for I am privileged to have been part of the work force at what is now Holloway Prison and Young Offender Institution.

Hilary Beauchamp
April 2010

Introduction

The words 'Let this place be a terror to evil doers' written over the doors of Holloway Prison remained there until the old building was demolished in the mid-nineteen seventies. Many other things have also changed. In the past, women inmates 'slopped-out', wore prison-issue floral dresses and remand prisoners could have food and wine handed in by relatives or bought for them (with their own money) from local restaurants. The old building held some 300 inmates, including a handful of lifers. Still the largest women's prison in Europe, Holloway now has a dedicated Lifers Wing and a total inmate population of over 500. There are en suite loos, a swimming pool, Avon make-up and indeterminate sentences for some offenders.

This book charts my experiences as a teacher working inside the prison. I have tried to picture the impact that a place like Holloway can have on the women it holds. It tells of some of the many women prisoners I have taught over the years, their backgrounds, problems, issues and preoccupations. It describes their often tragic lives which may be affected by such things as abuse, deprivation, the use of prohibited drugs or over-medicating, personal breakdown, mental health issues, low self-esteem (or, as the reader will also discover, on occasion inflated notions of self-importance), self-harm, disadvantage, poverty, deprivation or lack of anything that might be seen as ambition. It looks behind the public mask, the bravado and fantasy at things like vulnerability, lack of a decent home life, fragile hopes and recurring fears. At the same time it takes in the effect which the prison had on me as an outsider, telling how I survived the rigid demands of a regime steeped in security, control, regulation and obeying orders (of necessity I must accept).

In many ways (and whether or not 'evil-doer' can ever be an acceptable description), Holloway remains 'a place of terror'. At least it is somewhere that any self-respecting woman would wish to avoid. Once prisoners pass through Reception they become part of a different world, experience a new language and fall into the distinct culture that exists within this hidden world. I have tried to bring out all of these features in the text, as well as explaining how creative pursuits can help women to come to terms with their enforced confinement. But I have also tried to record those 'golden moments' when achievement, success or self-realisation strike through against all the odds. The personal stories of the women are fleshed out by my own observations of their problems, foibles and charms, gleaned whilst working with them at close quarters in the relatively relaxed context of the Art Room.

I have also described how just being inside a prison can make people feel guilty whether they have done anything wrong or not and whether they are a prisoner or an outsider, such are the security checks, monitoring, surveillance, power imbalances and air of suspicion. Sometimes my mind tricked me to returning to the prison at night because it was such an overwhelming institution. I felt guilty in that after every action that might conceivably be viewed as 'subversive' I imagined myself in the dock delivering well-rehearsed explanations of my behaviour, however benign it may have been in reality.

I describe all of this in the book, as well as how it affected me as an artist attuned to 'picking up the vibes'. I learned to live with and to survive the system and events around me.

Throughout (and except for historical figures), the names of people have been changed and in some instances the staff or prisoners described are composites or have been endowed with an amalgam of traits or behaviours which may have registered with me at different times. I have also left time vague. Occasionally, I have relied on artistic licence to protect individuals or emphasise given points, but the stories and descriptions are real not fiction or fantasy. I do hope that something of value to observers of prisons and imprisonment, seasoned or otherwise, emerges from all of this. What follows is designed to be both an enjoyable read and to convey a true sense of the nature of imprisonment for women.

Hilary Beauchamp
April 2010

Dedication

For my children Gabrielle and Danny Beauchamp

The book is also dedicated to my three sisters, Avril, Suzanne and Colinette

CHAPTER 1

Lisa-Shirley

Burial grounds, subterranean occupancy. That's what the planners had in store for the area of land which is known today as London N7 ONU. When the cholera epidemic of mid-nineteenth century England was killing far more people than expected and the cemeteries weren't big enough to cope with the dead, then these few acres along Parkhurst Road were designated as an overflow graveyard. But the sickness never reached the catastrophic proportions expected and abated. Instead the new crisis came in the shape of criminals, even more contagious than cholera and with there being nowhere to confine the lawbreakers. Bridewell was full. So was Newgate—and the Tower of London was overflowing with all kinds of bad folk, undermining society with different degrees of gravity, all flung together in chaotic overcrowded cells. That's how Holloway Prison was born. It served as the overflow, built a little after Pentonville Prison and in the same style.

If you could ignore the fixtures and fittings in the old Holloway then what was left was a spectacular piece of architecture. It could have been recycled into a covert institution albeit dedicated to some Saint of s & m persuasions. A gatehouse was visible from the road, built in high gothic style with turrets, arrow slits and a barbican housing a massive portal, all of which was modelled on the gatehouse of Warwick Castle. No moats though, just double yellow lines to hinder invaders and evacuees, and with a vast grey stone wall encircling the whole prison. A small opening for pedestrian visitors and staff was cut into the wooden doors at the front opposite to a garage and a greasy spoon café.

So the grandeur could only be perceived in glimpses when the dreariness of that part of London was obliterated, just at the threshold with your back to Parkhurst Road and your eyes upwards towards the turrets where a flag with a crown and another with a Union Jack waved everyone inside. A dark stone floor led across from the wall to the main prison. Two stone griffins with keys clenched in their claws clung to the outside of this front wall and looked down from above to where yet more wooden doors welcomed you at 'Her Majesties pleasure'. The words 'Let this place be a terror to evil doers' reminded you of the real purpose of this institution—so don't you forget it! Prisoners arrived in vans driven slowly along the stone floor; just slowly enough for those words to be read, then swiftly the driver would manoeuvre the new residents round the back to the less exclusive quarters that would become their home.

Inside there was a central atrium with four wings radiating outwards and with high ceilings, solid walls and stone floors that could these days provide some Holloway Road yuppies with their pad of all pads. There was plush mahogany panelling along the administrative corridors and impressive marbled landings. Wooden floors were polished relentlessly and walls were continuously scrubbed and wiped. Only privileged prisoners were entrusted with the care of these prestigious parts. Up through the middle of the building rose a highly decorated cantilever staircase which swept right up to the top of the prison.

Uniformed staff kept an eye on all passing traffic from a goldfish bowl of an office right there in the centre. The walls were bare except for emergency buttons placed at regular intervals and they were painted in high gloss Home Office,[1] Civil Service cream. Natural light didn't venture much inside the prison what with the small windows, the bars and the closed doors. Most of the time electricity illuminated the gloom, giving long-term inmates the prison pallor and they emerged from their cells like etiolated plants. Holloway had become the largest female prison in the whole of Europe housing approximately 300 women.

If a panic button was pressed by some member of staff too out of their depth to cope, then other prison officers would lunge en masse from all doors, careering towards the crisis. More often than not it was a fight breaking out, threatening to bring chaos into the highly formalised life inside. These little

---

1. Prisons are now the responsibility of the Ministry of Justice

metal pimples attached at calculated intervals on every wall served as reassurance that help would come to those who pushed them. Non-uniformed staff like me were perceived as useless obstacles, invisible and irrelevant, so I flattened myself against the cold walls until the stampede disappeared. We had no obligation to respond to emergency bells so that it was best we were not seen and not heard. There was never a tranquil start to the working day. It was always frenetic somehow.

On the top floor, four stories up, lived the lifers. A relatively stable group, they knew their fate and mostly rolled up their sleeves and got on with it. They created their own neighbourhood, availed themselves of all accessible facilities, learned about their rights, got themselves a job, budgeted, decorated their rooms, and settled into their new home. Underneath them the remand inmates rattled, angry and loud. It was a tense wing, perpetually disrupted by new prisoners whose days were interrupted by appointments with solicitors, court appearances, family visits and it was a place of endless anxiety about not knowing when their cases would be called, what charges they would face, and what was happening to their families and their homes.

Further down lived the teenagers in the Borstal Wing—the 'borstal brats' as they were called—living in their boarding school and getting into trouble. Then there was the Hospital Wing housing women with mental health issues and physically sick women. Those withdrawing from drugs wrapped themselves into their beds for as long as they could while their cramps eased. Deep in the bowels of this main building was a small wing for women who, for whatever reason, needed to be segregated, usually due to the nature of their offences. They shared it with women kept 'down there' for breaking prison rules who awaited the prison adjudication process before they were punished and returned to their normal location on other wings. A separate building was set aside for the mothers and babies. The former were allowed to cook their own meals, push their prams in their own exercise yard and live together, separated from the rest of the prison population.

Holloway was a self-contained city, a bit like the Vatican, only less holy. It had its own kitchen, laundries, gardens, shop, hospital, church and gym.

A Works Department maintained the establishment, more often than not by retrieving broken sinks thrown out of smashed windows, mopping up flood damage and reattaching toilets torn from pipes gushing putrid fluids. There were corridors of archives packed with case studies, hospital notes, court papers and files with names, photos with prison numbers and 'proofs of existence' documenting the lives of women who passed through this part of the penal system. Justice was being seen to be done, courts were being obeyed. It was the Queendom of Holloway, just off Parkhurst Road, an independent country, a women's world dominated by female staff, with a few male workers dotted about here and there.

Holloway seemed to have its own gravity with a unique pressure squeezing at a different rate to that of the outside world. Inside those thick walls my senses always seemed to be crushed by officers who had the upper hand. This ultimate power from those in uniform towards those of us who wore civilian clothing defined our relationship from the outset. We were viewed as being less effective, less important and more bothersome. They had keys, we didn't. My own access to any part of the prison was barred unless doors were unlocked for me and locked after me. It was gratitude and dependency every few steps or you didn't get anywhere. Even if I didn't break any rules I always felt like I was doing something wrong. Surrounded so closely by a kind of police force all the time unnerved the spirit and was a continual reminder of some rights and wrongs that were particular to the institution and of which I was ignorant.

For every prison rule there was a compulsion to sabotage it. For everything that was forbidden, the obsession was to acquire it. Suspicion kept the cameras busy monitoring the inhabitants and searches kept the officers busy making sure that no-one was up to no good. So I tried not to look anywhere that I shouldn't, see anything but my job and connect only with those people I needed to work with. This resolution didn't last long, it was impossible to adhere to. Everything overlapped, became fuzzy, so that flexibility became a must in order to survive. But for the first few months I was repeatedly confronted to explain my presence, my reason for being somewhere. The claustrophobia of locked doors that I couldn't open or close on my own account intensified the smallness of being a nobody. It aggravated a guilt that always seemed to niggle away somewhere along with other feelings of belligerence to combat it. But big issues of right and wrong were a preoccupation of the working day of everyone inside Holloway. It was Society's Safety Net, its punishment, its protection. Social change was reflected here. It was a barometer for the state of the nation, a test of the country's success as a society and its failure. So I felt that it was no good me being anything else but passive as they locked me in or questioned me, or looked down from sharp uniforms. The sense of oppression would lift as I left at the end of the day, and I could open my own front door and close it when I wanted to.

I dreaded walking along the Remand Wing. As I passed the toilets, used sanitary towels flew across my lower limbs as they were ejected from under the doors. The large gaps at the bottom of the toilet doors ensured a visible body count for all passing officers checking on numbers. However intimate the procedure they were interrupting, security always came first. Knickers could be seen flopped over ankles and the soundtrack of evacuating efforts accompanied these visuals. The stench was putrid. On the damp floor of the toilet recesses, scrunched up lavatory paper festered together with the odd used tampon. Legs fidgeted avoiding the foul smelling water which sloshed along the open drains as some inmate flushed away their excrement. Nobody stayed long on the Remand Wing—nobody cared. The prison landings were narrow and at the times when I needed to visit the more segregated parts of the place they were often full of marauding inmates, wolf-whistling, cat-calling or just hustling by giving the odd shove. A single railing prevented passers-by from falling over the edge onto wire mesh that separated the landings. Down below, if you lurched against this railing, you could peer through veils of wire mesh all the way to the ground floor and the officers like blue blobs in the goldfish bowl.

Nobody seemed to talk in prison. Everyone shouted. It still seems like that today, a relentless din at all times with never a break. The huge ceilings kept the ranting alive with echoes. Sound was butted onto the walls of one wing and kicked up to another landing. It never went away, not even at night. It was punched from one woman at the top of the prison who spun it off the walls to her mate three floors down. With only wire separating the wings, the noise ran amok, free from all constraints. Keys clattered as the officers moved around clashing them into the locks, opening and closing heavy metal doors. Screams and shouts revolved around in a never-ending relay.

Even if I went outside into the prison grounds to get to other wings, the hullabaloo would rage on. If it was not a couple of separated lesbian lovers swearing undying affection or having a domestic tiff, it was a conspiratorial ensemble arranging an illegal trade in some banned substance or other. Sometimes I could hear every word as they swung their parcels with professional, well-practised accuracy from one window to another. Otherwise cockney backslang made translation impossible.

Vain efforts from the moon to naturalise this walled edifice by softening its edges, spreading gentle moonbeams and reminding us of some natural order to this world were thwarted mid-journey. Stars sparkled elsewhere. Evening light no longer faded out into the darkness, calming away the day for rest and renewal. The national grid, accessed by a timer, powered the huge prison arc lights, dragging black shadows onto the prison gates, illuminating the walls with a chemical yellow and obliterating the night sky.

A block of flats opposite to the prison provided evening entertainment. Inmates who had recently left the prison came to renew old friendships with those prisoners still serving their time. They would throw them the odd present or two, making use of well-chosen spots inside the perimeter wall, capitalising on the black angles created by the false darkness. Seedy and unsavoury males staged a performance on balconies of the flats, profiting by the theatrical spotlights as they wiggled their genitalia around hoping some sexually deprived woman was gagging for a looky looky. Some women reciprocated by putting on a strip show and waggled their sexy bits for those male wankey wankers.

It was raucous and it went on all night and other parties went on as I crossed the grounds. The prison vermin partied under the night sky. Shimmying their tootsies in the moonlight, the prison rats danced, playing with the detritus thrown out through the bars by the inmates. The worst things that got flung out were the 'shit parcels'. No plumbing in the cells meant a choice. If the occupant needed the loo after lock-in at night, then she had to tolerate the smell in the potty or get rid of it. Parcelled up in socks or any other appropriate wrapping it would be flung out through the cell window into the night. Sanitary towels, red and heavy were also lobbed through the bars and fell onto the earth below. Unwanted food mingled in amongst it all. The outside cleaning party, nicknamed 'The Wombles' attempted to keep up some standard of hygiene but it was a struggle as well as being dangerous. At any time a missile, wet, soggy, solid or liquid could fly past and even hit those poor cleaners.

The Education Department existed in theory, but in reality there was no 'department' as such. It was run by a prison officer at that time and she worked from a cell along the administration corridor. That's what we then used as an office, a base: just an old cell with one desk and a couple of chairs. We shared the corridor with other non-uniformed staff such as probation officers. The rooms were small with rounded thick wooden doors, the corridor immense and at the bottom was a kitchen and toilets. There were no classrooms, just free spaces which we could use because they were of no use to anyone else. On one wing we used the dining room, on another an empty cell. Old deserted lavatories were usurped as storerooms. Sometimes classes could be held in empty offices—it was all 'make do'.

My main workspace was at the top of the prison, four floors up, in an old storeroom with no plumbing. Water had to be carried up winding staircases in huge jugs and brought back down dirty at the end of the class. If inmates wanted to go to the loo mid-lesson, then they just couldn't. Shortage of classrooms meant teachers were peripatetic and roamed around slotting in wherever they were needed and whether there was a classroom or not. The Occupational Therapy Day Centre provided the most teaching hours. It was all pretty hodge podge, a couple of us used to be employed to spend time with the women in the morning and afternoon. There was a pottery teacher who worked in cramped conditions and had to lug the finished creations to Pentonville Prison for firing. Then there was me and an occupational therapist who supervised knitting, sewing and other needlecrafts. We were all supervised by a clutch of patrolling prison officers who ensured that security was maintained. Occasionally the officers helped out, were supportive, helpful and formed good relationships with the prisoners. Sometimes staff formed too good a relationship with the women and they suddenly left, were transferred or even dismissed amidst a lot of gossip.

A cookery teacher was employed too somewhere. She taught the 'Arts of the Kitchen' and was really popular even if she seemed to focus a lot on pineapple upside-down cake. Another couple of teachers taught English, but that was it. Evening classes provoked the most activity with teachers coming into the prison and putting on slide shows, having discussion groups and that kind of thing. This was the old guard of teachers, not taking it too seriously, entertaining their students rather than educating them. Oh—and there was another evening class devoted to teaching the 'Art of Hat-making'.

City and Islington College, the Holloway education provider, had started to hire new day-time lecturers, pioneers of prison education, fired-up with enthusiasm, fervent and bent on making a difference. I was one of them. The newly appointed education officer was straight out of Ruskin College, Oxford. Another new teacher was connected to the Claimants' Union. More teachers gradually joined our ranks. We were involved individuals who were prepared to revolutionise the syllabus, innovate and drag it into the twentieth century, though little guidance was on hand to help us. We were paid by the college and answerable to it, but we were also answerable to the prison, so we had two masters which gave us a lot of trouble. We learned on the job and made mistakes. As well as fixed teaching hours on a sessional basis (no holiday, no pension), I had one-to-one commitments to visit women who needed special attention, or who were segregated on security grounds or sick. Part-time teachers were not allocated keys so that much time was wasted hanging around waiting for uniformed staff to open doors in answer to buttons that they never seemed to hear. That was why the buttons were tough metal structures. They were often abused, pushed inwards violently and held down until the sound reached unbearable levels, enough to awaken the most indifferent prison officer. Too much passivity got you nowhere. You needed a strong thumb and a streak of belligerence or you couldn't even arrive at your destination.

I received 'a referral' from Sister Grey who was in charge of the Segregation Block. She said that she wanted me to visit a particular young woman. There were only two residents in that block at the time; one of them a convicted woman called Shirley who had been accepted onto a full-time education course studying home economics as a substantial subject. She was a middle-aged woman with a thick Liverpool accent who had numerous convictions for drink-related offences. On the outside she lived a derelict existence, with no permanent home, no family and no friends. This time she had come back into prison after throwing a bottle through a police station window and then assaulting the first policeman to appear on the scene. Maybe she had just become tired due to the effort of her daily life. Happiness in prison was not that unusual because the institution provided companionship, warmth, food, activities, care and shelter. But nobody admitted to such benefits, not publicly anyway.

Residing on an ordinary wing with huge numbers of women upset Shirley because her vulnerability advertised itself. She couldn't read or write and had other learning difficulties. Nobody wanted to befriend her so she became withdrawn and susceptible to bullying. Isolation suited her and the Segregation Block protected her. It was small and she could relax and receive individual attention. Her transformation took place from the time she rolled out of the prison van. This troglodyte, with enough wildlife on her to restock a small planet, gave her name to the prison reception office as Shirley McNally. Her stench was so vile that the staff collided as they dashed in and out of that confined space to grab fresh air as her fleas, disturbed by this activity chased after them. Bodily fluids cemented Shipley's clothes to her body. She spat out her curses and peed on the floor to mark out her territory. A good de-louse, a shower, clean clothes, plenty of sleep and she started to metamorphose. If she felt the pull of alcohol she would head for the church at Communion. Dissatisfied with a quick glug from the wine chalice she had been known to grapple with the priest for the whole eight pints of Christ's blood. In the block she settled down, her alcohol level dropped, yearnings eased and her mind cleared. Her humour returned and with her plastic Home Office issue rosary round her neck she pulled up her cultural roots from her childhood spent in Ireland and planted them in the Segregation Block, below stairs, in Holloway's dungeon.

Shirley's cell was immaculate from hours spent polishing and scrubbing and the staff appointed her the cleaner for the whole wing which boosted her weekly spends. She traded her hand-made paper roses and carnations and revived talents from her travelling youth to further enhance her standard of living. She could roll a perfect cigarette with one hand at the same time as mopping the wing with the other. With her nicotine stained, crooked fingers and a pin she could divide matches into quarters, extending their life fourfold to accommodate her addiction. Orange peel kept her tobacco moist. Her life was never so rich, nor so comfortable. She had the place sussed.

Her literacy skills improved and her cookery lessons supplemented her bland prison diet. Shirley did her 'bird' business class. There were many seams of gold running through the grey stone of Holloway—she was one of them. She wore the prison issue dress of blue flowery fabric and flip flops, her tobacco and Rizlas in her 'dolly bag'—a draw-string prison-issue cotton handbag—her face made-up like a theatrical mask. She was never so happy. For Shirley prison was a good, positive and rewarding experience, her wits and mind became alert, all her senses were reactivated as she moved further and further away from her time hibernating in some London tunnel. On Fridays she set her hair when out came the cardboard Tampax applicators, which were tightly rolled into each tress and she queued for her porridge the next day all curly and wavy, acknowledging the compliments like the Queen on a royal walkabout.

Her next door neighbour was a teenager who was being kept down the block for assessment. The teenager would spent much of her day with psychiatrists, psychologists and doctors all intent on creating a case study of her mental and physical status for the courts to decide on her future. Meanwhile she would be kept in isolation so that she needed occupying. I was new and still had no keys as yet. I was therefore perceived to be rather unreliable, 'just a civilian' and therefore not to be trusted. I didn't qualify to fill in any forms; nobody needed my signature, my views or my professional advice. I rang the bell to the wing and waited, a third rate entertainer, a Home Office redcoat on sabbatical from Butlins. Sister Grey turned the key and let me onto the wing.

'I'd like you to see Lisa, she needs something to do. You can't issue her with anything unless I see it. You've got an hour before lunch'.

Nothing was said about why Lisa was in prison—I was told nothing at all on this score. I was too far down in the pecking order to even ask and I could only speak to Lisa through the hatch in her door unless two members of the wing staff were there and no other inmates were out of their cells. Then she could come out and I could teach her in the centre of the landing. Those were the rules. It was all I was told.

Sister Grey, the chief nurse, was not only in charge of the Segregation Block, she was in charge of another territory, which was the most coveted and desirable item in the whole prison: four wheels carrying a cupboard with a lock on it. It went by the highly appropriate name of the 'Jolly Trolley' or 'Pills on Wheels'. The trolley attracted stalkers, muggers, dippers and any other inmate who wanted a quick downer, upper, sleeper or keep-me-awake. Sister Grey held the keys: she was God. She was divine, and she knew it. Harsh institutional lighting gave the entire wing the look of a colour transparency, unreal and spooky, and too long spent in the bowels of Holloway had given Sister Grey the same prison pallor as the inmates, which she compensated for, unwisely, with orangey foundation, heavily applied to her face and neck. Excess powder stuck to the rim of her nurse's collar and as the day wore on more and more of it dripped onto her uniform. Sister Grey wore high heels; impractical suede things that were ill-fitting, and every time she walked along they would frill out on either side of her feet.

A table was already set up in the centre of the wing and two chairs had been arranged opposite to each other on the patched lino which shone from Shirley's elbow grease. At the end was a glass office with, clear, 360 degree vision. The two officers, startled by the sound of the metal door, jerked themselves up straight before collapsing back into their seats as they saw as I entered my lack of authority to effect their progression up the promotion ladder. Cigarettes were revived along with their customary, relaxed seating arrangements. Shirley was off the wing doing her cookery class.

Sister Grey reached for her keys and unlocked Lisa's door. From the top of my eyes I watched Lisa as she walked towards me, She had close-cropped hair, a boyish face and wore tight jeans, a shirt and socks. She reached for her boots, left outside her door as if it was a five star hotel, only they weren't left outside to be polished. Long laces could strangle, boots could inflict pain, block doors and conceal contraband, so that's why they were left outside, and never were polished.

Lisa took ages to put her boots on, unnecessarily slowly, a show put on for an audience. Sister Grey shuffled inside her suede shoes. Lisa felt the tension and sniggered to herself. I looked towards her but she missed my glance. Lisa smiled again and looked up momentarily. I smiled again. It missed. Her smile was for her alone, not something she wanted to communicate, certainly not to me. She finished putting on her boots, making sure both laces were fastened exactly to match. They were adjusted and readjusted until the bows balanced perfectly. She smirked towards those Home Office cream walls and sauntered towards me. Her movement was so slow I was forced to wait and watch. I smiled. It was an 'I am going to try and teach you something, helpful,' kind of smile saying 'I am a nice person … I am not your enemy'. Lisa grinned on. She sat opposite me, sidewards on, like Whistler's Mother.

So 'Miss Free-to-walk-anywhere-with-a-desire-to-do-a-good-job-and-inspire and-with-a-clean-criminal-record' met 'Miss All-the-time-in-the-world-and-going-nowhere-young-teenager'. I talked to her about what she could do and perhaps what she might want to do, but my words got stuck somewhere in the air because they couldn't be heard. They never landed. Lisa smiled on with no response. I was embarrassing myself by overacting, by my over-enthusiasm and my earnestness and wish to please. There was no response. I had no idea how on earth I would get this young woman to start being creative in such a dismal dungeon of a home. Her attitude confirmed that she had not initiated my visit, nor did I now stimulate her interest. The decision to invite me was, so I imagined, to make life easier for the wing staff whilst at the same time providing some distraction for this bored and sullen young woman. But I couldn't find the trigger to start her off. Despite displaying colourful materials, vivid papers and numerous pencils, temptingly resembling children's sweets wrapped up as presents, her apathy stared back at me. She didn't want anything I had to offer. My other audience, sitting in the glass office, was not impressed either. They too remained unmoved, expressionless as they puffed smoke above their heads, lifted their chins and looked down their noses.

Towards an hour after my arrival Lisa had still not shown any signs that I had made contact with any of her senses. I had delivered an empty monologue. I had tried to demonstrate some ideas but they seemed to have looked so bad that they would not have inspired anyone. The more I talked, the more foolish I sounded and as my efforts to communicate stumbled on the less meaningful they became. Nothing in her expression, nothing in her body language convinced me that she had paid the slightest attention. I was not to be speaking English any more, just some incomprehensible gibberish. She smiled on though, slightly mockingly, making me want to give up and go to find a more willing student. But I had to be seen to be doing my job so I stayed and took the humiliation.

I tried to negotiate, to start her off on something, to show her pictures, to encourage her, and she smiled on and the audience smoked and Sister Grey shuffled her papers. I knew I had a good product but my selling pitch was dire. At the end of that long hour with absolutely no results I gave up and sat waiting for Sister Grey. The materials lay as I had arranged them, untouched, unused. The highly coloured intensity of the art equipment brought freshness to the faded gloom of an oppressive scene, but nobody seemed to have noticed it but me. But I decided to leave them for Lisa as at least some pathetic evidence that I had spent an hour of my life there. Sister Grey checked them over, examining each item with a thoroughness disproportionate to security risk involved. Then with a telepathic understanding born of routine, Lisa stood up and followed Sister Grey towards her cell. In utter silence, boots were removed and put neatly together. Lisa entered her home and her captor, Sister Grey, smoothly locked her captive inside the cell. It was all so well-practised and carried out in absolute harmony.

I reached the end of the wing distracted by my own thoughts and lack of success. The last cell before I could get away, an arm was sticking out from the slit of a hatch. It was pushed out by a body that could not be seen and it was a mangled kind of human extension with deep groves scratched into the lower half from the elbow downward. It was a joint of pork on its way to the oven.

> To prepare crackling, score the skin well, if you do it yourself, use the tip of a sharp knife and cut the skin with quick jerky movements
>
> Delia Smith

A nurse was outside the cell, cleaning the arm with cotton wool and disinfectant. An officer was standing by with arms folded supervising this 'medical procedure'. To rid herself of the pain in her head, which she couldn't deal with, the woman had inflicted upon herself a pain that she *could* recognise, that she *could* deal with. It was a visible tangible pain, administered with a bit of broken glass that she had somehow found. The arm was still being treated as I left the wing and I never saw it again.

I was released from the wing with complete indifference. Sister Grey's voice was slightly whiney with a high pitch and a slight lisp as she patronised my performance along with gestures of helplessness. She let me off the wing while chatting amusingly to one of her colleagues, already moving on to the next stage in her rigid routine. I was the cat being let out at night. I took Lisa home with me that night and the following day, and for the rest of the next week. Maybe I was 'Miss Out-of-her-depth-coward'. Lisa frightened me.

Later that month and in answer to another invitation from Sister Grey, I set off again for the subterranean location of my failed performance. It would be a luncheon slot this time. The travelling saleswoman rehearsed her script, collected more props and set off past the 'public loos', down into the hospital unit and further on down heading under the earth, where pure daylight was just a slit at the top of narrow windows and where every footstep echoed the isolation. Without keys, I always had a slight panic in the dimness of the Segregation Block.

Knocking loudly and ringing the bell on each dividing door, the journey was too slow for my liking. A couple of young female officers laughing from their office saw me approaching and came to meet me, smiling at my enthusiasm and urgency. One of them grabbed my hand and walked me down the wing, further down into the catacombs towards the next door. The other talked of being locked in and asked how was I coping. 'Of course it is a daunting place,' she offered, then asked, 'Are you finding it all a bit frightening'. 'Wouldn't it be awful,' she said, 'to be locked inside'.

We turned a corner. All I'd got with me were a few pencils and paper, 'No, absolutely nothing else really … nothing, look.' They still asked to check and they were officers after all so I complied. 'Lisa,' I am going to see Lisa … I've been invited by Sister Grey.' I volunteered the piece of paper validating this. They knew of the prisoner concerned, they said. They'd worked on her wing the previous week. 'Yes, I would hate to be a prisoner, not be able to go home … scary.'

They unlocked the door and I walked through, their keys locking it shut behind me as they giggled at me from the other side of the hatch. My gaolers had led me into a security cell with soft walls, one especially designed for the most disturbed kind of prisoner. They had asked reasonable, attentive questions and I'd replied, following their lead. I'd bleated my way into that cell with the mindless prattle of my answers without being aware of it. I started knocking and shouting to be let out, louder and louder. Not enough terror, no response. I kicked the door, screaming louder and there were a few more giggles. After begging and pleading for my freedom, I heard footsteps advancing towards me along the corridor outside. There was more laughter and teasing jiggles from their keys. Then they were both there peering through the hatch watching my distress for a while longer. The keys turned. 'Oh that was bad. I'd thought I would be locked in forever. How terrifying …

It was really scary to be locked in,' I panicked on convincingly as my liberators laughed with reassuring pats and hugs. Then they released me and sent me on my way. When I retold the story to my colleagues later, I was met with shrugs and shaking heads. It happened; that kind of thing happened.

Institutional food in huge quantities is repellent. Like school meals, it isn't seductive or attractive. Crossing a prison wing at mealtime, this vile smell is mixed with the staleness of re-used air, that of too many bodies living too closely together, of medication, sickness and unhealthy living. Lunch was in full flow.

Meals were brought up to the wings in trolleys packed in vast stainless steel containers. The 'muck trucks', as they were fondly called by prisoners were wet with condensation and dripping with fat or whatever was inside that had shaken about in the journey from the kitchen. Over-cooked and with colours as artificial as Blackpool Illuminations the food looked and smelt bad. Fluorescent green peas, transparent water-logged potatoes and sticky, fizzy meat provided the main course that day. Pudding was yellow currant cake. Some borstal girls tried to make hooch using the currants. They found ten currants in the cake for forty women! On one of my first visits to the kitchen I had to see the chief tea-maker. She was standing over a vat of frothing liquid about five feet in diameter. Bending over the boiling liquid, both of her hands heaved at a spoon the size of a spade which she stirred with great effort. Brown scum clung to the sides of the vat as a pillowcase of a tea bag rocked and rolled in the middle.

If I breathed in only through my mouth I could get through the wing without inhaling the lunchtime smells, but it was an effort and unnatural so I tried to hold my breath to avoid being sick. I descended the last stairs to be met by Sister Grey.

'Lisa is not allowed out of her cell today ... there's not enough staff. If you want to you can go in and see her, but I'll have to make sure the door is kept open . . . Lisa you've got a visitor.'

No response, louder: 'LISA YOU'VE GOT A VISITOR!'.

'OKAY … OKAY'.

Lisa's cell was the first one past the stairs, it looked empty to me through the hatch but she must be in there somewhere. The door was opened for me and Sister Grey flicked the lock so that Lisa couldn't bang us both up together. I passed by the bed and sat on the only chair. The voice that had replied to Sister Grey had wrapped itself inside a sheet and was feigning sleep. My attempt at engagement this time would be more measured.

Leaning back on the seat I observed Lisa's home. The same lino as the corridor, the same colour on the walls. I could still have been in the corridor except for the socks drying on the thick, institutional radiator. The wall opposite peeled old glossy magazine pages, dripping down pictures, some left stuck to blobs of glue, like they were helping to plug up some kind of seepage. The whole wall looked like a neglected face, badly shaven and sickly. Most women attempted to personalise their imprisonment, but Lisa's room looked as if the occupant had already vacated it. Everything looked rejected. There were no photos to revive memories of an outside existence, no letters from friends or family sent to keep her cheerful. The wardrobe with the door open revealed nothing more than an old pair of jeans and a couple of bars of prison soap. There was nothing on the sink but a tube of toothpaste, far away from the toothbrush which lay on the window sill. Wedged to keep the window closed was a box of paper knickers of the kind issued to inmates who lacked personal clothing. So the light was trapped outside and the air was trapped inside, stagnant and sour at the very bottom of the prison. It made breathing-in an effort—or was I just starting to feel anxious?

Opaque plastic windows prevented anything like clear shadows or bright sunlight. The dull gloominess imposed a dirty grey on all objects. Even the art materials I had left last time round had been infected by this and seemed to have lost their colour. They lay abandoned on the floor, in the corner with a dirty blue plastic prison plate and mug. Nothing seemed precious to Lisa, cared for or important. Nothing had a special place that meant anything.

Lisa still feigned sleep, though with fluttering eyelids as I turned towards her to check every now and then. So the pretence continued—and I wasn't going wait this time. I got up noisily, scraping my chair on the floor in the process. I reclaimed my possessions, shovelling up the pencils and crumpled paper, clattering ever more loudly in my efforts to reclaim the initiative. Lisa's eyes jerked open and looked over with the same babyish stare. Blankly she watched me press the paper flat and sort out the pencils, or was she just staring through me to somewhere in the distance? Then, twisting herself off the sheet, she rolled from her bed while I completed my task.

'Come … see,' she said.

She bent over and carefully lifted up the edge of her prison blanket, which touched the floor all around her bed. Why hadn't I noticed that? It was only when she got up from the bed that I saw how the blanket was only half on the bed, to allow it to overflow onto the floor. Reluctantly I joined her on the floor, my side against hers. Underneath the bed were a group of objects, hardly discernible in the dim light. As the curtain was lifted up further, light started to define the images. The objects were arranged in lines with equal space between them. I knelt next to Lisa to see them. Now we were both on the floor. She was watching for my reaction. The objects were now in full view as she tucked her blanket under the mattress. They were figures, about eight in all, each around six inches long. They were lying down flat, in roughly made coffins, with crosses decorating the lids, painted black with bits of red here and there. They weren't men or women, just kind of people, not as rough as stick people but well proportioned yet lacking in gender. She was still watching me.

'Yes,' said Lisa, 'You can pick them up.' I lifted them gently into the palm of my hand and turned them over to see more detail. I could tell that her smile re-emerging. I saw her watching my expression. I didn't want her old smile. I lowered my eyes and threw that untrustworthy show of friendliness back onto the prison lino. Here was a profoundly strong collection of images, directly constructed, and simply made to fit in perfectly under the bed. The whole installation had been considered with the creative profundity of an expert sculptor.

'How were they made?'

'I wet that paper that you left on the table and mixed it with porridge, it makes them all stiff Miss. Then I coloured them with that paint you left… once they had dried on the radiator. Good aren't they?'

After that I couldn't stop her talking. She lifted each figure up and played with it like a real person. She gave them characters in a creaky, weak but menacing voice. They were victims, frightened and trapped and she had control over them so that they did exactly what she wanted them to do. They resisted in their squeaky screams and fell back into their graves. Then she would start on the next victim and repeat the drama. She played with them like toys. They spoke back. She resurrected each one in turn using the blanket as a makeshift curtain to bring them into the spotlight, and then shoe would rejected a figure back into the shadows as interest waned, moved on to animate another of them.

'You can just stay there,' she scolded and dropped one figure back into its coffin. 'Don't do that or you're finished … you fuckin' idiot'. She lined-up another against the wall. 'Frightened are you … You cry baby … Cry baby!"

So it continued, vindictive sinister ramblings, spiteful and savage. I was in the presence of a macabre ventriloquist's act that I dare not interrupt. They were staggeringly strong sculptures. Porridge figures, sexless and morbidly snug in their cereal box coffins, black and red, in the graveyard beneath her bed. I watched with morbid fascination, repelled yet compelled by it all. Whether I should say so was another issue. And was I being in some way complicit in the violence? But they were only porridge toys, harmless and fragile. Yet there was a reality to them that had twisted that ordinary, dull cell into a place of tragic drama, of improvised acting, impersonation and fatal endings. Lisa had invigorated a new reality into existence. She was the set designer, stage manager, actress, wardrobe assistant, director and scriptwriter.

To admire that meant I was enjoying them, and to enjoy them would have meant I praised her simulated violence and cruelty. What I actually did was nothing to do with art in the end.

What was happening was nothing about showing off her artistic skills. It was to do with something else, which is also what made it so creative. But it was also something more and I got that bad feeling again which stifled me. Her cell had been turned into a horror show of petrified, static figures. All around us had been forgotten, this reality felt dangerous so I looked towards the other reality outside of her room and tried to leave, but she was in the way and she knew it. She wasn't going to facilitate my departure. So I settled back on the floor, into my front row seat in the stalls as the intimacy of her closeness aggravated the intensity of my thoughts. We were squeezed together and her voice got quieter and quieter and we seemed to be getting smaller and smaller and closer and closer. She was virtually lying on the floor now under the bed still playing with her figures, blocking the exit to the door. I was stuck in the cramped space between the bed and the wall. I couldn't go anywhere without the cooperation of Lisa and she didn't care how I felt. Then I saw those wonderful floppy shoes resting against the door. Sister Grey stood there chewing a biscuit and with her other hand holding her cup of tea. She peered down to her bosom where her nurse's watch hung.

'Times up … You'll have to go. What are you doing on the floor … and what are those things? Oh, they're horrible. Is that what you teach? Is that how you spend your time?' We were both being told off. 'They have no faces, or clothes … they're nasty, why don't you draw something pretty and colourful? I need some paintings for the office, but I don't want those ugly, depressing things.'

The tension broke and the show was over. Lisa brought down the curtain, turned away from me and faced the bars of her window, her back to us both. I staggered up and out into the corridor. Sister Grey scurried me out gabbling about her taste in art and asking whether I could paint her portrait or some flowers or 'A nice sunset'. What kind of art was I teaching? What kind of a teacher was I? The wing clock pointed to twelve, which motivated a fresh bout of activity. Unlocked doors produced the muck trolley for Sister Grey to distribute meals from. Officers scrambled into activity, pressed and twisted their cigarettes violently to extinction in wobbling ash trays. They sprang up from their seats to greet the stainless steel vats. Lifting the lids released billows of steam that forced heads backwards and caused eyes to tighten closely. There was that smell again.

Shirley was let back onto the wing from her cookery class; humming and carrying high in her hand a plastic plate laden with buns. I passed her on my way out as the doors grated shut. I trudged along back to the education office with Lisa's figures still in front of me. This was a long way from those art college classes about tonal values, harmonious compositions and colour wheels. Holloway had thrown up something way beyond my experience. It was challenging and dreadful at the same time.

An officer shouted at me to hurry. She wanted her lunch and her shift had ended, she was off duty and wanted to get home. I quickened my step, but only slightly. I was still in the block and couldn't end it in my head. The uniformed magnet tried once more. She screamed again urging me to 'Hurry up, for pity's sake!' Impatiently, I yelled back at her as I speeded-on towards her past the cell doors. 'I'm coming, I'm coming' as a plaintive voice from behind one of those doors wailed in reply, 'I wish I was, Miss ... I wish *I* was!'

Those four little words jerked me away from the horror of the block and it lightened my mood bringing relief. The hidden voice finished my day off with a contagious cheerfulness. The guardian of the huge wooden doors crossed me off his books, freeing me to make for the tube and home. At some point along Hillmartin Road, my attention crossed over from the events of that day to the present. A vile smell seemed to be following me. I checked the soles of my shoes for dog dirt, the pavement for overflowing refuse; or maybe the drains had burst and were discharging noxious fluids. I stopped and took in deeper sniffs, but it walked on with me in my own little bit of atmosphere. It was a souvenir from Holloway. That institutional pong had escaped, hidden in my hair and my clothes. It hung around me and I hosted it all the way home.

Christmas was coming and I was in demand from staff who recognised me as having something to do with art, didn't know my name but knew I was part of something creative. Decorations were thus *my* department so did I have any to spare? For a while my head was turned by my popularity, even though I knew full well this would come to an end on Boxing Day. Nevertheless, such interest could be nurtured with generosity, and besides the establishment badly needed decorating. Christmas was the ideal promotional vehicle for my efforts in the Education Department.

The block needed jazzing up so I took down some paper and red and green paint. Lisa was allowed out of her room to work with me. Maybe if we coloured the white paper we could make something festive and start out from there. We could work together as a team. And so I gave Lisa the large pot of red paint and a brush and I had the green. She responded immediately with an enthusiasm I had never seen before. This was the breakthrough, I thought. Contact had finally been made, we were communicating. That was until the paper constricted her ambition. As I painted my paper in long even strokes, she rolled her brush off her paper towards the walls, dripping it along the floor in concentrated fascination. Adding more scarlet paint to a still over-weighted brush she painted indiscriminately on any surface that got in her way: chairs, walls, along the floor. Her brush waved like the wand of a sorceress, swirling redness around in spirals. She did this silently at the beginning apart from some strange noises that said nothing and meant nothing but ran out of her in spits and spats of moans and cries. She twisted more frenziedly then, blighting the room with more splashes of scarlet and dancing footprints and smears on Shirley's polished floor. She closed her eyes and ignored my verbal intrusions. Only her physical presence remained.

'More work,' that's what their expression said as the officers looked over to her, At first they remained seated, still smoking, until Lisa's movements forced them out of their chairs. Stretching their stiff backs and shoulders, they creaked into the vertical position. 'More work, no more sitting down,' and Sister Grey wouldn't be able to finish her newspaper either, though at this stage she didn't consider it a medical matter. Nor could it be remedied by me. Any kind of talk was too late. I couldn't bring Lisa back from wherever she had gone. An immense energy had been freed, too big for me to quell. One of the officers still arching and flexing his back muscles strode closer; the other held his hands together and pushed his arms out straight in front of him clicking his knuckles loudly to awaken them ready for action. Both ready and in unison, they edged closer towards Lisa so that her arms couldn't flay around anymore and slow her movements down. Her eyes remained closed as her became more monotonous. The paint brush hung from her straight arms and dripped down.

With Lisa lodged between them, the officers shuffled her inside her home and locked her door with a big heavy key. Sister Grey never budged, nor did the 'Jolly Trolley', the medicine cabinet on wheels. My innards twisted with guilt. Nobody paid me a glance, nor gave me their time, and I was left to my own devices. The only way of redeeming myself, I thought, was to get a bucket and clean up. I was safe cleaning-up; I couldn't cause any harm.

Why was I excluded from any explanation or information? It would have helped me and it would have been an acknowledgement that I too was professional like them. The secrecy of Holloway reduced such conversation to a minimum. Most talk took place on headed notepaper between specialist departments, with numerous copies being sent to the right channels or appropriate hierarchy. It never arrived in the letter boxes of teachers. The information that did come usually lost impetus due to difficulties of, and delays in, communication.

So I decided to clean up. I could do it, I knew that, because I did it last time. It was a mundane activity with a clear beginning and end, uncomplicated and simple. The buckets were kept in the sluice room together with disinfectants, soaps and cloths. How much I emptied into the boiling water I can't remember but I do remember sliding the bucket along the floor, Sister Grey moving out of my way in silence and the two officers resuming their sedentary positions. I had to drag it backwards and forwards renewing water till the cream walls emerged again and the water ran clear. My panic abated with the physical effort of scrubbing, which also cured me of my shivers and kept my insecurity hidden. Nobody spoke to me, discussed the events or came near me. I'm sure they regarded my lowly cleaning-up operation as a penance richly deserved. The officers blew their smoke rings, rocked backwards and forwards in their comfortable chairs, drank their tea and laughed. All the while, unnatural whining sounds from Lisa disturbed their conversations and they nodded to each other now and then, perhaps to signal that the should prepare for further action if necessary. Sister Grey, still a vigilant spectator, realised her entrance was perhaps overdue and took up her rightful place in front of her Jolly Trolley. My hands hurt, swollen by the hot water and strong prison detergent which had sucked out all the natural oils. My fingerprints were dimply with dehydration. The prison disinfectant reddened my skin and broke it in several places. But I'd recovered and I wanted to see what was happening in that cell before I replaced my bucket and folded up my cloth.

Not that I could resolve anything, but some unknown trigger had been fired by me and I felt responsible. Why shouldn't I go and see Lisa now? The whole situation had involved me. Despite my apparently marginalised position, I was concerned. I would learn from it and educate myself not do whatever I had done wrong again. I walked over to Lisa's hatch more quietly than usual, hoping that my interest would not be perceived as interference or something counter-productive.

Red paint scarred a naked torso, the bedsheets and Lisa's throat. Her mesmerised eyes were dim and trance-like. Her noises sounded painful, but without the stress of hurt–more to signal an intense pleasure. They were less repetitive, but still incomprehensible. Hands slid down the walls forming red lines to the floor, then her head lolled back on her pillow and rested in slow motion. Whatever world Lisa was in, it had cut her off completely from noticing any other individuals, hearing any other words or communicating with any other people. I was nowhere, looking without being seen, voyeuristic and uncomfortable. Peering at her inside her room caused me to have further feelings of culpability. Suddenly, without bothering to look at me, Sister Grey revived barked an urgent order for me to move away. I jumped backwards, startled at the ease with which I obeyed. The mop seemed to have grown taller when I resumed my manual labour and the mop bucket had become far heavier.

The sudden noise of the doors opening drew my attention. I'd forgotten all about the other resident. Singing distractedly, Shirley returned to the wing from her cookery class holding tightly on to a plate of freshly cooked food. Shirley couldn't compete with Lisa's echoing groans, so she stopped accompanying her own cheerfulness. That was the first source of her confusion; she didn't feel like finishing her pop song because those weird noises were ruining it. The usual welcoming party wasn't greeting her arrival. Nobody was interested in her cooking either. Her home had been invaded by a strangeness that she didn't understand. She made little twitches of her head lifting one ear and then the other. Frowning and cutting to the quick her good humour of a few seconds ago, the groans drew her towards Lisa's cell. I wanted to warn her, but what could I warn about? After all who was I and what did I know? I wanted to protect Shirley but couldn't–I was just the cleaner. Stretching upwards on tiptoe she peered through the hatch and watched as those groans persisted.

I looked over, hoping that Sister Grey wouldn't think I was involving myself in matters that didn't concern me. She was filling up a syringe with some antidote. Shirley's head peered inside Lisa's room, wrinkling up her eyes to see better. She turned her head from side-to-side through that narrow hatch as if the image would become less baffling from a different viewpoint. Howls squeezed past Shirley's head, then more moans and howls. She watched for a few more minutes, pushing her face further through the hatch, just looking and staring. Then enough was enough. She withdrew her head and turned away from Lisa's cell. Lifting up the plate of cooking, she pushed it through the hatch and with immense pride and a huge smile called out to Lisa, 'Eh you you're fuckin' mad, ere 'ave a pasty.'

The screeching stopped: no laughter, no hysteria, no movement, absolute silence. The officers prepared themselves as the shadow in the corner mopped the floor. Sister Grey stopped beside the medicine cabinet. They were all caught up in the same photographic still, posing together, in readiness, rigidly calm. Lisa's face came to the hatch, her red stained cheeks pushed against the slit; as she eyed up Shirley's offering. Out came a hand and she grabbed a pasty. 'Cheers babes.'

The two women transformed that cell door into a garden gate. Munching away they yattered on about the latest gossip that Shirley had gleaned from the other prisoners in her cookery class. Lisa was transformed. She asked questions, added a joke or two plus the odd expletive. Questions were asked, answers given: who was going to court, what sentence would they get, what had Shirley ordered from the canteen, what were they having for supper. The rest of us carried on with what we were doing. Sister Grey closed the drugs cabinet and rejoined the like minds. We might have communicated some visual relief to each other at the peaceful outcome, but that would have made us equal and so it never happened.

Shirley became all serious and pointed at Lisa's eyes, shaking her finger up and down.

'And you'd better clear up that fuckin' mess you've made … I'm not clearing it up, you messy bugger'. You'd better have a bath as well, and clean that bath out afterwards . . . I have enough to do.'

And that's how it ended. Sister Grey re-established her authority in the office surrounded by her bodyguards. Lisa called over for a cloth, Shirley got locked in with the rest of her pasties and I collected up my things and they locked me out. Lisa was soon allocated to another institution. I wasn't told where, but apparently her assessments were near completion. I was never allowed inside her cell again, nor was she allowed out to see me. Paintings *were* accomplished inside that room, but I became a mere delivery service providing materials, renewing pencils and brushes. All I could do was to squint through the hatch as Lisa showed me the results of her efforts. She never did much. Sometimes I visited and materials hadn't been used, and nothing was accomplished until a few weeks before her departure.

This one time she had produced something substantial. She was standing in the middle of her room waiting for me and holding two paintings in front of her. The black figures from under her bed had been replicated in paint. Dripping red oozed along their bodies and fell into their tight containers. Her hands moved the painting round, bodies floated across the page as if in a kind of tank. Upside down, another figure lay trapped. A huge black dagger dripped red paint on all sides. The painting turned a complete circle until the first figures set her off again, causing her to move around but with little talk. She was more interested in my reaction. I'm sure that familiarity had caused an uneasy rapport to develop, and I'd now become part of the institution and therefore part of her life. I was getting used to her too, I'd become less intimidated, more natural. I listened and suggested other materials and we even talked of other things. We became quite amicable though Sister Grey still waited for her portrait and paintings of flowers and 'nice little sunsets'.

Lisa still couldn't, or wouldn't, extend her palette from the two colours of black and red. Sometimes she would write words, such as 'Murder', or include references to crime articles in newspapers. Always, floating some-where, were those genderless, black people. Strange amoeba-like forms were added that balanced the figures in an abstract kind of formation. Once I first suspected that she would be transferred to another establishment and fearing she might destroy her work I asked her if I could keep the paintings; the sculptures she'd already dismembered and placed inside her rubbish bin.

'Only if you would put them up on the walls for everyone to see, in glass frames, around the prison.'

My duplicitous promise caused her to push the paintings through the hatch into my covetous hands. This promise which I know from the start could not be kept remained a cause of anxiety. Glass frames weren't allowed as they were an obvious security risk, and also dangerous if anyone broke the glass or tried to use it as a weapon. Then, the macabre content of the paintings meant that if placed on open view in the prison they might be perceived as an encouragement to create similar, morbid subject matter. As I walked away into the distractions of my outside world, I had to leave Lisa to her dearth of stimulus and time to brood over my trickery. Her confinement strengthened her tenacity.

She had the time to dwell on matters and the space to work me out. The following day Lisa asked to see her framed paintings. 'Not ready yet, haven't got any frames.' The next week it was the same, only with a different excuse as I wriggled and dodged her questions. I had dug myself into a large hole from which there was no escape. I bluffed, tried to deflect her questions, procrastinated and lied. Sometimes I hoped that the next time I visited the block she would be gone, then it would all become easy, but it didn't happen like that, she was always there. One lie went on top of another lie: I lied about the nonexistent frames and about where they were. I just wanted peace and for her to stop, and of course she didn't–and why should she? Each visit seemed to start off well with no mention of the paintings, but turning to go she would call me and repeat the same question, 'Where are the paintings hung?', 'What kind of frames did you chose?'.

So each time I hoped that she would have forgotten and each time I made to go she increased the pressure. Staff were making oblique references to her imminent departure so a crunch was coming, a final confrontation. I mumbled my explanation once again and made to depart, but Lisa lunged forward trying to grab me through the hatch. The rest of her body pushed against the door pressing it to open in an effort to eliminate the barrier between us and break the lock. My eviction from the wing was facilitated by Sister Grey clumsily grabbing my arms and my own personal escort of two prison officers, who I walked between.

I was terrified. I was scared, yet too mortified not to go back. I thought about my lies relentlessly. I knew I would be perceived as cowardly if I didn't return to see Lisa and explain everything to her. But more than that I knew I had persuaded Lisa to give me the paintings using false pretences. They were intensely powerful and I wanted them. The situation was of my own making and therefore it was up to me to fix it. There was only one option and the quicker it was dealt with the better.

The very next day I went straight down to the block without seeing anyone else. I wasn't invited there, nor had I been timetabled to see Lisa. I just went because I wanted to get it over with and rectify any wrong I had done. I saw Sister Grey and reinforced her bad opinion of me by explaining myself. Lisa was locked up completely, not even her hatch was open. I told Sister Grey about my lies and what had happened since. I had decided to come clean and tell Lisa all about my trickery. Sister Grey didn't react in the way I imagined: she wasn't shocked or dismayed. In fact, she needed persuading when I asked for her permission to talk to Lisa. It wasn't that she thought I might again disrupt the peace on the wing, she just wasn't particularly interested and couldn't understand my concerns.

Shirley was sweeping the floor. Lisa's face was right up against the hatch before it was fully unlocked, ready and waiting. Sister Grey's keys dangled limply alongside her crisp apron as she closed her office door leaving me alone with the face and a blank expression looking outwards. I took up a position far enough away that a fist could not attack my face and with Holloway's heavy door between us I began my confession. Neither of us looked away until I had finished. I admitted to every lie, explained how I really wanted the paintings and how I couldn't possible display them as it would upset too many people. They were too controversial and the prison wouldn't allow it anyway. Besides we couldn't use glass. I bumbled on with my guilty plea and extenuating circumstances, apologising again and again. Lisa was still staring outwards, eyes wide open, unblinking. I struggled on explaining, repeating myself to make sure I hadn't missed anything out.

All I wanted was a change in expression, some softness to appear. On and on I went speaking at a white, unmoving face and two eyes. I didn't stop my guilt-ridden diatribe even when Lisa turned away. On and on I went, following her inwards towards her bed and continuing as she spread herself over the blanket and stared upwards at the ceiling from her pillow. My face pushed itself up against the hatch now that she wasn't close enough to bop me one. I was talking now to the back of her head, to her hair and a bit of forehead. Was she listening? Should I go on? Had I left anything out? Silence, maybe she was going to throw something or make a quick lunge.

I thought about more explanations and different ways of saying the same thing. No sign of Sister Grey and Shirley was still sweeping-up. I watched the forehead and waited for sounds or movements, a reaction of some sort.

'I'm leaving this shit hole tomorrow, I want to take some pencils and paper with me that's all I can take . . . so leave me some. You can keep my fuckin paintings if you want, I don't give a shit.'

And that was that. I left the wing and never saw Lisa again. Amongst the papers in a bulging pigeon hole labelled 'Education', a few paint brushes and two half used tubes of black and red paint were wrapped up in a plastic bag. Scribbled on a sticky label from Sister Grey was written, 'Return to Education. Transferred to Broadmoor'.

I have rarely coveted any paintings as much as Lisa's. Maybe it was the fact that it was my first intensive encounter with Holloway that made them particularly important to me, I don't know. But I believed in them in a way that I could not believe in a lot of paintings now exhibited in modern galleries. They were truthful representations of a life directly interpreted. This young woman didn't want to become an 'artist', she just painted and made little sculptures, that's all. They added up, there was not a gulf between creator and creation like that which makes me suspicious of the 'art' in many exhibitions. They weren't just about her. There was symmetry, balance and an artistic skill that objectified the images making them more powerful and accessible to the spectator. I didn't have to read copious explanations either such as those which seem to have become more important than the images in current art. There was simple craftsmanship to the sculptures and they were invented out of nothing. 'Lack of resources stimulates invention': I'd read that somewhere.

CHAPTER 2

The Competition

Round the corner from Caledonian Road tube station and looking straight ahead, the high gothic-style folly blocked the skyline. Dots of navy blue trickled out of a small door set into the lowest corner of an enormous wooden gate, while other people wriggled past them in the opposite direction in order to get inside. It looked as if a shift change was in progress. Fifteen minutes quick walk and I would beat the dinner time rush.

The solid wooden doors opened, releasing a swarm of prison officers as blue prison vans entered beneath the stone portal. If the vans hadn't moved forwards slowly, one of those eager deserters would have been run over. Having delivered his own batch of detainees to Reception staff ready for their 'welcome packs', another driver reversed out of the prison, parked his van and knocked-off for lunch. Other blue uniformed staff looked down at me from the gatehouse and I looked up at them for permission to proceed. After much shuffling of papers and telephone calls, eye contact was made before an authoritative gesture pointed me on my journey to the next closed door. I was still early for my afternoon session and, even with the delays, the chances of my making it on time remained fair.

I had by now been issued with my own set of keys, a strange appendage carried on the lower half of the body. Given to me with intense seriousness and a frightening 'talking to' about security, they were contained in a shiny black leather pouch. The great key chain was attached to a thick belt around my waist. It dangled down and swung between my legs like a pendulum. Too shallow and slippery for its contents, the leather pouch was too small for the keys and they popped out as the press stud burst open under pressure. Often this happened when I was on the loo followed by a heavy splash as the keys anchored themselves in the lavatory pan. So I made my own marsupial with cloth, nice and deep, and it never happened again. At least I didn't now have to wait behind the doors to different wings and beg someone to let me through.

The administration corridor cleaner, a trusted inmate—a red-band—called over to wish me 'Good morning'. She pushed an immensely wide mop slowly up and down until the floor reflected her shadow. The grandiose spiral staircase stretched right up from the ground floor to the top of the building like elegant scenery from a Hollywood musical. That was the nearest I ever got to glamour, being the star turn, or in the spotlight. When I was on that central atrium, the stage lights focussed on my every step as I walked up and down. I'd crossed the pond and my name was at the top of the bill. Every time I ascended those iron circulating stairs I escaped into celluloid. I acknowledged my audience and listened to the silent applause, before the sound of keys, locks and other metallic prison noises broke down my delusions.

Right across my path, hoards of higgledy-piggledy prisoners disrupted the dignified atmosphere of The Centre, laughing loudly, singing badly and falling over each other with gusto. And I could see how those interlopers derailed 'Miss Blue uniform' in the glass office. She handed me my keys but looked across wishing that they would hurry on out of her territory. But the women were oblivious of her contempt. They were off work now until after dinner and all too soon they'd be packing plastic bags with pencils or performing some other chore in the prison workshop. Vitality was being rediscovered in this short period of liberation. I too needed to take advantage of the intermission. I dropped off my coat, picked up my list of students' names, declined an offer of tea from the red-band in the corridor, greeted a couple of probation officers and scarpered down to the prison kitchen.

Mainstream further education establishments invite students to study a subject within a syllabus for a given number of years. Those years are divided into terms, with breaks for study or holidays. Staying power is rewarded in the final year with some nationally accepted acknowledgement and the student moves on out, making room for replacements. They all climb up the ladder together and move away on completion of the course. Not so in Holloway:

no holidays, no terms, no predictable students, no time limits, no breaks. Just roll-on-roll-off classes, mixed abilities, endless years. Some prisoners stayed for days, others for weeks or years. We knew where every student lived and could visit them in their homes. Some focus was needed to punctuate the year, some event to engage the students in and most importantly something that the educationalists could count in order to monitor achievement so that it could be officially recognised. The actual process of education in prison seemed to be of minor interest, and it sometimes seemed we existed just for the sake of it, to fill in forms and other papers. There was no point in trying to explain the frustrations of being perpetually overlooked and ignored; the effort of it all led to compulsive moaning and grumbling which didn't improve anything and only made you yet more disgruntled and ineffective.

I found the solution in the bottom of an old filing cabinet labelled 'Dead Records'. Arthur Koestler with crumpled shoulders was stuck to the bottom of it looking up from the dust. So I turned him over and read the back of his head. That's when I first learned about the inter-prison art competition; an annual event which he promoted and largely initiated. It seemed to be the ideal way to motivate prisoners and provide some focus. Successful works of art would be exhibited at a venue in London. It was one way of letting a small breeze into this airless institution and it allowed eyes to peer into places never before seen. The problem for me right now was the proximity to Christmas. There would be a conflict of interests, and resources were being used for decoration, for cards and other festivities.

It was all banging, scraping, clanking metal and gushing steam down in the kitchen. The steam burnt my eyes, the noise grated on my teeth and I clenched them together for relief. My ears were being crippled again by institutional sounds. Just inside the swing doors I stopped and looked around the busy landscape of countless moving figures, clones of each other, each preoccupied with a joint mission to feed three hundred plus and growing. How could I find the women I needed to in this snow-blindness of white uniforms bent on a deadline? My search had to be completed quickly and with the least disruption. Maybe I should just have left, but here I was and I might as well stay. I interrupted the first worker I met.

'Do you know where I can find these women?' my finger prodded the first three names on my list as I placed it in front of her eyes in case my words couldn't complete their journey. Without even looking at me, she shook her head, and plunged her rubber gloves further into the grey soapy washing-up water, drenching the draining board and splashing water everywhere. Institutional resistance alerted some prisoners to an unfamiliar inquisitor on the prowl. Even if the inquisitor was known, it was safest always to say 'No'—and after all she and I had never met me before. 'No' was always the safest word in prison. A rogue splash ran down the names on my list and off the paper. I tried to shake and blow it dry, just before I was jerked forward by a muck truck which was impatient to replace me in a queue.

Each prison wing had a trolley and each trolley had a dolly and each trolley-dolly had her own muck truck. If anything was missing it would be the trolley-dollies who got aggravation from the other women on their landing. They stood around inspecting the day's menu, turning their noses up with disappointment; looking into each other's stainless steel vats for something more delectable or which smelled better than their own. They prodded and poked around sniffing and peering. Prison officers supervised the quantities and counted the portions, overlooked by their dollies who checked what the officers were counting just to make sure. Cauliflower was being strained and dripped over someone's white rubber kitchen boots as they screamed and swore at someone else who nearly slipped on the greasy floor.

Something brown and lumpy was being plopped into a tin vat by a cook with a white hat who then passed it along a line of padded hands. The hands lugged it past a trolley-dolly with a downturned mouth and squeezed in nostrils who recoiled backwards until the vat was safely in place on her trolley and covered with a lid. Long lines of workers replicated the same process elsewhere until all the trolleys were fully laden. The sound of screeching metal intensified in line with this increased activity. I found somewhere to stand against a wall. I knew I was in the way and I was being glared at as an intruder with no sense of timing. The cook was laying a table with a knife, fork and spoon, right in the middle of the kitchen.

'She's not working down here today love ... got some visit or other. Oh, the other one, well she's sick ... so she says ... and that other name ... what was it ... Amber? Amber's got a solicitor's visit. Not your lucky day ducks.'

He wiped his hands on a towel and flicked it onto his shoulder. Acclimatised by now to the racket of his kitchen, he seemed oblivious to everyone else's malfunctioning senses. I lip-read the cook's mouth and mimed a disappointed reply. He placed a plate of food between the knife and fork already laid out on the table before him, picked up the cutlery, frowned, gave it a quick wipe-over with his apron, replaced it next to the food and waited. Sounds slowly became bearable until they almost stopped as the kitchen workers chose to wipe instead of bang, whispered instead of shouted. Occasionally somebody would look towards the doors. The cook consulted his watch, pushed out his belly and carefully wiped around the edge of the plate.

The Governor One, boss of all bosses in the prison, entered the kitchen and marched manfully towards the chef, boss of the kitchen. After silently nodding heads in acknowledgement of their mutually prized testosterone, the Governor went to the place setting prepared for him by the chef. Still standing up, he picked up the knife and fork and took a bite out of the meat and two vegetables. The chef waited. The female workers watched, the mouth ate, the Governor concentrated, the throat swallowed. The taste buds responded favourably. Another quick nod between the alpha males and the rite of passage for today's lunch was complete. It had survived the Governor's tasting. Consumer tested by the head of Holloway Prison, the dinner was deemed to be edible by all. The starting pistol was fired, the cook nodded towards the hot, loaded trolleys and the race to feed hungry prisoners began. The trolley dollies gave one huge push, then threw their bodies behind the wheels to keep up the impetus. It was all part of the prison's daily regime. I left the kitchen and returned to the Education Department cell without anyone having been crossed off my list. I'd have to wait until the afternoon to continue my search.

Down in the sub-basement, the Christmas party had been in full swing in the Occupational Therapy Unit. The decorations I'd already made were nowhere to be seen. Of course they weren't. My good intentions had misfired and they had been locked away in a cupboard. I'd thought that a few large decorations would be more impressive than lots of little bits and pieces. It was a problem of size and I thought I had got it right. The ceilings were so high I had overachieved. With the help of a really sharp and bright prisoner (a part-time Womble) we set to work. She had given birth to five children and during every lesson she'd make cards for each one adding instructions as to how to survive without her and adding umpteen love hearts and glitter. She took her sentence for shoplifting casually in the same way she had taken an earlier one a couple of years ago, and another a couple of years before that and so on. Other prisoners came to her for advice which she dispensed with all the experience of her years in the system. She reckoned that she knew the good lawyers, the liberal courts and every scam available to fellow felons with opportunist brains and a cigarette or two to barter.

So we worked together to make three large cones, each six feet tall, architectural masterpieces of painted sugar paper. We stuck the paper together in double layers to make huge squares that could only be worked on if they were laid flat on the floor. At the end of each session we had to unstick them and Daisy cleaned it all up so that nobody could moan at us. Then when they had dried, I bent over and re-stuck them to make three huge cones. We made a Father Christmas for each hospital landing that could stand and smile at everyone, putting big black eyes on them and a thick black belt with a gold buckle. They grinned with sparkling white teeth and we painted all three scarlet. They had arms but no legs, so that they just stood on their bases. I couldn't think of anything to use for beards and neither could Daisy at first until we looked around the place and found a solution: sanitary towels. They came into Holloway by the cartload, of course they did, and they were stacked high in toilets in the unit.

Daisy brought the unopened packets in a plastic bag as if she was clearing-up something, so nobody would notice. She loaded up my cupboard with them. I stripped them down to their cotton wool and saved it (Holloway's pads never had much pure cotton wool in them). We stuck three lusciously thick white beards on their chins and the bits left over I put back into Daisy's sack—and when it was full she deposited it, with more front than me, at the end of the wing to await transfer to the prison skip. Over six feet tall, the three Father Christmases caused people to smile and skip round them with joined hands like they were in the school playground. This reaction confirmed that our efforts had been a success. We would deliver them to the landings after the weekend when they were completely dry. Everybody thought that they were great, really inventive and Daisy and I loved them even more because of those enterprising beards. Until Monday that is when I felt the blue uniformed people looking at me strangely and my education boss asked me to spare a few minutes to talk in private. Something had happened and it was related to something I'd done.

Day staff were still working, just before the evening changeover, and one particular officer at the main gate had nothing to do but wait for the end of his shift. He had given a last casual look along the prison wall and then another into the prison forecourt. Nearly dark now, the prison lights would soon be switched on. Silence and emptiness, just the muted throb of the traffic in the distance and a prison cat making tiger shadows against the wall. The officer gave another look and counted the minutes before he could be off duty and down the pub. Then there was a moving flash of colour and he gave the wall a second look. Around the corner, tottering and stumbling with a luminous grin, came Father Christmas, heading straight for the gate, jerking and rolling into the central yard and onwards towards those massive wooden gates. Whether it was a trip on the cobbles or the gate officers quick push I'm not sure, but a Father Christmas rolled onto the floor and then along it. Unable to right himself he just lay there on his back with a big fat grin and thick cotton wool beard. Surrounded now by a circle of officers, they stared down with folded arms at the grin on his face.

'Where's your sleigh?'

'A bit early this year aren't you?'

'Thought you came down the chimney?'

'Where's your reindeer, love?'

They all leaned over and spoke directly into the huge black eyes of the unseeing Father Christmas. He lay there with just a small pair of dainty feet sticking out, slightly crumpled and awfully still. His huge eyes stared back up towards the dark sky ignoring their smart remarks. The feet started to shuffle. A pair of feet in trainers wriggled outwards, then a pair of legs in jeans emerged out came body in a tatty T-shirt, then a head emerged and the figure sprang up from the concrete to the rhythm of 'Dah, de da, Dah, Dah ... Dah, Dah'. Throwing out her arms on the final Dah, Daisy bowed deeply to each of her captors in solemn persuasion, hoping that they would treat her leniently. Five officers bundled her off down the block—it was registered as an 'escape attempt', so she'd be down there for a couple of days. I never did get the whole story, but apparently Daisy had prevailed upon an officer so that she could get the cones early in case they were damaged by the cleaners. Somehow she had given the officer the slip (that's how the story evolved), she'd got herself under a cone and started her run. It was that simple. Without doubt Daisy could survive the block and even enlarge her client base. She'd increase her contacts and plot some new party trick to keep prison lethargy at bay.

The other two Father Christmases were imprisoned together in some dark cupboard because they were considered to be a security risk. I looked for them after Christmas and they had disappeared. Some prisoners said they saw them up on the Lifer's Wing, others that they had been in the gardens, but I never saw them again. Sadly the partying over Christmas had to cope without my additions. Just a bit of tinsel decorated the tables. Someone stuck a bit in her hair, but that was all, pretty dreary really.

'Take one paper plate, one bun one biscuit, one jelly and one tangerine then move along quickly to the end and you can take one plastic cup of orange squash. Then go and sit down.'

The mistress of ceremonies was really making things swing as she waved her cigarette. She dropped the nearly finished butt ostentatiously into an ash tray, silently giving consent for it to be finished by a desperate inmate who was in the throes of nicotine withdrawal. Two hands plunged in and the winner ran off into a corner straining on the ciggie. One behind each other, bodies leant against the trestle tables pushing against each other to catch a glimpse of the canapés at the top of the table.

'Jingle bells, jingle bells' over the sound system accompanied the energetic slurping of much diluted orange juice through cheap straws too useless to match the women's intense dehydration. The allocated biscuit was eaten whole before anyone else could steal it. The jellies wobbled into mouths from plates held by shaky over-medicated hands. Some well-organized inmates planned for the future and stashed a week's supply of goodies in amongst the folds of their clothing.

'Why don't you stay, we're going to play bingo next, the winner gets one cigarette, but if you've got to leave then do us a favour and take this down to the block, it's for the cleaner.'

No paintings here for the competition either, they'd all been used for Christmas cards, so I repeated my promotional speech, left more materials and smiled around like I'd caught their festive spirit. I took the plate of seasonal nibbles and descended even further down into the prison. Only male nursing officers serviced this basement wing and it provoked much controversy. It was small and intimate; too intimate some people thought. The dual tasking that mingled care with discipline and the chunk of male hormones caused the rumours to fly upwards into the main prison. The block cleaner was still scrubbing away in the kitchen and looked at the plate with suspicious interest. 'There's nothing wrong with it, it's for you, here try the jelly, it doesn't look that bad.' Picking up a spoon from the draining board I tried to tempt her.

'Fuck that, I don't use the spoons down here, I bring me own … that cow in that room over there wanks with them, I caught her at it the other day, mucky bugger, I bring me own spoon with me.' Out of her top pocket she showed me her very own utensils, carefully wrapped in tissue paper and as sparkling as prison plastic can get.

One of the women down the block was on my list and had to be 'ticked off'. There was some bread sticking out from her small cabinet and dried up sandwiches. Rejected and abandoned, they lay curled up on a paper plate near her pillow. She wouldn't be eating those; nor the apple turning brown on the window sill, nor the porridge solid by now in the bowl. This long-termer was down in the basement for observation. Her features magnified the thinning face and a bony frame reminded me of a peg bag hanging off a washing line. Anorexia was draining her down to invisibility under baggy clothing and her weight plummeted to even greater depths in that base-ment. I'd given her art equipment at her request and she had used it well. She needed it more than food, I think. Hers was the first contribution for the competition, a small drawing from out of her locker, made with felt tip pen, with intense patterns covering every corner of the paper. So at least I had something to send off. But I was putting my hopes on the more stable population. The evening session had begun so hopefully and they would be on the wing—I'd have to take the spiral staircase.

We'd all become mechanical travellers up those stairs. Hypnotised by our own movements, we fell into line, round and round, up and down in our dance routine. Our eyes vacantly distanced our bodies from the prison activ-ity. We escaped and pushed our imagination into pleasanter times although a surge of intense noise urged me not to lose concentration. I was getting higher and higher up the building looking down further and further. The prison spiral was navigating me upwards. 'The Bed and Breakfast Wing' got its name because it held short term remand prisoners. It was also called 'The Bronx'. Waves of heavy, throbbing music agitated the metal netting. The sound of shouting and screaming hurried me up the stairs; fellow travellers covered their ears and followed my quickened steps upwards.

I arrived at the penthouse suite at the top of the prison. This Long-term Wing held women who had been sentenced to four years or over, lifers and a few remand prisoners who had been waiting a long time for mortal judge-ment under the Scales of Justice at the Old Bailey. Traffic went more slowly at the top. It had been observed in some survey or other that women settled down after conviction—all their volatile behaviour evaporated as soon as Mr.

Judge (it was mostly men) had the final word. Men however did the opposite. Another survey had observed that women received longer sentences than men for comparable crimes. Some said it was men punishing their mothers for the let down feeling of seeing a woman in the dock. I don't know.

It was peaceful on the Long-term Wing and the absence of incessant noise made me feel deaf until I got used to it. On the whole, the women there had their own routine, kept their appointments. Yes, they had their issues to deal with, but they contributed in some way or other, made use of the facilities and were not destructive. This was their home, their neighbourhood, their village. In a way they ran the prison, they were the workers who cleaned and cooked in the kitchen, and they were often trusted inmates taking on tasks with responsibilities. An extra froth to the coffee, an extra tang to the tea, and extra crumble in the sugar, one particularly responsible trusty had been servicing the workers on the administration corridor as the tea and coffee lady par excellence. How good she was we all thought, and how economical. The teachers, probation officers and welfare workers started to feel quite spoilt and indulged. For weeks on end she'd pushed those comforting beverages in front of weary staff, with empathetic 'cooings' and 'oh dears' and 'mmmms' and 'poor yousssss'.

Disappointed faces peered around the empty kitchen one morning, no kettle on, and no cups ready—she'd gone. Where? Gone when? Up where? To Durham? Why? An impromptu room spin, the prison term for a search, had discovered bleach tablets under her bed, hoarded like nuts for the winter. Two and two had been put together and security had come up with a poisoner. Evidence had been collected, inconclusive evidence but enough to register enough doubt as to her real trustworthiness. Cups were taken away with other utensils from the kitchen and replaced by this year's new institutional plastic, this year's Home Office design and colour. Then the gap closed. The irreplaceable lady was replaced.

Now that I was up on the Long-term Wing I went on the scrounge for paintings, drawings, poems, writings; anything creative from the women. Door-to-door lobbying would get the job done efficiently. Liza was reading and greeted me as someone she had already seen that day. What a graceful lady, always controlled and articulate. The staff in the Education Department had asked her to help out teaching some of the women on a one-to-one basis. Liza being Liza had made a real success of it, the women liked her and she handled her rather ambiguous position with tact and sensitivity. Mavis in high heels and exotic underwear displayed beneath a transparent negligee was missing her evening class. 'Ask that Caspar chap to let me back into his hat-making class, Christ it wasn't as if I'd killed anybody!'

She lifted up her chin and clucked her teeth, eyeing up a couple of the wing's murderers. She'd caused a near riot the previous week and she was still seeing the funny side of it. Caspar the 'Hat Man'—as he was nicknamed—took his job and his class seriously. His formal attitude went well with his tailored suit and organized classroom. On the minus side he had too much spit, which boiled up and effervesced out of his mouth when he became over-heated. His class was loyal and attracted women who fantasised about Ascot and an ensemble made perfect by a designer hat. ; It was diverting and entertaining. Caspar was obsessive about security. He had several pairs of scissors chained to his belt, which he fastened tightly for safety.

Mavis was a regular in his class. There was something in Caspar that she recognised and understood. I think Caspar revived many a flagging dinner party on the outside with tales of his work and characters like Mavis. She was as controversial in the tabloid press as she was on the prison grapevine. Her business was done in the city, flexi-time, obligingly providing a 24-hour specialist service, satisfying all sexual tastes. Those full frontal implants had been a good investment and made her a rich lady. She needed a good gutsy laugh a day and prison wasn't going to change that, so she planned a comedy turn and Caspar would be the fall guy. This harmless bit of fun was essential to stop her feeling low and it prevented her feeling like she was in prison. Everybody could understand that surely!

Thrusting her enhanced bosom in front of Caspar, she posed and pushed to cause an earthquake of spit to bubble out of his mouth, and the more it came the more she pushed her investments into his face. Practised arms engulfed him and nimble fingers fiddled with his belt round the back. His attempts to carry on fixing some chiffon to a little pink creation couldn't possibly succeed whatever his protestations. It went on until he reached for his scissors. Then didn't his mouth dribble. Quite beside himself with confusion at what seemed like a lapse and maybe even the ruination of his security conscious reputation, he flew around the room in despair. Not only were all his scissors missing, but the belt was too. He searched and searched but without success. Just as he was about to press the emergency bell and go public with his failings out popped Mavis swinging his belt. His scissors were all present and correct but she had cut the belt off with one pair.

She laughed the night away. The story was good for a few days and the events of that night infected everyone. Caspar never did see the funny side. He banned Mavis because she 'wasn't serious enough' for his master-class. She didn't appreciate his skills and his professionalism. The ban didn't last long though. Mavis was the jam that attracted the lesbian flies. They stalked her and would even come to learn hat-making in order to sniff her exotic air.

The penthouse suite inhabitants were a talented lot, they were motivated to spend their time well, 'A-class' students, their skills easily tapped into. Most were articulate, talented and bright. This stable population could organize their own life. They planned their day to suit their obligations and during lock-in they had the peace and certainty of knowing that they wouldn't be moving house for a while. If I got to teach any of these ladies then it was a treat, top stream on the whole, motivated and eager. Even the teachers who taught these women were perceived as a cut above the rest so that in turn staff with less able women in their class were somehow perceived as inferior.

The long-termers had even started a wing magazine. It was called *Behind the Times* and contained poems, letter, and articles written by the women. The contributions included a review of 'De Profundis' by Oscar Wilde and a recipe from a Fanny Craddock cookery book for potato cakes. They also included a description of a wing event—'Bonfire Night'—only there was no bonfire, just baked potatoes and singing. With more than a squirt of relish the magazine decided to tell the story of the first Governor of Holloway,

George Wright, who had apparently come from the old Newgate Prison where he was the deputy governor. During the six years he was in charge he was susceptible to crossing the line between honesty and dishonesty. He'd cooked the books to the extent of £200 and been discovered in his greed by the town clerk. He wasn't prosecuted though, just quietly dismissed. The stories were interlaced with a selection of poetry, one of which was called 'Ode to a Con Man':

> Where are you now? In what strange bar?
> And outside parked my dented car,
> A bottle of scotch in your fighting hand,
> Your money tied with a rubber band.
> Or perhaps you're holding in your arms
> A lady with fast-fading charms.
> I wonder if you think of me
> Or if you're safe across the sea.
> Perhaps you've joined the IRA
> If so you'd better stay away.
> But if you feel you've done me wrong,
> Ten pounds would help my time along.

'How are you today Miss?' The door was lightly ajar. Underwear was soaking in a bowl just inside her door. Not to make the same mistake as when I last met this particular lifer, I smiled a bit too wide and promised her that I was, 'Fine, really . . . Really fine.' Last week she'd been the slowest to clear up in the class and had caught me flopped into a chair preparing myself for the grotty task of cleaning up the mess.

'What you need is a massage Miss' and she came over all businesslike, wiping her hands down her apron and heading right towards me. I couldn't have stood up quickly enough to refuse her, nor could I refuse her sitting down, I was so exhausted. Her clammy hands started to glide across my shoulders. They reached the bare flesh at the top and the just about crushed my ability to move ever again. My body stiffened, my bottom hardened onto the prison chair, my legs got lost somewhere in-between and my feet; they could have been anywhere. The more she kneaded away the tighter I became. The sweaty smell of her nylon overall shot up my nose and I tried to breathe it back out. Her hands wriggled away over my neck. 'MMMmmm you're so tense,' she whispered in my ear. 'I'm in for this Miss,' and louder, 'Did you hear what I said Miss? … I'm in for this … that's why I'm in prison.'

I felt her hair across my ear as Ann leant over me pushing her body nearer and pushing that smell right back up my nose. A slip of thought had got me into this weak situation and I had travelled from intense activity, to fatigue and now to feebleness in those wriggling clammy hands and fingers. She continued to knead away at my neck. Never has a scrap of paper on the floor consumed my interest with such intensity. Fixing on that paper was my lamentable attempt to block everything else out. Two grubby feet in plastic sandals smashed the paper flat under her rubber soles and got caught in some stickiness beneath it. Twin bunions oozed out between the plastic straps and knocked against each other. Dirt oozed out between her toes and got trapped under the straps. Her toenails were too long, too black and her toes rolled over each other as Ann's hands continued to writhe around my neck.

'You've got to get back to the wing now Ann, the lessons been over ages and you'll get put on report if you're late.'

She did hear me, although how I don't know. I could hardly hear myself speaking and I was surprised that I still could speak at all. It didn't sound like my voice, just a squeaky noise from somewhere at the front of my face. She dropped her hands to her sides and mumbled something about disappointment and she must do it again sometime. A rubbing together of fat thighs sounded as she moved away from me.

'What's up chuck … all been too much for you today? … I'm bloody knackered meself … She's spooky that one isn't she? All that greasy hair and those pussy spots on her face … they've thrown away the key for that one; she is never going anywhere.' Nodding in Ann's direction, an officer lit a cigarette, squeezing it to death between her lips and exhaling enough air for the both of us to be relieved the day was over. Dramatic gestures are decidedly less emphatic now that cigarettes have left the building. Everything seemed more animated with a Benson and Hedges. Lodged between fingers or grasped between a clenched fist, cigarettes could make patterns in the air, drop ash and get inhaled, enlarging nostrils to bullish proportions. Even more impressive were the heaving chests throwing out smoke and taking in all those poisons right in front of you. A heavy boot bashing and twisting flat a cigarette underfoot added a theatrical flourish; put an immediate end to unwanted conversation like a scornful full stop. Cigarettes were a social asset, always shared around, linking people together, until we found out more about them. Shamefully humbled now, evicted addicts group together outside buildings, furtively puffing on overprized cigarettes with death warnings decorating their packets.

I moved along to the woman next door and stood in her doorway.

'You can come in … sit down … dump those clothes on my bed.' Ingrid sipped a cup of wine from a plastic cup. Her large flat mouth curved up at each side and she glugged it down. She pushed away the remnants of a Chinese meal as I tried to take everything in without her noticing that I was being nosy. Such luxuries were the perks of remand prisoners in those days—a half bottle of wine a night and food sent in if you had the money, together with the telephone number of the local take-away.

'My compliments to the chef, although that wine was a bit too sweet for my taste,' she congratulated the air, smiled and came down to earth to stare at me.

'She's got a lot of stuff in this room, I thought, 'had I issued it all to her?' My face turned towards the window as easels drawing boards, knitting, paper, pencils, wool and drawings all stood before my eyes. My eyes turned back towards Ingrid via the floor taking further boxes, crammed full with creative materials. I tried to make all this visual curiosity part of my sitting down gesture, but I reckon my host had watched every twitch of my face. She was too bright not to notice my expression. If there was something in that jumble sale of activity that was forbidden, then she didn't care enough to attempt to hide it: just the cool aloofness and grace of the Lady of the Manor, ready to entertain. I didn't often visit the wings. It seemed intrusive I never felt comfortable. Ingrid could ignore such wariness, nothing much touched her, she had built a grey wall around herself, and she allowed no one to intrude.

Some of the inmates liked visitors to their rooms and showed off their private space and its contents. Their photos and the other bits of themselves would be exhibited proudly and often explained—something to do with the women wanting to fill up the void left by their sentence. It confirmed their existence prior to their incarceration. They needed something to be proud of, to make them smile and to bring back memories of the good times. They hoped their possessions might help reconnect them with some future life.

'How are you today Ingrid?'

'As you can see I am very comfortable, thank you.'

This was an upper-class inmate, and her superiority could be sensed through the uplifted nose and slightly sardonic smile. Behind her snooty gesture lay prejudice and intolerance and there was very little give in her words. She intended to use her time on remand constructively and this she certainly did, moving from one creative activity to another. Her hands wouldn't manoeuvre any brushes you couldn't paint with, so she turned down cleaning jobs, maintenance jobs or any others that might be viewed as remotely benefiting anyone else but herself. Besides, she didn't *have* to do it like the rest of the wing—she was still on remand, still innocent until proved guilty, and the jury and Mr. Judge hadn't yet decided her future. I never saw her succumb to the prison sloth. For every Ingrid cell you passed there were other cells of hibernating bodies, parcelled up in blankets, sleeping their days away. Half alive, they'd queue up at medicine time and beg for various pills to render themselves comatose so that they could spend yet more hours in bed. A lot of women spent their first weeks in prison like this, maybe some of them were coming off drugs but some of them just wanted to sleep their time away. I always felt that I could prod Ingrid a bit and push her humour around. Whatever else, she wasn't fragile.

'I wondered if you would like to put any drawings or paintings into the Koestler Competition this year … I know you're not convicted yet but I could be creative with the forms, we both know you're getting a long sentence.'

I didn't mean to be cruel. Ingrid knew that she was looking down a very long road when she finally met up with the judge. But that's the kind of thing I could say to Ingrid; somehow I could say exactly what I meant. And I had no qualms about my liberal interpretation of the rules governing potential Koestler exhibitors. To me it seemed madness to restrict the competition to convicted women. Some women on remand stayed there for months, even years. For the filling-in of the entry forms I was the judge and I sentenced the women myself to make sure they got a chance to participate. I too could bend the rules a tad.

'You can win prizes and sell your work … It's very fair … and a way in which you can get your work exhibited outside and earn a bit of money to boost your weekly spends. I was enthusiastic about the Koestler and it showed. There wasn't too much around to stimulate ideas, boost self-esteem and encourage prisoners, so I sold it as hard as I could.

Ingrid pulled up her eyebrows and, with the confidence of being on her own turf, turned towards her guest who was at this point having difficulty keeping her eyes away from the menagerie of muddle and activity displayed in her room. It would be so good to be able to view a wider perspective than is possible with the human eye. The chameleon fixes with one eye, giving the other the liberty to roam. If you had that sort of vision you wouldn't cause offence. It was just politeness that was stopping me from blatantly gawping , and the realisation that I might come across something that she shouldn't have or which she didn't want me to see, maybe something personal or private even. The notion that maybe someone was doing something that they shouldn't or were not allowed to do, or had something which wasn't permitted was part of the thinking of everyone in prison. What I made myself remember is that it goes on just as much outside prison, though it's less obvious, more diluted and doesn't seem so intense. Like when you're working out whether something is a con, or what the con is. Unless art materials were used destructively, then my tolerance ignored most other things that could be a bit iffy. It was a question of balance, like most things, and that attitude seemed to work. The institution had its own rules and the teachers functioned within different constraints; they had their own ethics. It was a shaky cohabitation where a dollop of commonsense was the most fitting attribute. Without that it would be impossible to find any creative ambience—some things had to be sacrificed. Such complicated clumps of consciousness always nagged away somewhere under my ribs. They came back from time-to-time, then I had to forget them, or I would have gone crackers and achieved nothing whatsoever.

Ingrid painted anything that she could see. Everything interested her and she tackled every project with a fierce will. Her best pictures were the prison scenes directly drawn from life, full of humour, distortion and truth. They were accomplished with confidence, fearless renditions that she didn't worry about, just enjoyed. Whereas others would hesitate about composition, perspective or other visual devices, she just blasted through those obstructions and discovered the real priorities.

'You see this watch?' Her arm rested on the table in front of me and her hand dripped over the side—her wrist lay exposed gently swaying to and fro as the watch caught the strip-lighting and flashed obediently. 'It's a Rolex, worth thousands, so I don't need the money … I have more than enough, but maybe I'll enter the competition nonetheless … it will look good on my parole reports, eventually.'

Her German accent slowed up the words, prolonged the sounds as she smiled across to me. Ingrid was far too cool to be enthusiastic about such meagre rewards as a few pounds, so the parole bit appealed to her. 'Go ahead choose something,' she said.

With my curiosity suddenly given sway to indulge, I scanned everything in her room: the paintings, drawings, sketches, collages, the lot—I peered and pried. It was such a creative heap of fascinating ideas, experiments, shapes and in-between there was research and study. Not to be glanced at briefly, I took my time, my own low budget Timex time, and left Ingrid to her after-dinner mints.

If you were Catholic, your name was on a blue card outside your cell, a Jew and you had a red one. If you were nothing in particular, your name got written on a white card. Mona's blue card had got her a special visit from the priest the previous week. She was a precarious resident on the Long-term Wing. Her state of mind put her into deep depressions and complex, introverted states of mind. The hospital wing had an open door policy for Mona and it comforted her to think that she got help when she was in need. Ever since she had been allocated her cell on the wing she had become convinced Ruth Ellis visited her at night. Everyone knew the story of Ruth and how she had murdered her lover and became the last woman to be hanged. The rest of the story was vague. Rumours rattled round the institution as to exactly where the execution took place and where her cell had been. Women scared each other with the possibilities and some staff reinforced the ghost stories with visions and sightings.

No one knew really knew where the gallows had been, nor the condemned cell where Ruth had last slept, but most people made wild guesses to big up the story. Tales of past dead residents got exaggerated, repeated and indulged in by present-day residents. Staff and inmates received sightings of ghosts and shadowy presences. It ignited the imagination of the vulnerable and Mona's mind was made for them—she believed any stories of the supernatural, in astral influences, in luck or fate. She would frighten herself even more by her choice of reading matter. Horror stories and science fiction books lined her shelves and others were reserved for her in the prison library. Finishing her cup of tea down to the last dregs she would read the soggy tea leaves too. When the officers weren't around, Ouija board sessions spread further fear, and if none of that worked, then out came the playing cards to unsettle the future. No wonder she was convinced the ghost of Ruth Ellis haunted her home. Poor Mona never seemed to sleep. One hand gripped her rosary and the other hugged her bible, but those malevolent spirits still inflamed her tortured soul.

It must have been their cold strength that kept Mona holding hands with the Holloway walls. One hand clung onto it even when she was eating. She walked up and down touching it in agitation, and the more she paced the smaller she appeared to be. Always the last to go into her room at night, her apparently decreasing stature was noticed with concern by the rest of her neighbourhood. Threads of wrinkles deepened as they gripped onto her superstitions and tightened her expression in a permanent knot of pain. Soon, everybody was worried. Everybody stared with anxiety as she passed by. There was a wonderful clergyman working in Holloway at the time, a kindly man and a tolerant soul who worked away quietly in his long black robes and shiny black shoes. So he was called in to help. And he followed his calling by blessing Mona's cell and exorcising whatever might be in there with his holy water and prayers—and it worked. It transformed Mona. She still found life too much of a puzzle, was still troubled and mystified and couldn't work things out, but Ruth Ellis had left her, Ruth had vacated Mona's room and moved on. Who knows what had happened. Whatever it was, it had worked.

A physical blast of heat forced my eyes closed. I squinted through the kitchen doorway and saw Mona organizing the wing suppers. Even in prison, the smell of singed bread is delicious and there was a conveyor belt of it on its way for distribution. In front of Mona on the stainless steel surface was a long, industrial-sized toaster. Slices popped up and down like piano keys. The hot bread jumped off her fingers and landed on a plate where it was trapped beneath a wedge of margarine, then grabbed by those in the queue before it got soggy and cold. Flippant wisecracks rose upwards as a descant to the intermittent dullness of the toaster. Mona kept control of both pressures, kept her nerve and kept everyone happy and amused.

Women were filling flasks with hot water, collecting huge plastic mugs of cocoa, clearing away the food trolley and disappearing back downstairs to the kitchen to join the queue. The evening ritual had begun. Women were gliding past me in fluffy slippers, wandering in and out of rooms, quietly moving from one task to another, slowing down as another day was ticked off the calendar.

'Night night, Sweetie-Pie.' Even the pet budgie on the wing had his own ceremonial ending to the day. A blanket was thrown over his cage—and that was that—a budgie doing time too. 'Oily Lips' slipped out a kiss towards the bird, while a big hand crammed itself into a jar of cocoa butter. She polished her magnificent black thighs, got into the many cracks and creases of her flesh, then made sure she hadn't missed a bit. With her other hand filled with more cream, she polished her other side and all its hidden bits. Yes, that calendar said her inter-prison visit was tomorrow. She'd circled it in red and chalked off every day before it. She inspected her red dress once again to make sure it was still there and held it up in front of her—that was to be a pleasure for her baby's father who was imprisoned in Pentonville Prison—pure hot pleasure! She wasn't going to wear her knickers on the visit—why should she, she didn't want to and she wasn't going to—no there was always a chance they might be left alone for a while, sometimes it happened. Officers guarding them might get called away and she wasn't going to deprive herself any more. She closed her eyes and, after a quick chat with the Lord, started thinking dirty.

It was a relief to be on this wing, it wasn't as loud and there was a kind of caring going on. Cells were decorated and attempts at home-making cosied the place up. Faith was knitting complex patterns with beautiful colours, her room a peaceful place with soft orchestra sounds from her radio. A pair of tights was dangling outside her window with lumpy white feet, heavy enough to ignore the slight breeze. This simple cheese-maker exemplified her self-sufficiency streak and green allegiances. In each nylon foot, white, curdy looking stuff drained between the heel and toe. To me it didn't look too like much of a success, but she reckoned it worked and it supplemented her diet with extra vitamins. She let me submit a wild, multi-coloured jumper to Koestler, but she didn't want it sold because it was for her mum. She didn't mind if it got a prize however.

'I'll fill in the entry form now Miss in case I don't see you for a while' She drew my eyes which settled on a fancy gadget from which she extracted a Biro. Decorated Tampax applicators had been stuck together accommodating a variety of pens and pencils. A tongue in cheek intention to patent this invention on release and a self-deprecating grin indicated the absurdity of the idea. 'And then maybe I could go into cheese production and make a million.' She shook out another grin towards the window and her dangling tights. We both grinned at her vivid imagination as I left her knitting ever more fantastic strategies for survival and continued on down the wing.

Pink light seeped out of the keyhole and I peered inside. Oh well, that was where my pink tissue paper had gone the other day. Dee had nicked it to 'up' the atmosphere in her den and attract a lover or two if they were passing by. It was stuck onto the light bulb with toothpaste. She lay on her bed, hands behind her head, waiting the wait of the trapdoor spider.

Serena beckoned me in quickly to her friend Usha's cell. Usha was sitting on the floor with her sari rolled up over her knees, taking the hairs off her legs. 'If you hang on a minute I won't be long … I've a couple of paintings I want to go in … they might win. You never know.' No razors were allowed—no wax, nothing was allowed in the prison that she could exfoliate with, but there she was doing it. There was a kind of cats cradle of cotton between her hands, so twisted that as her fingers moved up and down her legs the cotton shrank and stretched like elastic. The hands got closer and closer to her skin and as they did so the dark hairs on her legs were chopped off by the thread—it was an extraordinary sight.

'My mother used to do it this way and her grandmother—clever isn't it.' She dragged out some paintings from under her bed and asked me what I thought of them: 'Do they have a chance?' The first was of a man and a woman gazing longingly into each other's eyes, the woman with almond eyes, and the man a dark brooding expression, his mouth ever so slightly open. The second picture was again of a man and woman gazing longingly into each other's eyes, this time standing on a beach with the sun setting on the horizon. The third drawing was of a man and woman gazing longingly but this time under an apple tree in full blossom.

'I'm a romantic miss … Do say that they have a chance'.

'Of course they'll have a chance … they are extremely well drawn … of course they stand a chance'.

Donna was a talented lady, an eccentric and always smiling. She didn't want to be an artist, wouldn't know what they did or how they did it. She just loved painting, loved colours and animals. She laughed as she worked and didn't hoard her pictures. She gave them away to anyone who enjoyed them as much as she did. There she was in her room lolling on her bed giggling at something on the opposite wall. Coloured frogs appeared to be hopping up and down on her radiators. As one rose up another descended. It was a mobile display; a moving sculpture accidentally discovered and it was delightful. She'd painted the frogs on tissue paper and put them out to dry on the radiator. She'd made some green lily pads and they too had been put there. When the heating was switched on in the evening, the warmth rose, lifting the frogs up in the air and creating live theatre. She'd been watching it with fascination and I too became entranced by it all.

'You can take what pictures you like Miss, they're in that folder over there … take what you like, there's a couple on my pin-board over there.'

'What's this Donna?'

'Oh, that's got to last me the week, no spends this week, loss of privileges Miss, had a room spin, got found with a pencil sharpener.'

On the pin-board, propped up on top of a drawing pin was one solitary cigarette, measured with a Biro pen—like a ruler, but not in inches or centimetres but in days of the week: seven of them. So she rationed herself to segment of cigarette a day. It would be a bleak week.

'What a sad bitch I am, aren't I, one ciggie for the week?! … Have one for me when you're in the pub tonight Miss … Mine's a vodka actually Miss … Mines a lot of vodkas.' Donna turned back to her jumping frogs.

'Maybe that's all for tonight,' I thought as the corridor narrowed. I inspected a long line of brooms hanging onto a wall by large hooks.

'DEFLUFF ALL BROOMS AFTER USE.'

Each brush hung vertical to the floor, straight, erect and dust free. They were resting after their working day and in pristine condition as per the instructions. A frothy, filmy baby doll purple nightdress wobbled across my path with a hot water bottle clutched somewhere around the waist. Dee strode out of her cell dragging on a roll-up, in men's pyjamas with a cup of cocoa in her hand. There had been no takers, no-one caught in her web tonight. She was a bit pissed off, she said, but there was always tomorrow, yes there were going to be a lot of tomorrows. She was overtly in love with Mavis, who was wiggling her way to Mr. Sandman in leopard skin slippers, with three inch heels. A transparent film of silk hid nothing. With one hand on her hip, the other holding a lighted cigarette she blew kisses and shifted Dee's hormones into a state of tortuous anarchy. Mavis was driving Dee mad with lust. The compulsive gambler on the wing watched like she was at the racing-track and weighed the odds as to how long it would take for the one to catch up with the other and consummate her victory.

A dumpy figure in a candlewick dressing gown shuffled away from me. The bottom of her gown trailed on the floor keeping her feet out of sight as were her arms. She was just a beige mobile. Her head was made huge by jumbo pink plastic rollers. Heavy metal grips held them in place and they stuck out all over like television antennae. She could have been a clockwork toy winding down the day, jerking from side-to-side and disappearing into her little home.

Everyone started to move that bit faster. Up and down the wing, steamy figures wrapped for drying struggled out of the shower room with bottles of this that or the other in slippery hands. The sound of firm, solid, heavy shoes provided the bass beat to the flipping and flapping of slippers and bare feet. The grating metallic sound of lock-in formed the percussion signalling the enforced end to the evening's ceremonies. The curtain came down on the day and the house lights were extinguished. Rejoining those moving bodies, I looked down at the mesh suicide nets between the wings. These veils blurred the images above and beneath, but sounds surged through them to invade other levels and landings. Odd balls of this and that hung suspended in the middle, thrown there by someone, like pebbles into the sea. Bits of detritus dangled off the netting. Tissues and toilet paper could float down onto the next floor with an extra vibration to encourage their descent. It was a deep, deep descent.

I waited in the wings and looked up and down for a space to join in the chorus line. I slotted in, keeping in step and was absorbed into the composition. Holding tightly onto the central hand-rail I whirled round and round downwards, synchronising with a fellow worker. We exchanged nods and she slipped into my empty step and started her journey down swirling round that metallic maypole. Others waited patiently in the wings and fell into step. With no room to overtake, the dancers slipped into a routine choreographed to perfection. With superb timing we crunched on the iron spiral staircase, rhythmically rustling and swishing our costumes, ascending and descending. The official metronome for that day strained her neck upwards into the spotlight from her glass office in The Centre and assessed our performance. Nobody was out of line, pushing in, or spoiling the flow.

Now that all their front doors were locked up for the night, resourceful prisoners fraternised from their back windows. Pass the parcel wasn't strictly a game, it was more like target practice, a way to export merchandise on the end of a string along the outside wall to the customer at the next window. A couple of hands and knees were poking out of the bars that separated the narrow strips of transparent plastic. The swing of the pendulums had started to build up momentum until they heard my footsteps, then just a hushed silence. But I was not an officer, just a civilian so the parcel passing revved up again regardless of my presence. Inaccuracy and failure however were inevitable, dissatisfied grunts at their ineptitude disabled the steeplejacks; hysterical rage had the same effect because it was a skill made more successful with practice and without the pressure of discovery. The tension could get too much because it was a reportable offence, this independent postal service.

Officers were due any minute on their regular inspections. Apart from that it was a dangerous undertaking hanging half out of the cell window, legs, arms and face all precariously balanced to throw and catch swaying parcels. It caused all kinds of bruising, scratching and scrapes. The prisoners' verbal efforts would reverberate off the outside walls as in some slapstick comedy turn. My umbrella book always accompanied me on my outside sojourns to the Mother and Baby Wing in case failed deliveries dropped my way or, even worse, unsavoury refuse. 'Swinging' would become a dying art when the windows were all sealed up to make way for air conditioning. Little did we know this at the time or we could have looked forward to the new clean grounds, the lack of detritus and culling of rats.

The Mother and Baby Wing kept itself pretty much to itself for obvious security reasons. It was an independent society living life at a different pace from the rest of the prison. All visitors had to be vetted. I delivered equipment that's all, and classes were mostly post-natal and in childcare. No, I couldn't come into the wing, I might disturb the babies, but I could stand in the hall and wait in case any of the mothers had anything for me. Hushed and with almost an out-of-prison feeling to it, I waited amongst the prams. One lady came out with a drawing of her baby, taken from a photo, obviously traced and not very well done. She smiled up at me, looking for a positive response.

'Have you done all this yourself?'

'Goodness … how old is your daughter?'

'She's beautiful.'

I took her details, got the appropriate signature and was released from the wing. Ready for the return dash, my eyes caught sight of a pair of intrepid abseilers. A head was pressed against the plastic windows and bits of it popped out between the bars monstrously deforming the woman's features. The same arrangement was mirrored slightly further away. One hand held a long piece of string with a parcel at the end of it. But the woman was taking too long and getting nervous, her hands were shaking and her sight wasn't that good.

The pendulum continued to swing and the parcel kept returning. Nervousness was turning to anger and excuses defended the receiver's lack of skill. The string shook and quaked in the middle of the feud. It was the sender's fault, she was swinging too fast and the parcel had started to come undone. It wasn't near enough to the wall, so how could the other woman possibly catch it just by putting an arm out of her cell window. But she wasn't that articulate, she'd leant out too far and hurt her shoulder and her confidence was failing so it came out in abusive insults. Reciprocated abuse swung back along the trembling string and the anger shook it even more. Under frustrated breaths both tried to extend their short attention spans. I don't think it was skill that finally ended the game, it was the receiver's attempt to silence the humiliating taunts that fired her up to want to grab the perpetrator herself—and bugger the parcel! It was merely coincidental that the string twisted around her arm and she could haul in her bounty. With a triumphant pull she claimed her prize, jerking her friend enough to graze her face. Then the two figures bumped against their windows, damaged their knees on the stone walls and heaved their cramped and bruised body parts back inside their cells. Until the next pre-arranged delivery and collection. It was forbidden to play this game, just like it was to use the Ouija board. I raised my book again to protect my head and made my final dash. My shift was over.

It was such a relief to be outside the prison, refreshing and restorative. Opposite was the Holloway Castle. Perhaps the name paid tribute to the original design of the prison. I'd only been into it once. It was seedy and gloomy, just like the prison. Then there was the local café, where inmates enjoyed their first out-of-prison experiences or where visitors psyched themselves up to knock on those huge wooden doors to visit captive loved ones. I put my head down only wanting the repetitious pavement to occupy my vision—and trudged home.

'Don't tell anyone I work here … please don't say anything.' Strange figures moved around me, others in the distance were in slow motion, drinking out of cups and gliding trance-like around me. I was in some kind of Escher architectural folly—all staircases rising out of nowhere. Walls changed shape and rooms fell away from me in a maze of corridors without windows. Hands pushed in front of me then metamorphosed into legs that changed into steps rising up. The faces were all contorted but acting normally and to avoid attention I'd try and join that comparative ordinariness. But the catacombs prevented me. However hard I tried to work out the complex walkways and tunnels I could not leave. 'I shouldn't be in here, I really shouldn't, so don't say that you've seen me.' I tried to hide but one person after another watching me in my disturbed state did nothing. I tried again and again to convince them; they kept seeing me but saying nothing. None of the rooms made sense. I'd been sent to the wrong place but could do nothing about it. Everyone could see me, however hard I tried to hide.

It didn't take much to analyse this as just one of those midnight horror movies that haunts the mind in the middle of the night when you're asleep. The little scene with Ann wasn't going to be forgotten—it was still shuffling morbidly around inside my head, nestling in some secret corner ready to reproduce itself in the darkness. It is so familiar now to me that I can find my own way out of that maze. I can eject myself from its horrors so that I won't slip back into those corridors or climb those impossible stairs.

Arthur Koestler visited the Long-term Wing in the old prison. He came in on his own and was just left there—something in itself momentous. He was to hold a discussion with the long-term inmates and it would be accessible to all residents on the wing. Anyone could go in for a chat if they wanted to and all the women did, there was no selection. Nothing was choreographed to put on some false show or impression. He stood alone, without minders. I certainly wanted to go and just before the event I sneaked in next to a cupboard by the door. The talk was animated, the questions freely spoken, the answers direct and a good discussion finished the session. There was no awkwardness, it was all very easy. He talked about his life, and the competition which he had started. Women listened and he listened to the women. My hand went up in the queue to ask questions. As I steadied myself to start my question, my back pushed the cupboard door open and everything fell out over me. Laughter engulfed the proceedings. Women shrieked and giggled.

I remember Arthur Koestler's words on the different types of humour in his book, *The Act of Creation*. He devoted a whole chapter to this and in my embarrassment I read the one bit in my head that applied to that very moment. It is where he describes the humour that is used to put someone down, so that others can rise up. The humour that ridicules, which is used to humiliate people, so that the audience can feel superior. And this *was* such a situation, it was made for that chapter and I was the fool and I hated that. I had made such a bad impression. I looked across at him through my confusion and embarrassment as the shelf emptied over me. He never flinched, not a smirk, nor could a hint of a smile be seen. His face just signalled a dignified wait whilst I recovered enough to carry on. I was aware of the jeers and the laughter, but there was not a hint that it had destroyed his composure. So I was grateful for that and held onto that look until all the falling stopped and I could ask my question. And that's another reason why I would always support the competition that he started.

CHAPTER 3

Occupational Therapy

'Mary Reid's back.'

These words were moaned despairingly along the line of grey Home Office tables and the Holloway Prison reception officers sagged over them in unison, turned their heads and peered down the corridor as Mary, recidivist par excellence, re-occupied her time-share in Holloway for the holiday break. Two blue uniforms stepped out from the police van handcuffed together by two skinny arms. From somewhere in the middle a clattering and scraping hopped and jumped between their long determined strides. Rebellious little kicks protested ineffectively, so did the spits and oaths but they missed their targets and went ignored. The two enormous officers unlocked their diminutive captive and abandoned her inside the prison to wait for the welcoming party in Reception. Mary rubbed her wrists, readjusted the straps on her shoes and prepared herself for the familiar faces and the routine she knew only too well.

There was nothing subtle about Mary. A dog's hind leg of a parting separated the grey hairs growing out of black raven dye which had been administered too long ago. Her violent black eyebrows had been drawn in, badly, over purple eye shadow. Yellow false teeth jiggled around and fought to stay in place as she gave her details and answered familiar questions in-between clicking noises. Her lipstick had leaked from her mouth, filling in the furrows around it. As she filled in the boxes with a shaky pen and a face that could just about see over the counter, strings of white spit formed bars from the top lip to the bottom and stretched thinner as the teeth slid around her gums. An earthquake of coughing rumbled up from Mary's ribs now and then in an effort to dislodge the tar deposits caused from decades of smoking. Shrunken tattoos decorated the folds of her skin; blue wrinkly pictures which had shrunk over the years from clear images on her once youthful arms.

A last ciggie was suffocated in a prison ash tray with bony yellow fingers. Her own mobile light show, she glittered in oversized simulated leather trousers which sagged over her droopy backside. Through a feathery camisole, silver stretch marks wrapped themselves around her 32A empty cups. She clattered along the corridor in gold high-heeled shoes that badly needed mending, stilettos which prodded the floor and dimpled the prison lino with their metal spikes. She tottered haphazardly, bumping into one side of the corridor and then back and across into the other, zigzagging her heel prints as other prison officers waited behind a curtain for the next stage of her induction.

Mary was stripped; more thoroughly so than any other inmate. She was also searched more thoroughly. Everything was taken from her except her basic clothing. The bottom set of her false teeth was extracted with a slick flick of her tongue and slipped inside a plastic bag held by an officer with out-stretched hands and flared nostrils. Extra leverage eventually unlodged the top set as two bony, yellowy forceps wedged firmly behind the half-denture and prized away the suction. Mary's closed eyes couldn't witness this proce-dure. They were kept scrunched shut until the extra weight delivered them. The teeth were given a name and number and 'bagged' on a shelf together with the rest of Mary's property. Finally registered as a *bona fide* resident of Holloway Prison, she was escorted to her sleeping quarters. The two officers who brought her in sighed with relief that their responsibilities for this noto-rious new intake were now discharged. They could officially pass the buck.

Mary's first night in custody was spent doubled up with Ruby. The door banged behind them both. An officer peeped through the spy hole and moni-tored Mary's reaction, slowly locking them both inside for the night. The door clicked shut but the eye watched on. Inside, Mary first perched on the edge of her bed then propped herself up with a pillow and some bedclothes to remind herself of the comfort of her new apartment. Balancing more securely, she looked around and fixed on Ruby's tobacco tin which stood out of reach on Ruby's locker. A hawk with black dyed plumage, her eyes contemplated the tin as her toothless mouth rummaged around her gums like a neutered beak. Ruby lay back on her bed, perfected her roll-up, lit it and blew out an explosion of smoke. She was irritated by this intruder who was trying to destroy her privacy with stares. Prison wasn't about making friends, why shouldn't she ignore her? The eye through the hatch observed a silent peaceful tableau. Numbers and names outside the door corresponded accurately with the two silent occupants, both resting on their respective beds. The eye observed the scene for a while longer. Mary moved her head towards Ruby then settled on the tobacco tin, then back to Ruby and back to the tin. God she hated being watched, it was bad enough to have the spy hole in the door. Someone was always snooping, always spying, and on top of that some fixated roommate was now staring and gagging for a ciggie.

Ruby's irritation grew. Her rule was not to give thing out without knowing for definite that she'd get it back. So she was going to stick to her resolution. 'Fuck 'er', she thought, 'I don't even know the woman.' It was *her* tobacco, nobody else's and it was going to stay that way. She drew on a deep breath and blew out a ferocious gust of smoke, emptying her lungs. Mary watched as Ruby dimmed her eyes in nicotine ecstasy. But Room 19 was safe and secure now and the other dormitories were the same. All that was left for the officers there was for the diary to be written up. The patrol officer clinked her way back along the corridor to her office.

'Maybe I could give the poor bitch me' butt,' thought Ruby, a sense of benevolence germinating somewhere in the smokescreen, now the eye had moved on. 'No, fuck it, no way . . . not even twos up; don't know if she's got something catching'. Then she sneaked a stare at Mary and saw that desperate longing for the old cancer stick. Mary was twitching nervously, still fixated on the tobacco tin, then Ruby took another quick glance at her roommate. 'Ah Jesus, can't bloody well relax even on me' own bed … in me' own room, for Christ's sake' Ruby tried to forget and rested her head back on her pillow, but took yet another peek and Mary was still there, 'Effin' intruder'.

'Take it then, just bloody well take a roll-up then, just get off me back and give it a rest.' Ruby heaved herself up, leant over and shoved the tin onto Mary's bony lap. Her strength knocked Mary off balance and the tin nearly slipped onto the floor. Ruby returned to her ciggy and decided to regain her prone position facing the wall. Scrawny hands with bulging veins slowly examined the tin and emptied all the tobacco out on to the table. 'Bloody hell she'd better not be using up all me baccy on one bleedin' ciggie,' Ruby looked furtively over her shoulder. Then, with all the strength of her ageing frame, Mary bent the lid, again and again, pressed it flat on the table, bent it, folded it , then pushed it between her gums and with great effort and a series of gulps she swallowed it. At one point, she lurched forward making as if to be sick, her eyes filling with tears, and she stopped breathing for a moment. She turned her face directly at Ruby with widening, panicky eyes and waited for her lungs to start up again. Ruby caught her look and widened her own eyes too and waited for Mary not to die. After further contortions of her throat, grotesque sucking-in noises and the complete disappearance of her lips, Mary's body relaxed, the tin moved down to the roomier compartment in her chest and her breathing resumed its regular rhythm. She then took the bottom of the tin and repeated the procedure. Ruby had lost the capacity to blink. Her eyelids had locked open at the monstrous scene she was witnessing. Her eyes stuck open wider than they had ever done in their life. The whole Golden Virginia tin had descended down that human pelican's neck and into its digestive tract.

Ruby slid against the wall and pressed the emergency bell. Her eyes were still rigidly open and so was her jaw. It clamped hold of one explicit profanity and repeated it over and over again. Whereas all her breathing equipment seemed to have become paralysed, her mobility had compensated with uncontrollable spasms. Mary just sat on the bed readjusting her mouth and throat as if to get comfortable again, she wasn't looking anywhere, just had her eyes down frowning until a trickle of blood oozed out from between her lips. At this Ruby hurled her battered body at the bell again, upping the volume to an unbearable level. She screamed, threw her shoes against the wall, tried to lift up her bed, rattle it and bang it on the floor. She wanted the noise to muffle her shakes. She needed to knock out of her mind the image she had just seen—anything to replace the sight of Mary devouring her tobacco tin. What she really wanted to do was run, just run anywhere but she couldn't, she could only make more noise, crash things together and exhaust herself of energy. The rest of the wing caught the anxiety and joined in the percussion, banging whatever they could lay hands on. Anxiety turned to hysteria as an entire prison orchestra caught the rhythm without knowing why they were performing. They only knew that they were nervous and trapped and so everyone banged, harder and harder.

At last somebody responded, the landing officer, the evening patrol, the eye, first on the scene unlocked the door.

'Fuckin' muppet ... fuckin' muppet, fuckin' mad bitch, get 'er out of 'ere, fuckin' mad bitch! ... She's fuckin' swallowed my baccy tin, all of it, swallowed a fuckin' tin, look at 'er she's effin' bleedin' get 'er out of 'ere ... get 'er out of 'ere!-fuckin' mad cow'. Ruby's chest thrust into the officers uniform, the nearness providing some safety and normality. Only then could she point over to the crisis. Mary was sitting on her bed with the blood still trickling down from her mouth and Ruby continued to squawk around her calling her a 'Fucking muppet', screeching about the whereabouts of her precious tin and swearing at the officer for not coming sooner. She hated the prison, yelling, 'It's done me head in ... being doubled up with this, mad bitch!'

'I'm going to sue, I am, I'm going to sue'. A second officer flew round the corner and collided inwards. Ruby threw herself at his chest and clung on. 'She's swallowed a tobacco tin,' she screamed again and buried herself in the rough blue jacket.

'What ... the whole tin? ... How long ago?'

'Just now ... I bleedin' watched it go down.'

'Keep her airways clear.'

'What! ... Keep her airways clear ... you jokin' or something ... she's swallowed a tobacco tin!!!'

'Have you rung the ambulance?'

'Course I have'

'Look out … catch her, catch her'.

Too late. Mary flopped and slid off the bed, dragging the sheet down between her sinewy fingers. Room 19 was filling up now with officers and nurses. Relieved of their boredom, the rest of the prisoners on the wing were screaming too, but without knowing why or what for. The panic quickly stampeded its way through the whole prison, each landing catching it and adding to the mayhem with whatever objects made the greatest din, still in ignorance of the reason. At the top of the Holloway Road the Whittington Hospital was preparing to accelerate the sound levels and join the prison percussion section. The ambulance was crewed up and already responding to an emergency phone call.

'I want compensation, she's done my 'ead in, it shouldn't be allowed … I want compensation'. Ruby, angry one minute and terrified the next, always had a canny eye for the main chance. 'For Christ's sake grab her, don't let her fall, catch her,' one officer screamed hysterically to the other. Too late—Mary slid down even further, still entangled in the sheet she landed in a ragbag of folds on the prison lino. Desperately trying to disentangle Mary from the sheet in one quick move, an officer assessed the situation. It would be quicker to take the whole lot. The bundle that was Mary swayed in the arms of one of Her Majesty's prison officers, still caught up in the prison sheet: It trailed behind her like a wedding gown. The sound of an approaching siren urged them to quicken their pace. They raced off the wing and down to the main gate which was by now lit up by blue flashing lights which reflected off the walls of the prison and gave the watching audience, peering from their narrow windows, an intermittent view into the prison yard. The white bundle was passed over to the medical experts, doors banged; doors opened and gates grated shut. The ambulance sped through the night, through red traffic lights, over zebra crossings, past the Nags Head and up to the hospital.

All alone now in the darkened cell, Ruby rummaged on the floor for her tobacco which lay scattered all over the place due to the hurricane just departed. The after-shock was still affecting her; it was still making waves along her quivering body. Whatever she found she was going to smoke, she didn't care what it was, she needed a cigarette. Mumbling on nervously she vowed vengeance. 'Well that's mine now.' The redundant blanket was transferred across from Mary's bed to warm up Ruby's feet. 'And I'll have that as well' The extra pillow would cushion he head nicely. She took Mary's soap and flannel and anything else that would help to settle the score. 'I want compensation, she's done me 'ead in, mad cow, fuckin' hell, swallowing *my* bleedin' tin … cheeky bitch, *my* fuckin' tin … I'll sue, I really will'. Pushing her findings into a kind of lozenge shape she rolled it in a Rizla paper and made a weak effort to stick it together with her dry, frightened mouth. She covered herself in the blanket and pulled her knees up to her chin. The eye shone a torch through the hatch onto the lit ciggie and located Ruby's head at the end of it.

'OK Ruby?'

'Fine Miss, no problem … cushti,' The twilight chorus no longer distracted by the chaos reverted to their familiar evensong. Ruby listened calmly as inmates reconnected with their previous raucous conversations, window-to-window, across to the flats opposite, chatting to the night sky, making plans with the moon and cursing guards on night patrol. Her shakes eased now with the comfort of Holloway's own particular lullaby.

So many operations on her stomach extracting other metallic meals had left Mary with scar tissue and little else. During her many visits to Holloway—all for minor offences, she had devoured various items. She could eat anything from drawing pins to nuts and bolts or bed springs. She had eaten her own false teeth so many times that they were always taken off her on arrival, her repeated new dentures never fitted properly, and they wouldn't last anyway. Efforts to evacuate glass, pins and needles 'naturally' were made using damp bread soaked in Marmite. If this did not work then yet another operation on her poor, scarred stomach would be needed. For long periods of time she functioned fairly normally on the outside. But life got lonely, especially at Christmas and Mary would behave in some anti-social way to manoeuvre herself back into either Holloway or some other institution that would take over her life for a while until she felt able to reclaim responsibility for herself.

After the incident, Mary was returned to prison with yet more stitches holding her fraying stomach together and was given a single cell down in the Segregation Block, below stairs. Her clothes were replaced by a strip dress made out of grey padding. She had a mattress on the floor with an equally grey padded blanket and a cardboard potty stood on the floor. The room was bleak and dark, a subterranean eerie where graffiti decorated the walls. Mary was now at the bottom of the prison chain, a real class system, alongside other criminals who had committed offences inside the prison. Her neighbours were the worst in the hierarchy, the rejects of rejects, including women who had committed offences against children. At the top were the white-collar criminals. The more money they had tried to get away with, the higher-up they were on the institutional rungs. Many women prisoners were isolated in the block from time-to-time and for different reasons. Mary had now joined the mass of lost souls, rattling around the pit of the prison, offering their mouths up for repeated medication and their bums for repeated injections.

Going to the dungeons of Holloway meant a whole different lifestyle for inmates previously on normal location. Their days were spent in occupational therapy where they would associate with other women who were sick and heavily medicated, or those coming in from the courts with long, long sentences who were kept there for observation prior to medical reports. Their evenings from four o'clock were spent locked up in the castle dungeons. Some women where even further down in this stony strata. They were the ones still shivering with the cramps of drug withdrawal; whilst yet others were isolated because they might be a danger to other prisoners or themselves, or too vulnerable to tolerate any kind of social interaction.

Excesses of rage and all life's injustices were heaped on the women imprisoned for offences against children. In such a brutalising place they were sought out and hurt, often by women who themselves had neglected their own children. Staff had been known to take part in such retribution. Blind eyes pulled blinds down in offices providing a no-witnesses–no-go-area for institutional revenge down some deserted alley of a corridor. Subsequent facial damage was appropriately noted down in the 'Accident Book'. The well-heeled inmates rarely escaped without some antagonism.

One tabloid front pager arrived at the front gates warmed by her lush mink coat. Black plastic lashes curled up and winked at the cold grey griffin door-men. Out of her cell one day, the coat was left unattended and 'spontaneously combusted'. Mysteriously it happened without witnesses. Only the collar could be salvaged. Unperturbed by this setback, the lady in question incurred even more jealousy and envy by appearing in the dining-room that evening wearing just the fur collar, together with a shimmering little black number and the highest of high heels. Not used to her dark roots showing, this pharmaceutical blond outwitted the prison rules, which strictly forbade any change of hair colouring while in custody. She could charm the pants or knickers off anybody with her mascara hedges, provocative eyes, long legs and low bodices. She kept up her blond hair by bartering for bleach tablets from the kitchen cleaner and mixing these with her own urine. She reckoned it worked and certainly I never saw a dark root on her head. What favours she did in return she kept to herself, but she never went without during her entire prison sentence.

I passed Mary's home on one of my grim voyages to the Occupational Therapy Unit—'fun-time' for the occupants living below stairs. I saw her standing in a dreary patch of light. She was absolutely still, with her head down and her hands to her side. Her strip dress was stained and hung off her. Her medication was so strong that it had ensnared her in an invisible space. She was pale and thin. Her little legs stood uncomfortably together, oddly shaped. I peered closer. They were both heavily scarred with blue-red wounds, which stretched and twisted around both legs, like roots growing up from the floor, trapping her into immobility. I looked away and upwards towards the piti-ful light source. Pigeons were trying to hold on to the bars of her broken windows, but deformed claws from some man-made poison kept them from getting a good hold. White dribbles of pigeon excrement stained parts of the wall. The room stank. Her carers in the office looked up from their paperwork at the end of the wing. Mary's legs, oh they had been damaged in a fire. She had got depressed, wanted to die and had rubbed shoe polish all over her body, and then set light to herself. The fire had only affected her legs by the time help had arrived. No, she couldn't have any visitors yet.

'You don't know me, at least I don't think you do, I'm the art teacher, and would you like a drawing book and some materials?' If I wasn't going to be allowed to see Mary then someone else might profit from the art packs I was distributing. The hatch next door was open and I spoke through the slit to a mound of material on the floor.

'Did you knock?'

'No, sorry,' I tapped a knuckle against her door. 'Who are you … What do you want?' I repeated my introductory speech. 'Never heard of you … What have you got?' The voice spoke out from behind a strip blanket which was draped over a head on the floor—the body completely engulfed and the woman looking straight towards me. Well I thought it was a body. I could just about discern her form under the thick material. Her arms were resting on her knees and her head sometimes dropped forwards and sometimes lent backwards moving the blanket into ghostlike forms. I explained my wares towards what I thought might be her face. Someone underneath the blanket spoke, puffing the fabric in and out as it got trapped in her mouth after each word. 'Well if that's all, no fags or sweets, then you can bugger off. I'm not at home today, might be in tomorrow … get lost whoever you are.'

Segregated by the institution from the rest of the prison, for whatever reason, the woman had constructed her own world and gained control over her social life. What else could I do but leave her alone? Continuing on, I passed down the wing, eyes peering at me on both sides through hatches in the doors, voices asking for a light or a cigarette. Those slits in the door were only big enough for a third of the face at a time: foreheads pressed out, or noses, or eyes, Holloway's battery hens. Lunches were being distributed, arms reached out and plastic plates heaped with plastic food disappeared into open mouths in dark cells. Plates of unwanted food got slung through the bars for pigeons to continue the food chain before rats completed the process. 'The Muck Truck' got pushed along and unloaded its culinary fodder.

Two wobbly, plaster moulded Alsatian dogs sat on the floor, roughly painted and placed on either side outside a cell door. Leftovers from occupational therapy recreational hours, those dogs were two of the few I'd managed to pull out of their moulds with all four legs intact. That surprised me. The dogs' legs were the most difficult to remove because they were too long and thin. I tried to get a closer look but was stopped by an imperious command from on high. A pair of eyes emerged through the hatch.

'You come a step further towards this door and I'll set these dogs onto you, they're killers, real killers they'll do anything I say. Once they get a grip they don't let go, I'm warning you so clear off now.' I looked at the eyes to find the voice. They must have seen my whole presence from that slit. Did she know me? Who was she, had I taught her? Did I know her? How had she acquired the dogs? I didn't recognise those solitary eyes, not without the other features, it was impossible. I stood back and wondered if it was some joke. Was she laughing? I couldn't tell.

'Clear off over there, don't come near me … I won't say it again.' I backed away to the opposite wall and did what I was told. The two Alsatians remained outside, silently keeping vigil and I looked down half expecting them to growl. 'Stay … good dogs. Stay.' Further instructions weren't forthcoming, just a pair of eyes staring outwards. If I could hold onto her eyes she wouldn't notice that the rest of me was moving on, that was my plan anyway. We watched each other and I slithered along the wall. Her eyes moved along the slit following me and we kept moving along like that, staring into each other's eyes. With silent shoes I slipped from her vision keeping close to the wall. I tiptoed onwards until I heard the faceless eyes congratulate her loyal Alsatians and I realised I was off the hook. 'Good dogs … Good dogs.'

'I'll have one of those, if there's one spare.' An unfamiliar inmate stopped me and asked for a book. The officer standing next to her nodded approval. Dipping bread into a huge mug of what seemed like hot soup the seated prisoner gulped heavily and swallowed.

'You must try and eat it all,' said the officer, closely supervising each mouthful.

'This is disgusting, really disgusting.'

'Just eat it ... leave that stuff in the office, and get it checked.' She gave orders to both of us and continued to gauge the consumption of the bread.

'Can I issue these to that lady there in the corridor?'

'Is that all ... absolutely nothing else?'

The wing officer closed the door so that we were in private. She sat down and reached for a big book and made an inventory of my presents.

'No, that's it, that's all, nothing else.'

'Take the staples out of that drawing book, then she can have it ... she swallows things, there's a couple of drawing pins inside her somewhere, she just does it all the time, those staples could do damage.'

'Are the pencils and eraser OK?'

'No problem ... I'll give them to her after she's had her Marmite and bread, it cushions the damage, we just have to monitor everything ... if it doesn't work she'll need to have an x-ray ... are all the staples out? Put them in the bin then, wrap them up first though.'

Further and further down those dark corridors I arrived at the underground entertainment with the occupational therapist as the compère. I pierced the door with my key and uncorked Hades. It was a cacophony of captive wildlife trapped together for meaningless activities. As the courts dispensed punishment, so the birds flocked inside. As one species migrated out to different institutions, others would replace it as justice was seen to be done. It housed forty women (often more), three officers (sometimes), an occupational therapist and two teachers (sometimes). Too few staff and too few resources, too many inmates in too small a space. Too big a job. Women paced up and down, paced up and down again, wild and deranged, in long strides, Other occupants rocked on their feet, or rocked sitting down, whilst others shuffled heaps of crumpled paper in front of them, making it into piles, then crumpling them further, then straightening them out, then crumpling them again, then straightening them out, repeatedly. Others stood up, shifting from one leg to another, swaying from side-to-side.

During the chaos of moving house, a few young women on the Borstal Wing found themselves sent down to the Occupational Therapy Unit for a day's activities. Eighteen year old fire-crackers, they were frightening some of the more vulnerable souls and angering other women into near punch-ups. It was up to me to give them the attention they sought and that would otherwise be gained by being troublesome towards the other inmates. In a small alcove off the main room I spread out paper on a couple of desks and some on the floor. Energetic, mischievous and irritating those young offenders were to the other worried souls who were trying to find tranquillity. Children, really, progressing up their empty educational ladder from their equally empty home life. They'd get used to the prison, even get to enjoy it, making memories which they would later recall with nostalgia, like people remember their days in the army.

The alcove they were in had once been used as a sluice room or toilet. The open drains remained intact, but the door connecting it to the main hall had been removed. One student lay down on the paper while another drew round her whole body. Conjuring up any role model or fantasy creature that inspired them, the idea seemed to be that the student would create her own full-length portrait. Not exactly what I had planned, but teamwork was involved and the thought that it could support the rest of the staff and help to accommodate the exuberance of the young offenders presented an opportunity for me to demonstrate my flexible repertoire and my ability to rise to any occasion. 'Just use up their energy, tire them out, keep them away from the rest; just deal with them'. That was my professional brief.

Through the alcove, the swaying reeds of demented souls rocked and paced in relative peace now. Inside, multi-coloured drips slipped down the walls onto swirling puddles. Hand prints climbed along the paper, red flame coloured kisses pouted and screamed primitive print-marks on to the white cartridge paper. Then getting more adventurous they took their socks and shoes off and walked footprints around and compared and contrasted their efforts. They mixed up all the prints and danced on the paper, so that the paints intermingled in pearlised silver and gold. Two eyes remained fixed and steadfast absorbed in our activity: Gladys the knitter tucked well into the back of her chair, watched from a room outside. The distracting movement of her fellow patients didn't change her vigilance, nor did her rhythmic, oscillating hands which were creating a masterpiece with variegated wools. Intermittent jerks for more wool didn't cause her to cast her eyes down, nor did she need visual proof of accuracy. She could knit blindfold. Squinty eyes regarded me suspiciously. Her fingers knobbly with arthritis, they flung the wool up and around, strangling the needles. This audience of one sat motionless knitting and watching. Puffs of white hair popped out from a turban scarf tied at the back with a knot. It trembled a bit with the rapidity of her hand, especially when she yanked on the wool. From time-to-time she crept back and forth in the doorway, then hovered like a nosy bee whirring her needles. Just like a compass, she would twist on her axis, her eyes always pointing north towards the occupants of the alcove and me. Her bottom set of teeth stuck out in front of her top set, making her lower lip protrude in the form of a shelf. Propped on the shelf was an old deflated roll-up which she would smack with her misaligned lips in an attempt to revive it. The chipped varnish ends of her fingernails added a flash of scarlet to her knitting. You could work out how long a woman had been in prison by the stage at which the varnish had grown out, half-and-half, about a month—it was like counting the age of a tree by the number of rings. Those deformed fingers created soft intricate patterns, exotic stitches, exquisite workmanship. But inside her head was a malicious demon making mischief and she had targeted the activity in the alcove.

The borstal girls powered on with their alter egos determined to shock the lights out of all of us, with images of enormous breasts, scanty clothing, anything provocative. At the end after all the clearing up each teenager rolled up her fantasy image to take back to the unit. We waited to be let off the wing. 'That went well,' thought I, 'a success.' I had allowed those tormented souls to pace up-and-down in peace, allowed everyone their space, segregated the borstal girls from the others and entertained those of a more potentially destructive nature. No incidents—a good session's work. Then I felt this almighty kick to my rear and twisted round to catch Madame Desfarge executing her own brand of punishment with her foot to my behind. Still knitting she would have inflicted another kick if I hadn't swerved away.

'You're an apology for an art teacher you are, you're a disgrace, you shouldn't be allowed.' That sort of achievement you keep to yourself. But it was an awesome kick even in slippers. My lurch forward had slightly disturbed the woman in front of me but her poor mind was elsewhere. It was an inglorious finale made less humiliating only because nobody witnessed the assault. A month later I was helping Gladys parcel up the most beautiful pair of knitted white downy socks of delicate filigree. We wrapped them up in soft tissue and enclosed the whole in strong brown paper. I addressed the gift on the instructions of Gladys with a little note from her wishing him well and sent the parcel off addressed to 'His Holiness the Pope, Vatican City, Italy'.

During the two-hour sessions down in the Occupational Therapy Unit there would be fights, arguments, epileptic fits and asthma attacks. Deals would be organized, substances subversively exchanged. Inmates were counted in, counted out. Equipment was counted in and counted out. Inmates were counted to the loo, counted in the loo and counted back out again. They were watched every minute they were down there. Scissors were lost and found. Tears were shed in copious quantities by staff and inmates alike. Activities were limited to basket weaving, embroidery and knitting dishcloths mainly and I was supposed to spice things up with a no spice budget and rubber moulds of dogs, gnomes and footballers that had been ordered a long time ago by someone with few expectations. There were a few drawing and painting materials but that was it. I tried to hide the moulds, not only were they cretinously, boringly uncreative, but they were so badly designed that, as with the Alsatians, legs, heads, or arms always got left behind in them due to design faults (or maybe there was a design fault in me). As women waited impatiently for the plaster to dry I could sense tension mounting on already tense nervous systems. Extracting those creatures from their rubber coats with shaky hands meant that I was usually left to pick up the pieces of three legged dogs, headless footballers, or armless gnomes all of which had been thrown on the floor. The knock-on effect was that disappointed, angry women would leave the session even more agitated, and demanding, needing more medication from the 'Dr No-No' (so called for his lack of generosity in response to often spurious requests).

A twisted bent figure was lingering near the doorway. Stooped over with a rigid neck sticking out of a thick jumper, only her eyes could look straight ahead and her head seemed to be clamped down to her shoulders. The exit door remained locked shut.

'Would the Hunchback of Notre Dame please come back here?'

'Miss Come Dancing', shouted with a voice full of fatigue. She sipped her own imported tea out of her own bone china cup and saucer delivered to her by her own chosen prisoner. 'Would the Hunchback of Notre Dame come away from the door and come over here?'

It needed a second order to distract the opportunist escapee from her dream of liberation. A long finger crooked itself beckoning her over. Angela smiled to please its owner. She moved closer towards the authority but sat down on an empty chair hoping that was far enough. But the finger egged the frightened smile nearer. She found another empty chair, but there was a slow shake of the head. The beckoning finger would decide the ending, not Angela. By now she was outside the office looking down at the floor because looking straight ahead was physically impossible.

'Angela,' The finger curled her right inside the office and kept curling round slowly, Miss Come Dancing sighed and tutted twice before she shook her head again. She turned Angela around and gave a last look at the poor hunchback's deformity. Pulling downwards from inside her jumper she released a wooden tray, with a flowery picture, one beaded handle and a mass of half woven cane. She was miraculously cured. Two little empty pokes of woolly jumper stuck up from her shoulder, even the officer couldn't flatten them down, they just popped back up. Two corners of the tray had been left behind. Not only had that sharp sleuth prevented a theft, she'd sabotaged an escape plan—Angela had to abort her mission for freedom. The same hand waved her out of the office and further out of sight. Less misshapen and less crooked, Angela was able to sit down at last. Miss Come Dancing smugly settled back into her seat behind her plastic window where her eagle eyes missed nothing. She crossed her legs with an audible squeeze of her black stockings, and inspected approvingly her dainty feet, neatly cosseted in their three inch high-heeled black patent shoes. Those feet would prance rhythmically around the dance floor of her local Palais every Saturday evening in her pink net gown of a thousand sequins, her hands twisting to the tempo, her eyes twinkling, lovingly reflected in her partner's own twinkling eyes, while at the top of this dance Goddess, her monumental pink candy floss hair stayed rigid, as it did from week-to-week, day in day out, ballasted to her head and held by a thousand metal hair pins. This officer, whose nickname was known to everyone but herself, had witnessed most scenarios, coped with everything. When she was on duty the rest of the staff felt fine, assured that everything would be alright—and she never took her work home with her. She took it down the local Palais and danced it away.

A pair of boxing gloves clumsily took pencils and paper off me. White, cold, swollen hands started to draw. There was not a vein to be seen capable of transporting warm blood to those enlarged hands. They had been punctured to death by dirty needles, feeding them bad gear. A pair of arms stretched out in front of me and reached for the scissors. Abscesses had left blue holes near the elbows and track marks walked themselves up the woman's skin. A yellow face peered straight at me, suddenly, too close. Too much alcohol had impaired her liver and given her a bloated appearance. She sat down and talked to anyone who would listen about her last binge 'on the out'. Next to her was a hunched figure with a bashed forehead, a skimpy bandage over it and patchy hair. It staggered towards a wall, attracted like a magnet and I steered her clear and gave her a chair before more self-inflicted bashings did further damage. Several asthma pumps were laid out on the table beside the inmates; a table couldn't be laid without them. One young woman sat shivering away her withdrawal symptoms. Another was crying her life away.

I was nearly pushed off my feet by one distracted, excited woman who was pacing to and fro. She clipped my shoulder, shoving me off balance yet again. Her eyes, immobile, were fixed on some point in the middle distance as she walked her walk, backwards and forwards. Something was simmering inside her. She was right in front of me now, with only a paper width between us. I moved my eyes around her face, purposely avoiding eye contact.

'You know they never let me out to attend my father's funeral, the only link with my mother, he was murdered and the prison wouldn't let me out to his funeral … the bastards.' Off she went again slamming her feet on the floor with every step she took. Back she came again. 'The only bit left I had of my mother. He was my stepfather, my mother's fourth husband; my mother was murdered by her fifth husband.' She went to get herself a pencil and paper, hitting the lino repeatedly as she banged into a chair. She flung the paper on to the table, but wasn't ready to sit down yet, and back she came. 'I took that bastard into the forest and slashed the arteries in both his legs … I made bloody sure that bastard won't walk again!' I strove to divest my face of all fear, moral judgement or any other emotional inflection. By this time she was right up against me again.

'Have you got an eraser?' I nodded. She walloped the floor with her feet, went over to her chair and sat down. 'I'm in for Grievous Bodily Harm now; I'll be going down for a bloody long stretch.' That was that. Vacant eyes around the table watched for a while unmoved, it was all so humdrum. And so Life continued down in Hades serenaded by a crackly sound system playing Engelbert Humperdink singing, by popular request, 'Please Release Me.'

All the women squeezed themselves together around the table like a warped jigsaw puzzle left out for too long against the elements and who were now like dislocated pieces, possibly forever. Count scissors, count needles. Erasers were forbidden, red pencils were illegal, care had to be taken with pen nibs which were used for do-it-yourself tattooing on the wing. I could never pace myself elegantly or placidly through these sessions but was led by the nose due to demanding women with short attention spans and a keen eye for taking advantage. I exhausted ideas and projects on women who were motiveless from jumbo prescriptions of Largactil and other stupefying sopo-rifics. I exhausted myself on women exhausted with life. I slogged up a down escalator. I fizzed away trying to dislodge that omnipotent apathy which lived inside Holloway until the end of a session left me like a damp firework, burnt out in some corner of the room. Sometimes Rip Van Winkle stirred and awoke, from fog-dependant, smog sniffing, crack-smoking addictions. The drug addicts, skeletons of parched bruised skin, shivering and aching, mouths sunk into gums with insecure teeth, were left abandoned, dotted here and there, crumbling from a diet of pure sugar. De-toxed they would be fattened-up on the prison starch, gums would stretch out to accommodate new prison teeth, and monthly bleeding would mark their rehabilitation into womanhood.

Most of the time I never knew why women had been forced to take up resi-dence. There wasn't time to find out, or nobody thought to tell. I just kept to my allotted timetable. I was ticked off as part of the staff to inmates ratio so as to comply with Home Office criteria and regulations. It was crisis management, knee jerk survival. Progress was not monitored, but numbers evened themselves out with a bit of creative mathematics.

There was Jean, a six foot tall stork of a woman whose skin was sore and flaky. Her lips peeled from the dryness of her mouth and her hair was brit-tle and lifeless. She sat in a corner of the room with her long legs wrapped round each other knitting dishcloths. There wasn't much choice then, just wool skills, a bit of sewing and me. Jean didn't want to stop at dishcloths, she had another idea. She was knitting a rope ladder to climb over the wall and get home to Ealing. The idea was ignored; nobody confronted Jean head on. But every night the occupational therapist would unpick the knitting unbeknown to Jean and so sabotage her ambition. From the time she cast on the first stitch Jean was going nowhere. Forever hopeful of a cigarette bonus or a coffee reward, she always volunteered to clean up at the end of the session. She would leap up and grab a broom. Rearing herself up to her full height she would push and poke with the broom, crashing into chairs and tables, fiercely and without too much artistry. She'd smash the industrial broom onto the floor, then pull it within an inch of its hairy ends, scratching away the rubbish and wearing out the lino.

Then there was Terry, a rather androgynous young person who sat throughout the session rocking backwards and forwards. To cut out the noise she had shoved a tampon in each ear and as she swayed too and fro their strings swung like pendulums on either side of her face. There were fewer and fewer Muriels, but there was one with her head scored with lacerations, cuts and scars. A lobotomy operation had left a deep line on her forehead and the years of electric treatments had resulted in her slow speech and barely conscious disposition. She couldn't live for five minutes without creating some kind of fire in a tube and infusing her inner workings with smoke. She was a spayed old vulture scavenging bins, old ashtrays and the floor for squashed fag butts. If she couldn't find tobacco, then she would try and smoke anything, from banana skins to tea bags. She smoked pencil shavings once and these went off like a fuse, nearly burning her nose off. If she didn't have Rizla papers she would use the thin wrapping from a Tampax. Down time couldn't have got any worse the night of greatest drought and despair. Last day before pay day, one match, and a few threads of baccy, no papers. Kneeling down beside her bed in prayer, she turned to her favourite page in the Bible and smoked it. When she sat down to paint, she chose the same seat every time, the same colours, and she painted the same shapes—circles within circles within circles.

A Tinkerbell flew into Heathrow on her way back from the warmer climes of the West Indies. She was greeted by dedicated customs officers and excited sniffer dogs leading to the discovery of a Louis Vuitton with a false bottom and six kilos of undeclared excess luggage harvested from some Jamaican cannabis plantation. Grounded and handcuffed she took the non-scenic route around London in her reinforced meat wagon up the Camden Road and into the cosy care of Her Majesty's civil servants to await trial. This Dutch nymph lit up the bowels of Holloway like a bird of paradise lost mid-migration. Floating into the occupational therapy unit she sparkled and shimmered in her own designer dresses made from the waste of that diabolical place. She used the junk found in waste bins and transformed them into fringes, bows, stars and flowers. Bits of paper, she sewed to her dress, wool she made into tassels to decorate her hair. Sweet papers she found on the floor or in the exercise yard she twisted into adornments and attached them to her coat. She recycled dried orange peel, and seeds from fruit and made necklaces and bracelets and found leaves, dried them and fixed them to her suede boots. She made her own buttons, hair bands, skirts and dresses. Using the debris of the prison, her drab dungeon was transformed into a fairy grotto.

Marie was a flower child, a magpie, a truly creative individual whose imagination could not be dulled. She told me that she had danced at Stonehenge, camped overnight at music festivals and had hitch-hiked everywhere. She medicated herself on the outside with plants and herbs. She lived in a commune with other like-minded folk. Holland was her favourite country because she thought it was much freer than England, more liberal. She found small bits and bobs that caught her eye, and reinvented them to make her cold stone cell a gentler and softer place. She always seemed alone, yet she was ever resourceful. She painted on anything she could find. Letters to friends were full of coloured patterns, envelopes too were painted with curves and shapes, colour upon colour, always luminous, psychedelic colours recalling some clandestine drug trip she had negotiated or a mushroom-picking nature ramble when she had imbibed. She must have devoured every kind of pill in her short life and experimented with every mind-changing powder and potion. Excavating the damage caused by such abuse, there remained a spark of pure creative energy to be discovered. She painted, slowly and intensely from the beginning of the session to the end. She was a puzzle, an enigma. Inmates left her alone, she didn't push or pull anything and she neither gave nor received any sexual favours. The officers in their crisp Persil white shirts, their stark navy blue uniforms and highly polished leather shoes were bemused by this foreign lady, and merely lifted their eyes in disbelief.

Occasionally they would search her room to keep the fire risk down and to monitor her acquisitiveness, but all-in-all they had bigger dangers to deal with. She stood directly in front of me, suppliant, with arms folded and cautiously, making sure that no-one else could see, she reached inside her rather floppy blouse and produced in her hand an intensely, beautifully painted, decorated egg.

'Would you varnish it for me?'

'Varnish isn't allowed … you shouldn't really have an egg either.'

'Would you varnish it for me, you could do it couldn't you?'

'No, I really can't.'

'Please.'

'I can't.'

'Please.'

'Leave it in the cupboard I'll think about it.'

I knew I would varnish it; I knew I would take it home for her and bring it back polished and shiny. Like an actor rehearsing the script, from then on I imagined the repercussions of my decision. I planned my answers to likely questions. It even went as far as a courtroom, a judge and punishment. Should I tell anyone else—get a witness as to my harmless motive? Should I write something down—just in case? At the end of the session I collected the egg, took it home and varnished it. The nature of the institution had trapped me into its unhealthy sense of proportion. I'd become embroiled in its subterfuge, thought about possible allies and discovered a whole new language. The next day, I returned the egg to a pencil box in my store cupboard. Moments later Marie opened the door and in its dark corner she found it, looked over its new, tough brilliance and expertly replaced it inside her blouse. Accomplished so professionally, I thought and I was congratulating myself on the smoothness of the whole operation when the alarm bell went.

'Didn't you get the memo?'

'What memo?'

'A training afternoon, new officers, a practice search. Everyone had to be searched, we had not done a full search for months, so that it was long overdue, 'These new officers have no idea … there's no problem is there?'

'No, except Education doesn't seem to have been told.'

'We'll remember next time, get all your women up at your end, they can wait over there … we'll start with the borstal girls first, get them out of the way.'

I was back at school, waiting outside the office of the headmistress. It was an immediate and a unhealthy reaction. I remembered my rehearsals and my prepared storyline. Either I would have to leave or find some way of coping. If the egg was discovered—that harmless inoffensive egg—then for sure I would volunteer my part in its presence. That's what I had decided to do. I simplified the whole issue, forgot all about any other tactics. If I was made to feel even younger, then I'd resign from this unhealthy lifestyle and find another job. There was no alternative.

All normal work stopped as every prison officer joined in the search. Staff organized themselves into groups, put on gloves, instructed women to stretch out their arms and started looking. More officers came into the room from other parts of the prison and replied to the prisoners' questions with blank shrugs. Surprisingly there was little resistance, so docile had they become that any deviation from routine seemed merely a mild annoyance, that's all. The women just waited for instructions, came forward when they were asked, stood how they were told to stand and for as long as required. Then they moved away to where they were ordered to wait. They queued silently and stood behind each other against the wall. No-one could go to the loo, sit down or do anything but wait their turn. I was moved away from the women and watched this quiet drama as I shuffled magazines. Marie looked calm. She had put herself nearly at the end of the line. Beside her the rest of the women leant back and rolled their heads resting them on the wall until they were called. Marie looked straight ahead, still and acquiescent.

Each woman was taken into a small room for the her search. They returned dishevelled, rearranging clothing and sat down relieved it was all over. It would soon be Marie's turn. Turning away from the woman beside her she folded her arms so that she appeared to be even more relaxed. Then, with one of her hands, she slowly pushed the egg along her blouse to the front fastening. In one movement she appeared to fiddle with a button, then take the egg out of her blouse into her other hand. She straightened her back against the wall with her hands at her sides. Soon it would be her turn. Then a fist tightened and a trickle of crushed shell floated downwards. A confetti of colour shimmered and floated over her flimsy skirt, trickling on down past her legs until it rested, camouflaged, on the speckled institutional lino. She allowed her dress to brush against the wall from time-to-time; blocking the view and distracting would-be spectators. But I was the only sightseer, nobody else suspected a thing. All that beautiful work, all that effort, initiative and energy she destroyed in a moment.

The queue formed and she took her place, impassively waiting her turn as the women followed each other, obeying instructions to keep in a neat and orderly line. Her name and number were called out and the routine search completed. Returning in the same impassive manner, she was replaced by the next woman in line until all the prisoners had provided sufficient practice for this prison officers' training exercise. The room slowly emptied and the officers returned to their designated work in other parts of the prison. Jean's broom started its journey down the room, pushing along under each table until the tidal wave of muck unknowingly joined up with that delicate wreckage of an egg and shoved it along with the rest of the waste. Marie never lost her motivation, never stopped creating her beautiful designs and she didn't stop in Holloway for long. Curiously her charge of importing six kilos of cannabis was somehow reduced to three kilos. It was a puzzle to her because she knew exactly how much was in her suitcase and had pleaded guilty to all charges. But somehow the amount was reduced and consequently her sentence.

Sitting on a table with her back to me was a new admission, engrossed in a large heavy art book. She was chuckling to herself as I moved to sit beside her.

For the next few minutes, she showed me the pictures in the book, pointed, laughed, questioned me and immersed herself in paintings by Titian and Rubens. Her favourites were those of feasts and parties. Huge paintings of Bacchanalian revelries in forests full of nude ladies, cherubs, men drinking, lying on cushions, having fun. 'They look like they are having a good time, don't they? … Don't those children look cheeky. I bet they get up to a lot of trouble … What do you think they are drinking Miss?' And so it went on about each character. She was endlessly fascinated by the paintings which she had never seen before. Inspired to paint, she took a large piece of paper and worked her brush around it recreating the party, the festivities, the zest for life and the fun.

Familiar with all farm chores and the husbandry of sheep and cattle, this unknown quantity in the penal system charged with arson and refusing to give her real name, age and address on arrest, discovered paintings. A dearth of a formal education and extreme learning difficulties prevented Millie from reading the accompanying text, so her response was direct and invigorating. She loved Picasso, all his paintings attracted Millie, including his depictions of massive, all-powerful women, running along the beach or sitting around in simple clothes which fell seductively from their shoulders. Inspired to paint by these works, Millie vigorously recreated such scenes. Those larger than life creatures fell off the history pages and onto her paintbrush, accompanied by love and passion. She rolled towards me, always the first in the queue for attention at the start of the session, obscuring all others with her size. With her denim dungarees, checked shirts and Wellington boots, bright red cheeks and thick black hair, she was a large and impressive woman with a voice commensurate with her size. She'd collect her materials, push books under her arm, pencils behind her ears, paints in one hand, brushes in her mouth, and install herself in her habitual burrow at the head of the table. She moved on to the classics as her collection of paintings grew to ten. They were something to be proud of, a creative success. I wanted to show them off so I pinned them up on the walls of the central atrium of Holloway—allowing maximum exposure for staff and inmates. Everyone had to move through that area; I was going public. Thumbtacks just about secured them in place as blue uniforms watched me. Out of the glass office window, someone stood with arms folded looking on. Excited by Millie's paintings, I celebrated. The audience stood back with pride on Millie's behalf. Those paintings were beautiful. Slowly walking back I reflected on that exhibition. Ten pieces of paper said I'd been here, ten paintings said I was more than a box ticked off in a staff register; ten paintings beat a knitted dishcloth. They proclaimed that I was more than just a diversionary tactic.

As I closed the door which released me from The Centre I heard loud ripping noises. That noise was something to do with me, I knew it. I remembered once going down to Reception, I heard a wailing, a pain that was big and grew bigger as I waited there. Someone was being beaten up, some fight was going on—I approached an officer with my fears. 'Oh that noise, it's nothing, just a new arrival. She's deaf and dumb ... that's the only noise she can make.'

I was relieved to hear that, and then I became appalled at my relief, at what I feared was the first symptom of institutional immunity. One sense could compensate for the loss of another sense, so they say. It must be true because prisoners, locked away out of sight could read the sound of keys and footsteps and recognise individual officers by such limited signals. Unconsciously, I had developed this skill, the skill of translating sounds. I knew that ripping noise was mine just as I recognised my home and possessions, so I retraced my steps to The Centre and claimed responsibility. Gone was the exhibition, the images of parties and colours and cherubs and trees and goblets of wine. They were being swallowed up into a filing cabinet, trapped by locks like everything else in the prison. Practised hands twisted keys on chains that swung with the excitement of yet another incarceration. The officer returned to her glass hide, surveyed the walls and relaxed at the emptiness. 'I'm not looking at those disgusting paintings, naked women with children and half-clothed men, disgusting. It's a disgrace to see them on the walls for all to look at. Absolutely disgusting ... and if you want to take it up with anyone, then mention my name, I'm Miss Agnes McFee MBE.'

Rights and wrongs, scoring points, complaining, attacking, defending, asserting rights, depriving rights, justice, injustice were all ribbons of molecules built into the DNA of Holloway from the first day it was built in the nineteenth

century. Since inmates were arguing and being argued about, while officers were debating matters, while the governors and the medical staff and all
those humans rattling round the institution throughout the day and night
were chewing over their rights and those of others, I threw my hat into the
ring, got my argument together and got stuck in. Too dumbfounded and
too pathetically slow off the mark to go head-to-head with the officer at the
time, my only recourse was to put it all down in writing. I penned state-
ments in triplicate on green, red and pink paper, any paper that was required
of me, I put memos in pigeonholes, checked my rights, and got as much
support as possible.

They made me wait and wait for a reply. Almost a month later, a memo
arrived. My problem would be dealt with at the next Governor's meeting. It
would be number nine on the agenda. It would be discussed in my absence
and I was not invited to attend. I heard via my superiors the result of that
wise council—the paintings *would* be displayed . The decision had gone for
me, with a few reservations as to their number and how they should be presented. But it was a progressive step and I appreciated it. It would also make
Millie happy. On my way out of the prison with memo in hand I confronted
Miss McFee OBE. Yes, she had received a copy of the same memo. She didn't
agree with it but she knew she had to comply. The next day, before the lesson I went to see her.

'Can I have the paintings please?'

'You know I've searched and searched for those paintings and just can't find
them anywhere.'

'You put them in the filing cabinet.' An arm pulled hard at the drawers to
show me that there was nothing in the cabinet but a few envelopes and
paper clips. 'You know what this place is like . . . so many thieves, things
go missing all the time, and I just don't know where they could be. I'll keep
looking though and let you have them back when I find them, but don't
be too hopeful, it is a prison after all!' The compass swung back down to
Eunuchland and I registered my citizenship. I walked away, twisting back in

the hope that this monster would turn into a pillar of salt. I saw Miss McFee tidying her desk, preening herself and her shoulder pips, having neatened up her life a treat. I pecked my way down the line, to the bottom of the heap, and I never did see those paintings again.

One transcription was framed and displayed inspired by a Max Beckman painting of the back view of a naked man. Other paintings lined the corridor, a new initiative, an optimistic venture for respectability. This time it was the Head of the Medical Department. She took the Beckman-inspired painting down, again without reference to me and without prior discussion. I never witnessed it being removed, I just received a verbal message informing me that the depiction of a male bottom would be unsettling for confined women. Again I contested the decision. This time I questioned the man at the top, the Governor One. 'Yes,' he understood my position, 'yes,' he understood my point of view, and, 'yes,' he could see why I was so cross. But, 'No,' he was sorry the painting could not be displayed because he could not overrule the decision made by the Head of the Medical Department in favour of an art teacher. I continued pecking my way down through the order.

A red brick prison was growing up in the vicinity of the old Holloway. As ancient bits crumbled so new bits rose up. The bulldozers were forever on alert. Preparations had started to celebrate the closure of the Victorian institution. Soon the old prison would be razed to the ground. Visitors increased since it would soon be part of history and people wanted to see it before it disappeared. They doubled in numbers, forever a queue of heads with name tags, being lead around, pointing and watching—day trippers—lunch included. They would come into the Occupational Therapy Room and stare around. Organized groups, with organized teeth, organized nails and fresh skin, surveying the crumbling walls and crumbling inhabitants. Important looking men folded their arms and swayed back thoughtfully on their heels, pushing out their groins and showing their sharply ironed trousers. Important looking women would smile with their heads on one side and clutch their handbags tightly. Others would look through the spaces from behind the front line of visitors and watch from a safe distance. No introductions took place or any explanatory statement. They never introduced themselves, they just came in and stood there and looked.

Some women would ask them for cigarettes, or sweets. Most of the visitors would mutter something about 'a zoo', or along the lines, 'like watching the animals'. The women prisoners hated them. One bright green dress stood out amongst the wave of grey men who suddenly appeared in the room. She was obviously the wife of some important male personage who was looking to gain a morsel of credibility by visiting Holloway. Powdered-up and with a scar of lipstick she decided to meander in and out of us, as if on a royal walkabout. With matching green hat and the finest of woollen dresses, she curved in and out, perfectly balanced, perfectly poised. She smiled and bent her head from side-to-side and glided between the tables. My paint-plopped, ink-dripped clothing watched this green little number strutting her stuff for whomsoever and whatever reason. She chose Muriel and stopped. Bemused at her circles within circles within circles, her repetitive swirls, she stared a bit too long and realised, in her socially-minded etiquette sort of way that she might be thought rude if she prolonged her attention further without participation. Muriel's arms repeated the circles of colour, weaving patterns and lines as she concentrated. The electric light overhead placed her poor scarred face in the spotlight but it refused to meet the visitor's eyes. A quick flick in between her thinning hair and Muriel caught sight of a flash of green. The dress moved closer, a gold ringed finger came down on her painting on a tiny blue and pink pattern, right in the middle of the page. 'I do like that bit'.

Muriel stopped painting, put her brush down on the table, and stared directly into that clear, outdoor, outside, fresh air pair of eyes and waited for the perfectly manicured finger to leave its favoured spot. She started to tear her painting, very slowly, one way and then the next, until the middle bit of paper was isolated, that small bit of pattern under the fingerprint. Muriel picked it off the table, it was just the size of a small coin that blue and pink pattern and she pressed it into that gold-fingered hand. 'Here you can have it then,' said Muriel.

Left in front on the table was her painting split from side-to-side, torn right to the middle, denoting emptiness. That grand lady had been trained from the womb to hide discomfort with the right smile and the right gesture. She accepted the paper gift with the likeable pattern. Her cashmere clothes, that green softness, swayed away, her bright shoes clip-clopped back to her own kind. The waves of grey people parted and she was swallowed up into the safety of the freshly laundered shirts. Muriel reached for more paper and swirled her never ending swirls.

Women were collecting their possessions and moving to new up-market digs. Black plastic bags got trailed from bad plumbing and cells condemned as unfit to bed-sits with en suite loos. The two stone griffins, doormen to all newcomers were lowered from high above those majestic wooden doors and moved to the new prison to perform a similar service. Now at ground level, they lost their awesome power. Unwanted food and clothing chucked out of the windows got lodged in their claws and eyes. Their former glory was lost amongst the porridge and mouldy bread. Gardening equipment was leant against their back legs and cleaners smoked a hidden fag and did a bit of business behind their tails.

The new prison was already partly in use. The couple of working wings in the old prison which were still in use would be vacated and abandoned over the weekend as the last stage of the move. Prisoners were either transferred across to the new accommodation or to other prisons. The last working day of that old gothic style prison had arrived. It would be remembered by a gathering of all working staff in the central atrium, the last bit of Holloway's remaining grandeur. Sherry and cake would be served, speeches made and the last person out would leave the key under the mat. I got a memo from the kitchen; they wanted a selection of powder paints for the celebration. I thought that perhaps they were making banners or flags.

The smell of institutional cooking floated down the corridor as I approached the kitchen and I automatically started to breathe through my mouth. The cook emerged from his office wiping his hands on his apron and I caught sight of two enormous glossy breasts from a calendar on his wall. The last bastion of male chauvinism within the prison emerged from his office like he had walked out of a page of a Beano comic. A Desperate Dan look-a-like, he grinned at me out of a stubbly jaw of monstrous proportion. Too few teeth forced him to talk in wet spurts from deep down inside that cavernous space. In fact he was always wiping off some moisture with his towel, some wetness above his top lip, a trickle on his forehead, or a shiny line of sweat trapped in the creases of his stubbly neck. The damp towel flicked over his shoulder intermittently in readiness for the next heat and steam induced drip. Taking the paints he set them down and led me over to a large table. In the middle was a heap of cake slabs shaped sculptured into a replica of the new prison. He'd seen the plans and it was as accurate a replica as baking allowed. It was huge and would be even bigger once the marzipan and icing was applied to it. It would be exactly like the new prison when it was finished, walls and all. The cook gave me a tour of the cake, chuffed with his own expertise, which enabled him to replicate architectural plans. Everything was there and it seemed to me to have been baked to scale.

When the last working day of the old prison finally arrived, the staff assembled, the sherry was poured, and a couple of kitchen workers unveiled that cake. Red brick icing smoothed over marzipan with a rich fruitcake as a base, and with the date written beautifully on the top to mark an historic day. At the end of the evening the somewhat tipsy cook beckoned me over and handed me back the powder paints. 'Thanks ducks, but I only wanted that brick-red.' He winked as he nodded over to the cake with its terracotta covered icing-sugar walls. 'I'd no other colouring agent to get it that colour, ducks, however hard I tried. That powder paint worked a treat didn't it?'

CHAPTER 4

Murals and other Enterprises

Her Majesty's Prison Service serves the public by keeping in custody those committed by the courts. Our duty is to look after them with humanity and help them lead law abiding and useful lives in custody and after release.

Her Majesty's Prison Service Statement of Purpose

Everyone criticised the new prison. Gone was that elegant stone building, replaced by a modern-day university campus-style lookalike, all right angles and conveyor belt architecture, economically viable concrete with purpose built windows and flat pack furniture. The relocation was completed in stages, so for a while the Education Department lodged in what would one day become a residential wing. With only a door to separate us, lived the young offenders or 'borstal brats' as they were still fondly referred to. We were at the end of the building. Beyond us was the prison wall, then Dalmeny Avenue and after that the local newsagents.

In comparison to the ceilings of the old prison, the new ones seemed to be only just above head height and space had also imploded due to overplanned gardens and airless square rooms that were more claustrophobic and oppressive. Prison officers said that they couldn't see anything but winding tunnels of corridors. They could see nothing from their offices, so they felt insecure and not in control. And other workers joined in with the criticisms, so it seemed that Holloway had become a colander with holes which only the Security Department could block up.

Reassuring meetings pacified people for a while and changes were made to address the potential dangers and the security risks until routines set in and everyone got used to the change of venue. They gradually forgot about the old prison and stopped making comparisons and in that way life became easier for everyone. Some prisoners carrying black plastic bags of possessions changed homes with much reluctance; others saw it as exciting because there

105

was going to be a huge gym, better accommodation and a swimming pool. But temporary accommodation had to be arranged until all stages of construction had been completed, so instead of moving in next door to their mates some prisoners were directed to a bus, stacked their plastic luggage into the boot and migrated up the motorway to other prisons. The changes destabilised everybody for a while.

Four blocks, five levels and a 'trolley route' encircled the new building. Mobility sounded simple and straightforward. Ascending and descending was easy, a lift facilitated the journey from one level to another up the five floors, then down to the basement unit. The trolley route connected them all nicely, linking together residential and non-residential departments. Travel from block-to-block on the other hand reduced us all to groping rodents lured onwards to test our sense of direction. Winding passageways and dead-end spurs made lateral travel an endurance test. Contagious moaning rose up out of the prison's central heating in order to complain about another piece of modernity. Views on one side overlooked gardens that stretched out in front waiting to be tended. Concrete seats had been cut into the prison walls dotted around here and there under sheltered walkways as if prisoners would gently take the air as they sauntered around. The idea, some thought, was to emulate a hospital, that women didn't really commit crimes, they just got sick. Who knows? I've never seen anyone prevailing themselves of a temporary rest on any one of those would-be rural seats.

Views on the opposite side looked directly on to flats. That's if you were on a high enough level and could see over the wall. Then glass had been put in all the windows by planners who hadn't listened, so it all had to be replaced by plastic panes that couldn't be smashed, swallowed or used for slashing. So we muddled through until compulsive grumbling wore us out. Old cells collapsed under the bulldozers, forcing us to accept the new premises. The Education Department would soon be installed in a purpose-built block at the end of the prison, next to the chapel and until then we lodged in a half-way house opposite our designated premises. This temporary accommodation, part of a new residential wing, with half-a-dozen classrooms, established us as a spot on the map, a designated area that could be signed by an arrow and a notice.

My classroom was designed as a dormitory, with a loo which I camouflaged as a store closet. Just a bit more patience would be needed for the building across the way to be ready for occupancy. From my dormitory-cum-classroom I could look across and keep an eye on progress. Underneath the windows of my newly allocated classroom the deposed griffins stared out blankly and had to adapt to their new location. Close up, they had lost all that awesome power. They'd been lowered to ground level where their disreputable scars and blemishes gave them a more dilapidated impression. We continued in this interim state trying to provide a reasonable service in these limited quarters, planning for the future; a new syllabus and a new leaf. It lasted like that for quite a while but the Education Department was gradually establishing itself as a viable influence, meeting the needs of the institution and gaining credibility. Gently prodding and pushing its way into the general run of the whole prison experience, the department spread its offerings around and was represented at management and policy meetings, case conferences and planning forums, thereby making friends and impacting on the rest of the institution.

Erroneously purporting to be creative, nail pictures, italic writing sets, and plaster moulds of gnomes and footballers were the only evidence of any daytime artistic culture and these it seemed only existed in the Hospital Wing. Other than that there were evening classes during association time when prisoners could attend one of a small choice of classes such as hat-making, cookery, art and so on. Italic writing lessons had been introduced some time in the past, but were then abandoned. Amateurish designs had started to appear on the faces and arms of prisoners which became septic due to the use of old pen nibs and dirty ink. Badly drawn spiders' webs deformed faces and the names of lovers got etched on shoulders only to be crudely scratched out after a row. The borstal beauty spot tattooed high on the cheek evidenced a new club member. Those with skin infections filled the surgery, so that all the ink was rounded up and thrown out; and the wings were searched for stolen equipment to stop this unhealthy craze. Metal nails used for the pictures became tools for the self-harmers, also showing up on x-rays when abdominal pains needed investigating. No wonder they were outlawed. That left the rubber moulds to be chucked out with enthusiasm.

'You can draw me a pair of praying hands can't you?' The fearsome borstal officer confronted me mid-class and unfolded a black and white picture. 'I want you to draw me a picture like this, hands clasped together in prayer.' Only a door separated us from the Borstal Wing which gave easy access to to the Education Department for the young offenders but made us easy pickings for requests for favours from the wing staff, not yet used to the new daytime teachers and their serious commitment to educating women.

'If I get it photocopied then each of my girls can have one in her cell . . . I'll leave it with you then, let me have it as soon as you can.' Some staff had their own ideas about how to lead fallen females back onto the straight and narrow. She disappeared, leaving an anxious hush of students behind her. At least it was me in the firing line not them. My discomfort at this inappropriate behaviour had to be discussed, boundaries had to be set, and I'd be ready at the end of the lesson to repay the visit. But the education officer had got there before me and received the same instructions from the officer popping into the Education Department, which happened often now that we were next door. Of course he blocked the request, we were a strictly secular department, and it wasn't part of my professional job description to take on such casual commissions.

No current trends or ideas blew inside this hermetically-sealed community. Even security staff working on the wings lived above the shop in specially allocated flats and played next door in the officers' mess which was timetabled to suit their different shifts. This closed order received little input from the outside world. The perception was of a deeply anachronistic institution that was in need of a mighty push forward in order for it to catch up with the world. The new education staff could make a start on this and so we did in our new empire of half a corridor. The arts were one of the first classes to be introduced with a full timetable, and other subjects and new ideas soon followed.

A pioneering spirit took on board all issues to promote educational opportunities designed specifically for Holloway and its unique population of women. Little by little the Education Department was included as part of the institution. There was a feeling of growth and newness and of embarking on something important, with nothing to compare ourselves to and nothing to compete with. We were still a small department trying to be taken seriously. For a while progress was good, day classes were fully attended and new staff were employed. A wide choice of classes was gradually introduced. Examples of art work slowly started to appear around the institution, women had the opportunity to join the Open University and enrol on courses, and others who had missed out on any formal education could learn how to read and write. We started to be perceived as useful and as serving some purpose—we were becoming respectable. But a change in regime reminded us of a power over which we had no control and to which we were answerable—a reminder in case we got carried away.

A new Governor set a misguided stamp on Holloway's history by starting to change things around. Education was reduced almost to a standstill, resulting in months of class closures. No evening classes, no daytime education, no students. Other services came to a stop; in fact the prison virtually ceased to function. 'Security' was the key word. The metallic din of keys twisting and turning in newly constructed doorways bumped up the acoustics along those dark hollow walkways. Steel gates were built every few yards and the corridors were fenced in further with these obstacles. The unlocking, locking, pushing and pulling stunted everyone's progress. Wrists worked twice as hard, and fingers were bumped and bruised before staff had even reached their workstation. And it seemed like those doors not only inhibited physical movement but also mental agility. Inter-departmental communications slowed down, so we were all that much more isolated in our little offices, cordoned off from other departments, with little or no contact. Nobody knew what other people were doing, except for odd memos that arrived too late and were usually addressed to the wrong people.

Daily routines had to be abandoned as officers were re-deployed to keeping sentinel, which sent morale lower than it had ever been before. A skeleton staff just about provided enough escorts to keep the courts happy and perform rudimentary services within the prison. Rubbish bags piled up and basic cleaning was left undone so that the prison got dirtier and smellier. On a damp day I'd squelch along the outside pathways avoiding tampons and food droppings—on hot days the flies buzzed around spreading germs. Senior management blew downwards and the Education Department shivered ineffectually and had to adapt. We were turfed out of our temporary accommodation. We downsized to a caravan in the prison grounds which became the new 'Education Block', complete with wire netting on the windows and classrooms which I couldn't turn round in. The teachers waited, but nobody came. It was a salutary affirmation of our impotency predicting a future of similar slights. So we took to implementing a delivery service and taught through the hatches if we could, but it short-changed the women and deprofessionalised our skills—a bit of an insult really. The women were locked up for the most part of the day which didn't mean they were more controlled, on the contrary, too much locking-up unnerved the prisoner population, meaning more unrest and destructive incidents. It was a bad time and it went on for far too long.

Then there was a lot of publicity. Inspectors visited and took notes and observed and asked questions and listened and acted upon the information. So a new Governor was appointed and regimes started up again. New directives were sent down from senior management to the lower orders and we took notice and adapted. The new word was 'Yes' so we too became positive again. Classes re-started and productive projects got underway. Staff became optimistic as work got back to normal—and there seemed to be a balanced mind somewhere in charge. Hierarchies changed and people started to get to know each other. Talk went up and down the pecking order. Communications improved. We all seemed suddenly to become adults in an adult institution, not children being treated as infants. The new Governor regularly visited all areas of the prison; he walked around and spoke to everyone, regardless of their status and whatever job they had. His door was always open, so staff could pop in to see him. It humanised and civilised the place.

When the number one Governor himself asked me to decorate one of the rooms I said 'Yes, of course.' Who could refuse such a miraculous request? A new Mother and Baby Wing was being relocated on the ground floor and some imaginative soul thought that the intended day room could be painted. I was no longer the invisible woman, trudging for years along the corridors, teaching in the classroom and only coming out in December for the odd Christmas decoration task. Now I'd become visible as a professional—and it was only April! It would be a while before the wing in question would be ready for occupancy, so we could take our time with the painting. The only other people making use of the empty wing were a few male prisoners imported from Pentonville Prison to supplement the male work party and whilst in Holloway they were escorted by a male officer. They availed themselves of the new shower facilities at the end of the corridor before they went home to their own prison. Apart from that we'd have peace and quiet to work uninterrupted.

That's all that wing was being used for at the time. Fresh paint and fresh furniture would convert it into a state-of-the-art residence for mothers and their babies. It sounded a good project to get involved in; all I had to do was to look around for painters who were good enough. There was a good group of students around then, talented and motivated mature women. I knew them all because I used to visit them on the wings during the dormant period and give them assignments to perform to keep them sane. We had a couple of weeks to come up with ideas for the overall design, and then we'd decide on the best suggestions and work on from there.

The idea which emerged was that there would be a strong theme that could be translated into individual images to suit different women using different styles. It would not work for one person to design the whole mural, women didn't stay that long, and too personal a design would be difficult to translate for other painters who might follow. So we decided on a theme based on 'The Rain Forest' which meant that a central framework of exotic leaves and branches could form the main composition. Then individual students could choose different wild creatures: birds, frogs, animals, butterflies, etc. and paint them as they wished but with the structure of the forest linking them all together. There would be flexibility and the opportunity for many women to contribute in their own style.

We installed equipment and marshalled paints, brushes and of course tea and coffee makers. Security hadn't given me the freedom to work with just any prisoner; they insisted on reliability as a top priority. If they were not trusted inmates then I would have to be present to supervise. That was fine by me. I was happy with those constraints, which were both understandable and reasonable. Later, the original idea of a rather misty atmospheric rain forest had to be changed, and a somewhat flat, clear design replaced it. This was because it was easier for a group to interpret flat shapes: 'misty and atmospheric' was harder to translate. All kinds of leaves were drawn while exotic snails and butterflies began to brighten the room, which tended to be naturally dark and gloomy. Birds sat on the branches and frogs jumped amongst the foliage. Even the paint was bought specially, there was none of the limited Home Office range of powder colour or cheapo quality, and I bought the best acrylics with a brilliant colour range.

It was an uplifting exercise that distanced all those involved from the rest of the prison. From the time we arrived in that room we forgot where we had come from; and the women especially forgot the downsides of their lives which they would return to soon enough at the end of each day. We studied books, arranged different images, researched things, discussed colour and encouraged and supported one another. It was a wonderful experience for us all. The design crept up the walls and popped onto the ceiling. It was Holloway at its best and the exercise seemed to obliterate the nihilism that surrounded us. Maybe to an outsider it didn't seem too much to write home about, but it was, and it is important enough for me to write about it now. It showed that things were possible and that prison need not just be a waiting room until sentences end. It can be something else. Sometimes a woman would paint badly. At first it was hard to criticise, but it had to be done because we didn't want something amateurish and mediocre. There would be discussions and opinions sought that cushioned any such criticism. The more we worked together the easier it got, to the extent that we could become more direct with our views if we thought someone's painting deserved it. I got my fair share of criticism too if I didn't fit in with the right colour range or the right mood, and decisions were made together. The atmosphere tended always to be effusive and encouraging. Confidence grew, and so did their skills.

Two women in particular spent the most time working on the mural, Cleo and Maggie, an alcoholic and a drug addict respectively. Cleo was the better artist but the less confident of the two women. A delicate silk-like thread embroidered her cheek bone, winding upwards to her brow. The shard of glass had just missed her eye and she'd been left to bleed. The scar was faint now behind her hand which flitted across it self-consciously. It was a visible reminder of intangible memories that she couldn't properly recall due to booze induced blackouts. This visit to Holloway would involve only a short stay for her, something about a breach of probation and her two years of sobriety had earned her just a few months residency. That and her fresh lifestyle with a new husband, a flat in a different corner of the country away from former temptations, which all pointed to a short sentence. I knew she wouldn't be back after that and indeed she didn't return. It was something to do with maturity, hope, support and a strong will that for the first time in her life had all united at the same time, so she could move forward.

Maggie was much younger, less able but more confident—only four years of drug addiction, so she still presented reasonably well. Regular meals, early nights and the full medical service supplied by Holloway had washed out the white powder and woken up her failing bodily system. But her mind was still out there with the opiates, powders and pills, even though it was only theoretical. And her partner didn't help matters much on the outside. He was a fellow addict, her co-defendant and also now locked up somewhere in the prison system. The only chink that might have changed her ways was her baby, now on the 'at risk' register and being looked after by foster parents.

'I'll still take my drugs on the out, but I'll never let my habit get that big this time, so I'll be able to control it.' With this kind of self-deception her addiction would never be conquered. Cleo and I talked to her about this impossibility but we were unconvincing, so I expected her back, and she did return, but in fact only for a short while. How much we talked about personal matters was always an issue. In an institution of so many experts that in theory had made a success of their lives when the prisoners had failed in theirs, telling women things often inferred superiority. My role as a teacher became defined in a way that it would not have been in mainstream education. It seemed to me that unless I was prepared to talk with the same openness that the institution needed them to do as part of their rehabilitation, then I should shut up. But it never worked out like that, especially in this close work situation when a relaxed atmosphere facilitated easy unselfconscious conversations.

Maggie wrote to her partner every day but her letters were supposedly too obscene for the Royal Mail, so the officers handed them back for her to rewrite. They were highly literate scripts in which she role-played different erotic females with longings that only her partner could satisfy. This became her own special currency in Holloway's flourishing bartering system. You could commission any kind of a letter from her for the right amount of tobacco. Poems were a bit extra, they had to rhyme and that was more difficult. Such efforts satisfied her and kept her personal frustrations lubricated. Crude drawings illustrated each lustful detail—brashly-coloured full-frontal sexuality. Always assured a grand finale on the last page, they were smeared with some bodily fluid that convinced her partner of her full commitment. She'd talk a new story out loud to us and amuse herself in preparation for the next letter. Her fantasies were endless extravaganzas of lust and licentiousness. They called her the 'Wing Nymphomaniac', and she delighted in her ability to shock and provoke controversy.

Those two women became the most consistent workers. Other painters would join the group on a temporary basis because of their brief stay, but on the whole it was just Maggie and Cleo who coordinated the whole project. I'd help out with colour mixing or to demonstrate a way forward, give advice, or help out occasionally. But mostly I was a third point of view on subject matter, colour and technique. The women knew it was for them and they had the final decision at each stage. Sometimes I was just the tea lady, while the workers completed some special image before lunch and the prison routine forced them back to their landing.

The Mother and Baby Wing would accommodate mothers and their babies under the age of nine months, so we thought that the mural should be more for the mothers than the babies. Criticisms about our choice of design would be discussed as the inevitable visitors to Holloway came to see us. The women got irritated at predictable comments or questions about why we hadn't painted cartoons. Those big birds, they said, would scare the babies and as for that snake hiding down there, well that really would terrify them. The fact that the children were all still very much babies and wouldn't even be able to recognise the objects didn't deflect the visitors from their criticism. Both Cleo and Maggie justified the decision not to draw cartoons. So many times they were asked that dreary question that they began to ignore comments altogether, muttering that they were far too busy to stop and chat.

I got to know the women well; during the six months that we worked together it was an inspirational time, which stood out against the negative side of prison life. Sometimes Cleo would reminisce to the wall as she painted and each brush stroke seemed to wipe away another event in her past. She talked about how she'd lived on the streets, how much alcohol she could consume then, and how she had spent half of that time in a blurry haze. How many times had she awoken, scrunched up and bruised in some unfamiliar bed or some squat? The tremors were the worst, especially when she was alone and in the dark. Her local police knew her well; but at least they'd give her a cup of tea in the morning however badly she'd behaved or whatever state she was in. I think it was easier to talk to the wall, it was impersonal, neutral and it didn't judge.

So 'The Rain Forest' became a journal, a visual history. Her words fell out onto her brush, swirling their way into leaves, butterflies and exotic shapes. Maggie and me would listen and paint too, so that the mural wasn't just about form and colour. Those bad stories turned into beautiful patterns in bright hues. The process cured, it pacified and worked things out. And for Maggie it was like painting herself into the picture she said—and what she had painted had become her, somehow—part of her life—hidden in that forest. That's how she felt about it at the end of each day as she inspected her efforts. The more they worked the easier it became and the fewer mistakes we all made. Life seemed so normal, less prison-like. The women were spending their time creatively, changing their environment and giving something back for future residents of Holloway to enjoy. Even when we looked out of the window we forgot about the bars, so totally absorbed were we in our work. The view from the room was of a carefully tended and landscaped garden with flowering trees, neat hedges, flowers and tidy lawns. The rubbish never got to these parts; they were too well looked after by the gardening staff who had created that display in such a short length of time. A family of ducks had once more occupied a secluded spot and the mother was leading six offspring home to their pied-à-terre. One last coffee and a thorough cleaning of the equipment; that was the familiar routine at the end of each day. It was at this point that reality dawned and the dread of the evening lock-in and other institutional routines toughened the two women up. Their demeanour changed and they prepared for the culture shock.

At first the presence of the three male inmates using the same wing passed by with just a few interested looks. They weren't predictable visitors because their timetable was different from ours, but they were noticed as they came into the wing at the end of their shift. It added to the attraction of the women's day and certainly their work didn't suffer. It didn't bother me, all rather natural I thought. The project would soon be finished. It would be over in a few weeks and we were all kind of regretting the end of a special experience. Three o'clock and onto the wing trudged the testosterone. My back was to the door, so I only heard their boots walking past our room and them disappearing down the corridor. Then I heard the female hormones jump up and I heard their footsteps scurrying down those same corridors in the same direction and disappearing. Deprivation was making up for lost time. And I stood there in the room and wondered what to do next. There was something predictable about my isolation, I wasn't surprised, wasn't shocked but felt I should go and find them.

At the bottom of the passageway was the male officer in charge, a roly poly worker in navy blue dungarees and glasses that were worn so low on his nose they seemed pointless. They couldn't possibly connect with his eyes. They gave him a bemused look that seemed only to engage in something higher up the wall because he never looked at you directly. His eyes seemed to focus somewhere just below the ceiling. He was staring down another corridor holding a packet of sweets in his hand. 'Do you want one of these love?' He stretched out his hand and offered me a boiled sweet, turning his head up high in another direction. There was no point in asking where the women were or where the men were, so I didn't. In fact I never said anything. I could hear the noise of the shower, I could hear the noise of frolicking and giggling and I knew that the inevitable had happened—mine and his had met up. Testosterone had collided with oestrogen and peaked in some disused shower room in the largest female prison in Europe. So we just stood together each fulfilling our responsibilities of vigilance. We were still on duty and we waited. I leant against a wall whilst he stood centrally in the corridor, like two signposts facing in different directions. If there was no communication there was no collusion.

It seemed respectful that we said nothing and it felt like a mature decision, an exercise in discretion. Maybe the fact that the officer never looked at me was some way of denying the event, or of not acknowledging me, maybe he was embarrassed. Or had it all happened before with different women, different men while he was on duty? Who knows? Such intimate interaction between the sexes as was going on somewhere down that corridor was obviously not part of Her Majesty's intention when she sent offenders to prison. Yet it *was* happening. There was no abuse of power going on, just consenting adults of equal status consenting. I was thinking about all this as I hovered with indecision. I certainly had no intention of going down that happy corridor to separate them. We lingered a bit, then I began to feel self-conscious. I didn't like the idea of waiting for whatever it was to finish, or listening while things were happening. That seemed the wrong bit so I just turned round and went back to the mural room and pottered about needlessly with jars and brushes and watched the ducks.

Two wet haired, messy women returned eventually all smiles and bigger smiles and all flustered and giggling. They thanked me, which I hated and said so. I did not want to be in the position of allowing such behaviour and didn't feel as though that had been my role. But I didn't say that I didn't want to talk about anything that had gone on, I just didn't want to know. These were grown women and I didn't want their gratitude or any explanation or any information. Then I started to work it out, the moral implications: I analysed my reactions.

In no way had I done anything wrong—in theory—in that I hadn't profited in any way, abused anyone or used anyone. But it seemed subversive and I had been complicit in this seeming subversion. I hadn't exploited anyone or anything. On reflection I don't think that even a prison rule had been broken. I had never read a prison rule that involved this kind of situation although there was one covering 'good order and discipline' that sometimes seemed to cover anything that you can name. But there was this uneasy worry rattling around in my mind. When the judge had sent these women down at 'Her Majesty's pleasure', this kind of pleasure was not what he had in mind.

'Don't worry there's nothing to really worry about, if you know what I mean, God what an afternoon, God it was great! God my hair's soaking, God that was just great.' That's all that they kept on saying during the time that was left. They kept on and on, giggling and smiling, all shaky and stuttery, with fluttery eyes, knowing nudges and energetic adjustments to their clothes—reliving it all. In fact they were so excited, it was mostly expletives, sounds, sighs and murmurs—like they'd absorbed lemonade causing them to bubble and explode. They were far too wound up to make much sense. They'd say that they had spilt some paint on their hair so they had to wash it—that's if anyone asked on their wing about their wet hair. And so the cover up started. It would soon be time to return to the wing and they dried themselves off and tried to calm down and appear controlled. Then we heard the sound of the men coming down the corridor. We all stood up as we heard their steps. They passed the room in front of us in exactly the same manner as they had entered it, no different, no change. Heads up, eyes in front, marching onwards, in total control, like soldiers who had regrouped after a fray. Their supervisor followed them managing a ''Bye' and they vacated the wing. Cleo and Maggie on the other hand, waved that testosterone on its way with smiles, sighs, moony looks and a gentle swaying of their hips. The men never looked at them, never turned round, just onwards to the end of the corridor. They never flinched. But we seemed all of a mess, in complete disarray. I tidied the room, cleaned up and reminded the women of the mundane odd jobs that needed to be done before we left. I tried to ignore what had happened, but we all recognised that we had changed into conspirators. They were being so nice and helpful while I continued the chores and tried to work out the implications. I took the women back to their wing and left them there.

It was plain to see something about them was different; anyone would not fail to wonder what had happened to them. Usually at the end of the day, they'd be all tired and drag their feet anticipating the lock-in and the long boring evening that they would have to endure before the next day. Now they were effervescent and boiling-over with adrenalin. They were transformed and they couldn't hide it. With little else to occupy their day, such minutia were monitored closely by everyone on the wing, out of sheer boredom if nothing else. Everyone and everything was everybody's business, in case somebody was getting away with something or missing out on something. I never told anyone. I just returned to the Education Department, my colleagues and the rest of the day before I left to go home for the weekend.

Only when I was on my own and away from the prison did I relax enough to clarify my thoughts and work out my response to the whole business. I'd become subversive, embroiled in some intrigue particular to the institution, but not life in general, not life on the outside of the prison. 'Don't worry. There's nothing to worry about.' Those were the words that Cleo had said to me as if they were supposed to somehow reassure me. I was thinking about the incident and the heat started to rise as I imagined possible repercussions. The prison always managed to keep my levels of guilt topped up. The horror of suddenly finding myself locked inside was a picture that I carried around like a family photograph. It just seemed so easy to become a number, even just feeding the pigeons could get you a stint behind bars. Then I'd imagine a life without bills; shopping, traffic, cooking, rent and it began to look attractive. A job in the library would suit me. Education would be accessible and I could develop my interests and paint all day. My health would be taken care of and there would always be company. It could all be problem free—that's if I could control my routine. At this juncture my horror resumed and my thoughts became a little more realistic. There would be no privacy, I'd have to be perpetually accountable, and I couldn't just leave the building or go or stay somewhere when I wanted to—that would be intolerable. Then there was the brutality, the bullying, and the violence. Maybe I'd become part of that and spend my days down the block fighting every issue, or just fighting things because everyone in Holloway did it.

But I didn't feel like asking Cleo what that sentence had meant. These were adults and the fact that she should need to reassure me of something like that put me above them in some kind of way, as if they were indebted to me. On the other hand I had grown to respect her so it could have been said as a kindness to allay my fears. But I was still nervous. So the very reasons that had motivated me to enjoy teaching were now making me regret being connected to it. The fact that it was more than a teaching job and that it wasn't mainstream education had appealed to me. But now its complexity and its behind-the-scenes way of life had given me extra problems that I didn't want. I hated having to deal with this issue; it reminded me of school and detention. We'd civilised our workplace, acted towards each other like adults, we'd behaved normally, and forgotten where we really were. That was it, that was where it had gone wrong. They had been put into prison in order to deprive them of such a pleasure, they weren't supposed to enjoy it and they had for a while. And however much those scales in my head tilted up and down as I attempted to rationalise and sort it all out, I couldn't find any solid ground to ease my mind—just a doomed resignation of exposure which knocked out any rationality in the first round. Naivety caused me to imagine I could push it under the carpet and forget about the whole thing and pretend it never happened.

These two women had spent their lives dodging and evading issues. Their lives on the outside were full of deceit and lies. Now, for the first time since they both could remember, they had decided to tell the truth. Or was it that stereotypical theory concerning women and their inability to keep a secret. My Monday started off with a hint of what was to come. An inmate was cleaning one of the landings as I approached. Putting one of the yellow warning cones into place to alert oncomers to the wet floor, she turned her head and gave me a big wink. 'Could I put in for a job change please Miss and join the mural party, this cleaning is getting me down?'

That was just the beginning, I went to collect the mural painters, and was not only stared at by the officers through the glass but the rest of the women on the wing. They just couldn't keep it to themselves could they? My decision was to become a blank, a complete blank and not to refer to the incident at all. We acted normally, with excessive politeness and consideration towards each other. But they would stop talking sometimes when I was around and make me feel uneasy. Each day references were made to me by one inmate or another, with winks or gestures. As the week wore on, I got even more irritable as I realised half the prison, or maybe nearly all of it I guessed, knew what had gone on—or thought they knew what had happened. The prison grapevine had produced a bumper harvest with tendrils curling through the bars into every cell and dropping fruit onto every landing. This was a big scoop—and it just had to be published. It was just too good a secret to keep, too good an event to lie about! But I was still hopeful that it would go away and be replaced by some other drama that was massive enough to overtake it.

Part of me kept thinking that nothing had happened which wasn't normal and natural and 'What was all the fuss about?' Institutional exaggeration of what would be of no consequence on the outside was confronting me again. The nature of Holloway put this into the bracket of 'Forbidden' and so it had to be investigated. So it was. A governor-cum-inquisitor confronted Maggie and Cleo warning them that he would be coming down to the mural room to ask questions. So it was all seeping into an official enquiry. Those nudges and gestures had rattled a few nerves causing authority to react. First, Maggie was called out at the governor's request. Cleo and myself painted on in silence, and tried to hear what was going on in the next room. Maggie returned with a sly smirk and nodded to Cleo who went out to give her evidence.

'Mr. Davies, me! Having a shower with some men, now you know I love sex, I have been called a nymphomaniac and I do love it so. Those rumours about the men and me, Mr. Davies you know about the rumours in this place—mmm but I would love to share the shower with those men, it's a shame it's only a rumour.' Maggie lied with a skill well-practised over years of criminality and relied on her promiscuous reputation to fuddle the issue. 'Mr. Davies, I'm a married woman. I love my old man, we've been together since I was a kid; I wouldn't go with anyone else! . . . I just couldn't'. Cleo also lied but with the ease of an alcoholic. She relied on her own marital bliss to rescue her and Mr. Davies left the wing. Maybe that would be the end of it. Oh no—it was my turn in the dock. My head of department called me in and told me all about the story , the rumours and the gossip. I was a blank.

Then Mr. Davies asked to see me: 'I am running an investigation into rumours concerning relationships between male inmates of Pentonville and female workers painting on the Mother and Baby Wing. Did this happen to your knowledge?'

'No … it didn't'. His question was so arranged that I could say 'No' with conviction. I didn't known exactly what had happened. I had not actually witnessed anything, I hadn't asked and in theory didn't know. He asked me again and I denied it. Another blank. I wasn't sure enough of my own abilities to withstand pressure, so I didn't say any more. I didn't feel confident enough to decorate and embellish, I just kept up the denial and I'm glad the questioning didn't go on for long. But it was a badly constructed question easily slipped around. So I relied on what was really a technicality to take the heat off me in the hope that he'd close the case.

The thing about Mr. Davies was that he was a man with a good sense of proportion and was also perceived as a strong governor—a rare combination. Yes he had the reputation for keeping to the rules but not in a petty and small-minded way. I got the feeling that pressure had forced him to investigate and that he just had to do it but there were other more important things that he could be getting on with. But I wasn't that sure. Certainly, with me and the women he came over as extremely serious and driven to find out exactly what had gone on, so I took it just as seriously—it was the wisest thing to do. As for that male supervisor, we never talked again; we passed each other but never spoke about that day. He left soon afterwards, and so did the male inmates. They didn't come into Holloway after that.

Work resumed and after another couple of weeks the mural was complete. The three of us talked over our life together down there and all we had done, what we had learnt, how our work had improved, how really good the mural looked. We got into quite a nostalgic mood and of course we talked about that incident.

'Shall we tell her now?' Cleo looked across at Maggie.

'Tell me what?'

'Well we didn't tell you at the time because you would only have worried and now I'm not worried so we thought we'd tell you the truth.'

Of course they had had sex, the big deal the full works; they'd bonked themselves silly, every which way and more. They couldn't stop themselves and it was all so great, they said, fantastic, unbelievable.

'Then my period was late, a fortnight late, but I started this morning so everything ended up OK, didn't it. If I'd have told you that before Miss you would have only worried, so I didn't. Anyway everything is all right now.' Then the full implication of that incident dawned and I imagined how I would explain a pregnancy. The paradox between creative activity and control within a prison forced me to think about issues that would be irrelevant outside. The oppression of the system intruded and I resented having to cloud any future progress still labouring over the right and wrongs of the incident. So we worked on and somewhere hidden in the foliage was that clandestine playtime, somewhere amongst the birds was an interlude of anxiety and dread. Somewhere between the leaves, I waited as they disappeared, somewhere painted in was the excitement, the worry and the questioning. Then we completed it, finished it, and ended it all. It was sad. For months we had painted together, learnt a great deal, not only about ourselves but about each other. Word had got around about how good the mural was. The women were cheery with the compliments and confidence grew out of that praise. It enhanced the newly converted department and even more worthy was the fact that the inmates themselves had contributed and given their time.

When the Mother and Baby Wing opened, Princess Anne called in and saw the mural. Approval and appreciation reaffirmed that it had been a success. The women enjoyed it. It elevated spirits and the quality of it impressed the critics who thought that inmates of Holloway were only destructive and should be punished, not educated. Photographs were taken and it won a big inter-prison art competition that year. We thrived, going on to decorate a new Visits Room and a waiting room within the prison, involving different students, different subjects and other problems.

Cleo left the prison never to return and Maggie was transferred out to another of Her Majesty's establishments. She returned for a short while, but it was much further on in time and that past shared experience was reduced to just a fleeting remark, that's all. But at last there was a purpose-built Education Department, next to the chapel with proper classrooms and a small quadrangle of a garden. So we felt good and started to settle in. There were three floors for us to organize.

I was at the end of one of my classes in the old prison at the top of that spiral staircase (now scrap metal or in some reclamation yard) and chatting over nothing much to one long term prisoner. The days of the old prison were numbered, most were in a reflective mood pushing memories forward for comfort. We'd started on some ramble or two in the twilight at the end of an evening class when I decided to push aside the small window to peer through the bars. For once the noises of the outside world dominated and invaded that small quiet room, the sounds of the street coming right inside through the tiny gap. Across the road people waited at a bus stop loaded up with parcels and held out their hand to stop a double-decker. The taxis squeaked to a halt over the hill and picked up passengers The town lights were bright and busy. It was an odd feeling to watch and then turn around to that darkening interior of a community of people confined inside, free to look out but that's all. Sarah came over to join me and stared outward to the Parkhurst Road, but could only stand it for a couple of seconds. She withdrew her head, gathered up her things and asked to be taken back to her wing. Nothing else was said.

At the end of a corridor in the new Education Department on the first floor was a huge window stretching from the ceiling to the floor. Some prison planner had thought a good view of the outside world would be a generous gesture, or maybe he hadn't even thought about it much. Right in front, just yards away was an elevated view of London and a hint of its delights. Students would book their seat in front of the big screen and watch this real life documentary about Parkhurst Road and the life that was passing them by. Playing hooky from whichever classroom and huddling up to each other, they'd just stare out and readjust themselves to life 'on the street'. Then uncomfortable rumblings would replace the initial fascination as they remembered they were on the wrong side of that transparent barrier. So they got angry and it grew to rages from old grudges yet to be avenged. It caused a traffic jam within Holloway, blocking the corridor. Then the window got smashed and got repaired, so it was nicknamed 'The Wind-up Window' because it continued to have that effect on the women. That is until this Tantalus got smashed again. Finally the window was boarded up completely by someone with a modicum of sensitivity and commonsense.

My classroom was on the ground floor, with a view across to the demoted griffins trying to frighten passers-by on their way to the prison skips. It didn't work though. They were just 'in the way' and had to be skirted round impatiently. My new quarters seemed luxurious at the time, with their sink and storeroom and I was pleased to have a base for once. Two sides overlooked the gardens, which made the room light and airy. Inside a huge narrow store cupboard would be fitted with shelves and somewhere on the walls a shadowboard would be encased with a lock to hold scissors, a Stanley knife and other tools. A small stretch of corridor immediately outside my door joined up the outside back entrance to another door which led out to a small square garden; all the other classrooms were built around this tranquil spot with benches and flower beds. A stairwell led upwards out of that small corridor and the other classes were held on the first floor. Diagonally, across the other side of the building, was the students entrance and the office for prison staff who supervised them. I had the classroom furthest away from the office and for that reason had an internal telephone just in case.

We were allocated a studio to allow women to work on future murals, extending my territory to two whole rooms. The new mural studio was a deserted room, full of old filing cabinets and damaged office furniture. Thousands and thousands of vicious metal dividers had to be removed, carefully or they would cut the fingers. The one dark window looked out onto a dark wall—all pretty ghastly. It took time and a good imagination to motivate us. Chris was helping me right from the beginning. She was tireless and so supportive. Other adjectives like 'formidable', 'incorrigible', 'amazing' didn't quite do her justice. I grew to respect her energy and enthusiasm. She was a foundling, having been dumped in some doorway in a basket soon after she was born. But her past didn't take up much room and this prison sentence was going to be a positive time to learn and gain new skills then move on. She was cheerful and never felt sorry for herself, there were no obstacles, just solutions. Often her opinions offended people because she was so forthright, though never rude with it or aggressive. So we settled in to our new studio and became part of the sightseeing tour for visitors to the prison.

She talked, explained and educated them about everything, so I left her to it as she was so impressive. Our work was promoted with a brilliance that impressed them all, and spoken about with clarity and precision. Her first visit to the art room had been a reluctant one, but in keeping with her plan to use her time constructively and learn new skills. Now each effort excelled her last and her regular attendance showed commitment and staying power. Her drawings and paintings inspired other students to have a go and she became an extremely competent artist. She even did a course at the local college on her release.

We decided that to decorate the Visits Centre in the same way as the Mother and Baby Wing would not work. We couldn't paint directly onto the walls, so the murals had to be moveable. Huge pieces of blockboard were ordered and talented inmates were allocated one each. Chris painted three and they were good, very good. She also painted a magnificent Japanese-style screen. We did about ten in all, taking in different subjects. The mural room could only fit three large paintings comfortably. I couldn't visit often, what with my teaching timetable. But the room overlooked my class and all the women were trusted, so they were more than content to work alone and I could keep an eye out in case they wanted anything.

Chris was a strong woman who quite apart from being determined to make her stay a positive experience, wanted to give something back to the institution. She took advantage of every facility and sought out the Education Department as part of her renewal. There was sadness to her life and a hardship that often provoked days of quietness where she didn't say much and withdrew into herself. But there, waiting at the gates at visiting time, on the dot, came that gentleman caller. If it wasn't for him and his regular visits, I don't think Chris would have coped so well. It wasn't just the visit that absorbed her; it was the preparation, the pampering, the whole ritual, and the anticipation. All of the evening was spent making sure she would look her best for him and he did the same for her because it was important. He gave her intense joy, she adored him and his thoughtfulness kept her alive and invigorated during her sentence. She made cards for him, wrote to him daily and loved him as much as she could. What carried her through in times of stress and her down periods was her brooch. Attached to her overalls with a safety pin was a pair of her partner's underpants on which Chris had lavishly applied his favourite after-shave. This sexual talisman carried her through her sentence, lifting and soothing her spirits. From the back, as she was working, every now and again I'd see her brush fall, her work stop. Then her shoulders would rise and push up her body, her head would turn and there would be a sound of a deep, deep inhalation followed by an equally deep sigh. She'd pick up her brushes, relax her body and paint her guts out. If she liked you, then Chris couldn't do enough for you, but if you got on her wrong side then venom would spit in your eye. There was no in-between.

Chris appeared to be able to get what she wanted from any man. It was her voice; how she held herself and how she fixed onto a man's attention when all her assets were synchronised: completely over the top, so that it was blatantly obvious what her game was, so there was no deception—just sexual banter. Her style of speaking was precise and slightly challenging, and little noises in-between her words gave physicality to her voice. It was a seductive machine that should have been invested in on the stock market. I could hear her approaching; it was the clicking of those four-inch heels worn effortlessly throughout the day, and that height, the straight back and swagger—it made a formidable impression.

When I couldn't manage to wangle some extra resources from Bob in the stores, Chris would insist that I take her with me next time. I'd stand on the sidelines while she extracted from him material that he had so readily denied existed when I last asked. She could make a mop bucket sound like a sexual proposition. There she was on one side of the counter with Bob on the other side. She leant over and began her performance. It was all sounds and overlong expressions, subtle movements, sly overlong looks and sighs that drifted away lazily. The male victim drawn into the act knew he was out of his depth with this lady. So he clung on to his bunch of keys as a reminder of some kind of authority, kept to his side of the counter and let her have the bucket.

Anyone phoning for an appointment at the house of pleasure that employed Chris on the outside would have been completely manipulated. If he needed chastising and rebuking or didn't quite know what service would suit him, then Chris could get it out of him. She could summon up trade; encourage punters in their desires and tease out a cash only payment. She kept me in line with her organizational abilities. A list greeted me each morning of jobs that required doing, then she'd start her own routine, cleaning and polishing the room, and only after that begin painting. Every line she drew, she measured perfectly, redrawing things over and over again until they met her high standards. Materials were kept pristine, and hung on the wall according to size and texture. Every day her face was drawn and painted just as immaculately. There was never a slack day. I couldn't keep up with her and she often shook her head if I'd forgotten or mislaid something. She worked relentlessly with dedication spurred on by those underpants pinned to her chest and serenaded by one of Barry White's cassettes, 'Can't Get Enough of You Babe'. Sometimes work went on and time was forgotten and it was only the sound of the 'Muck Trucks' distributing meals to the wing that intervened to signal that she had better return 'home' for dinner.

Painters contributing to murals were chosen on ability. They might not be over-accomplished or over-talented, but they had to have the capacity to learn, take criticism, undertake research and work unsupervised in a responsible way. For the most part everyone fitted those criteria but Emily was an exception. She had a heap of talent: not necessarily of the creative kind, but that of the formally trained academic. But she was just as welcome as those more primitive painters who had not had the advantage of such an education. The first day all seemed to be well, and after a morning of teaching I zoomed over to see how things had gone. Less social than the rest of the group and partly because it was her first day, it still seemed to me that Emily's membership of the group could only be beneficial. She hadn't done much but what she had done was solid and good.

I was to be supervising the next day but arrived late. Little work had been accomplished by the newcomer who was sitting on the floor dozing. Normally the rest of the painters would badger me for opinions, criticisms, compliments and encouragement. They were silent and watched me instead of greeting me, leaving me to discover something for myself. They were leaving a space to point me in the right direction. So I stayed and tried to engage Emily in conversation but she only nodded over and over again. The next session she came late and in exactly the same withdrawn state, with not much being done and little communication. So I returned to the wing with her where privacy allowed me to illicit some reason for her condition. She was just depressed and thought she was getting the flu (she added carelessly as an afterthought). It sounded plausible. The rest of the workers wouldn't disclose any information but they were not happy with the situation; this much I could see for myself. Emily was never asked to join in anything. They never seemed to include her in conversations, so something was putting them off. Her work had got way behind, she had hardly done anything.

I confronted her about her behaviour, her fatigue, her flu like symptoms. In her room she lolled backwards with her eyes fixed like she was blind, or if she was not blind then her eyes had lost the ability to translate the images in front of her. There was only one explanation. Whatever noxious substances she had sniffed, smoked or swallowed had rendered her useless.

'Who grassed me up . . . which one?' Nobody had grassed her up, the other women wouldn't. I was experienced enough to recognise the signs and I didn't need any detectives to confirm my further suspicions. She didn't care too much either when I sacked her; she didn't care too much about anything. She just 'sucked at a wasp', that familiar insulting noise emanating somewhere between the lips and the teeth and as I left her room she sucked at another wasp, just to see me on my way.

As far as I was concerned my only worry was that work on the murals would have to be abandoned if there was any hint of drugs. I didn't want to be in the position of providing a safe haven for her or anyone else's consumption of drugs. The prison had set an important precedent by allowing us to work on our own and I was damned if I was going to let it go because of one person, someone who didn't seem to give a damn, had no loyalty and didn't care. The atmosphere changed immediately after I sacked her. The other women were relieved that she had gone and activity returned. Ten murals were completed. Huge paintings around three metres by a metre and a half—inspired by many painters: Gauguin, Rousseau, Blake, Patrick Caulfield. Then there were paintings of forests, Portmerion, the Taj Mahal, Chinese paintings; a good cross-section of taste and culture. The students in the Education Department have always produced work of a high quality and now efforts were being made to encourage all talents. As well as paintings, other skills were represented at the opening ceremony for the Visits Room, showing excellence in ceramics, tapestry, textiles, jewellery-making and poetry. Cards were made of this mural and it all came together in one marvellous display. The opening would not only celebrate the Visits Room but the work that was going on. It would also be a push for the prison shop.

Next, the women began taking their talents outside the prison, up the Archway Road to the Whittington Hospital. When more complicated medical procedures were needed than could be carried out in the prison, the sick women were escorted up the road and cared for on one of the wards there. Pregnant women gave birth on the Whittington's maternity ward, so that the hospital was important to Holloway Prison and still is today. If the women could paint something colourful, then the hospital would benefit, especially by brightening-up the maternity ward. Overlooking this ward was a small and tranquil garden, so the ceramics department joined in to make a bird-bath and a narrow tiled walkway. The paintings depicted different images of mothers with their babies and each woman who helped chose her own interpretation. If there was no room to work in the mural room at the prison then painting continued in the art room. It didn't even stop during lunch: permission was granted to carry on continuously throughout the day, just to get paintings done before women were shipped out or released. And it all got completed on time; everything giving an even greater reason to celebrate. The paintings and ceramics for the Whittington Hospital travelled out of the prison and up the road to where they would be displayed on one of the wards. This present was a thank you for all the care the hospital had taken of prisoners from Holloway.

At that particular time a casual and clandestine shopping system existed at Holloway. Half an ounce of tobacco could buy you a hand-knitted jumper. One roll-up could be exchanged for a painting, or a ceramic, but there was no consistency so it was often unfair. Women skilled in different ways could exploit their fellow inmates and staff. The reverse also applied in that those without skills became vulnerable. This subversive market wasn't (and couldn't) be monitored but everyone knew of its existence. It was a grey area and there was a cavalier attitude to the exchange of goods that exploited all the participants.

That was not the only motive for establishing a shop. If the women could supplement their weekly spends it would give them a certain independence and relieve their families from pressure. Also, if any profits were made, there was an opportunity to give something back, to contribute to a charity of a woman's choosing. It was accepted that a certain amount of 'unofficial' trading would continue, but at least with a shop there would be a structure so that people could defer to it. That was the way I was thinking before I came up with the idea that a level of true retail business might also work.

Hopefully a shop, supervised by staff but run by the women would regularise the dubious activities and do a bit of fair-trading to benefit everyone. It was clear that many of the women had extraordinary skills in many crafts. The multi-cultural population, national crafts, individual skills and the talent meant there would be no supply shortage if it could all be nurtured. Through the Education Department, women of all ages were discovering talents they never knew they had. Women with low self-esteem were given the opportunity to develop creatively, counteracting the negative effects of the prison system. Similarly, women with unrealistic self-esteem could re-evaluate their self-perceptions and learn a bit more about their true potential. The knock-on effect was that women became more interested in education generally and started to explore other subjects that they had previously found daunting.

After the tedium of institutional layers that stood between the idea and its realisation, the opening day finally arrived. It was a celebration of all the works completed over the months that had revitalised areas of the prison, places which until that time were gloomy and dull. Then there was the Whittington Hospital and the pictures there. It was to be a grand occasion. The women were superb; they behaved with dignity and were just wonderful. We all met the guests, talked and showed off our work. It was stylish and thoroughly enjoyable.

None of the influential guests let us down. We had support from the Gulbenkian Foundation and Ben Whitaker came to celebrate the evening. Judge Stephen Tumim opened the event and supported our aims in his introductory speech. The Governor of Holloway played host and showed the guests around the exhibition. It was a glorious evening. Holloway at its best. Even the artist Patrick Caulfield came to see Chris's transcription of one of his paintings. Her admiration for his work had driven her to base a picture on a still life he had painted, and she'd added a glass of wine and a nice bottle of red, which she thought was just what it needed! Other paintings hung on the walls and in the middle of the room different crafts were displayed. On the floors were rugs made by the women. Food was provided and everyone perceived that a good thing was happening, something quite unique. Of course there was the odd photographer who insisted that the rugs would be shown off more if one particular, rather voluptuous inmate lay down on them! But nobody minded that.

The shop opened from then on too. It was run by the inmates, made money, and achieved all that was hoped of it. There was a fair retail system regulated by staff and the charities the women chose to donate to were Victim Support and the Arthur Koestler Foundation. I'm not saying there were no problems, yes there were, from shoplifting to other dubious activities—and sometimes there was a bit too much under-the-counter activity. The shoplifters were given short shrift and banned eternally, sometimes for trying to take from women in prison for that very offence!

Despite the fact that the room didn't have any windows, it had been so well decorated and kitted out with light fittings that no-one ever seemed to notice. Inside, along one side of the shop was a small workshop where commissions were completed and sales were carried out. It became a splendid showpiece for visitors. Not everything was brilliant; many a time we had to tactfully reject some creation that sagged or bulged or was badly sewn or finished off. Cardigans made of wool like straw that caused the wearer's skin to itch went straight to the reject pile. but altogether it was a highly creative period, even down to the crutchless knickers and leather shorts. Among the favourite wares were Rastafarian teddy bears, all red green and gold with dreadlocks. We couldn't make enough of them.

Jasmin was the first manager of the shop. Convicted of some bank fraud, her numeracy and literacy skills were faultless, even if her other qualities complicated things. She lived on one of the trusted wings, without locks so that the inmates could come and go to their respective jobs around the prison without an escort. We had been allocated a small workroom on the wing and Jasmin was able to take some work home to her room at the weekend. So that is what I was doing, bringing the work to her. She lived on a small spur, separated from the rest of the wing and with only a few residents, a privileged arrangement in fact. There she was entertaining a young man. Not long in his job as a prison officer, he had in that short space of time taken to socialising and light coupling. They jumped apart as I entered the room as if something repellent had arrived. He laughed, but there hadn't been any joke. She laughed an open laugh with enjoyment at something pleasurable and at his lack of composure.

Jasmin seemed to be the most secure of the three of us. I was disconcerted and he was embarrassed. I gave her the work and left. It got worse after that and he never seemed to be doing any work, always just hanging around her. He continued to visit her on her wing and in the workroom, and I picked up whispers and mutterings from the other women who Jasmin shared her life with, not all in a spirit of goodwill or looking after her welfare. Rather it was jealousy: Jasmin was seen to be getting more than they were. The young officer continued to hang around and I started to dislike his presence because I felt he was putting on me—taking advantage, in a careless sort of way. They both were. Again, the prison culture pervaded my work in its unique institutional way. What worried me more than anything was the imbalance of power. One had the keys, the other no real freedom at all. So the relationship was open to abuse. That was a worry: the lack of parity. Frankly, I didn't care one way or the other about what was going on but it had become my business somehow, however much I didn't want it to affect me. This re-emergence of Holloway's complexities meant that I would have to deal with it. 'You're not working as well as you were . . . this project is new Jasmine and I don't want the opportunity squandered because of your indifference. He doesn't come down any more, too distracting, I'm going to tell him as well.'

'Have you got a minute?' I beckoned him out of his office and we stood in the corridor. Then I enlightened him about the institution and about its boundaries. To me it didn't matter what he did and with whom, it was his life and it wasn't any of my business, but did he know that if someone found out he would be asked to leave? No question about it. Jasmin, well what more could happen to her, the worst had already occurred—she was in prison. But for him, yes, he would come off badly. It was none of my business, it was his life and up to him what he did. But it wasn't going to involve me and I didn't want to see him in the workshop anymore. He could involve someone else in his intrigue. The project was more important than him, too many people had invested time to pioneer this new venture and any hiccups might sabotage the whole enterprise. I explained that he had keys and she hadn't and about abuse of power and exploitation all of which would be perceived in a bad light if it came out. He blustered and flustered and I think I must have appeared cold-hearted, but I just had to warn him about the implications of his visits. He never sought out Jasmine again. She found solace in the arms of another, some lady in her dormitory. That was the rumour anyway.

As I write this, the shop still exists in Holloway, but it had to leave its plush, custom-made venue and moved into a classroom. Then, when all the emphasis was on key skills, a new, smaller room was needed for a maths classroom. So it was downsized again to a toilet above the art room, on the first floor, accessed via a stairway. It always seems to be adapting to new and different prisoner populations and what they can offer the institution. And as to the Mother and Baby Wing mural, the 'Rain Forest', well rumour had it that they wanted the room for something else, so it was about to be painted over by a new Governor unfamiliar with the effort and organization that had caused that painting to spring into life. Nobody approached me to ask how I would felt. There was just a rumour, which I investigated. The mural symbolised so much; it had been such a positive and innovative project that I could not just stand by and let it be painted over. But gradually, no-one in the prison seemed to recall or understand its significance. New staff came and went as they rose up the promotional ladder, and I was still, after all, just a teacher. I sought the support of Sir Hugh Casson (as he was at that time). I cornered him one day at the opening of the Koestler inter-prison art competition. Immediately he responded positively and sympathetically. He actually came into Holloway with Lady Casson, saw the mural and put pressure on the powers that be to keep it alive and in place. It worked—at least for a few more years. By the time the walls were transformed back into Home Office cream I had come to terms with its mortality. Only photographs remain as evidence that it once existed. The continuing enthusiasm in the Arts and Crafts Department of Holloway owed a great deal to the support of Sir Hugh and Lady Casson. They gave of their time and took an interest in the department at a time when it was lacking within the prison.

Within the department we produced fashion shows and the inmates contributed in their different ways. If it was not making the clothes, then it was wearing them, or cooking at the end of the show, or just helping out with one thing or another. Different groups visited the prison occasionally for some event, maybe a theatre production, or some other spectacle. It has always been our policy to support such projects. But sometimes I wonder who they really benefit. I'm not saying that they should not continue, but some modifications should be made. I remember one theatre group that came into Holloway. They had a grant of thousands of pounds for their production. They were going to give a dance concert that would be performed in front of a specially invited audience. A selection of women were auditioned and the rehearsals began. Security was stretched in order to accommodate the theatre workers, the managers, soundmen, instruments, and the times they chose to start or end their work. A great deal of goodwill was forthcoming and a lot of reorganization took place to support them. Once inside the prison they needed to be escorted around and rooms had to be provided for rehearsals. So we invested a lot of time and energy in making sure we provided for them properly.

The women needed costumes and the craft teacher volunteered her services and those of her class. There were backdrops to design and make, and individual costumes to fit and sew and dye and design—it was all a great deal of work. With no money available from the main budget, the teacher begged old sheets from the laundry and recycled those. Eighty women worked on the costumes and some spent their dinner hours making sure everything would be ready on time. From the first day that the producer discussed the style and design of the clothes and backdrop until a few days before the show he never showed his head again. Then just before the show he decided he didn't like the main backdrop and rejected it—the work of eighty women! All the outfits had to be individually made to fit each of the sixteen women who would be dancing and they all looked gorgeous. A couple of other small backdrops were accepted, but there was no doubt that the women felt rebuffed and disappointed. They were treated very badly.

The show itself was a splendid affair, with many high profile visitors attending the final production in the gym; most of them invited for the theatre group's benefit. Not once was the effort of the behind-the-scenes-workers mentioned. No credit was forthcoming—no mention of backstage support. And in the video of the production, none of the women were given credit. There was an after production party — and if it hadn't been for the teacher gate-crashing towards the end, then those backstage workers wouldn't even have been represented in that celebration. As it was, it was so near the end of the event that there was not much left, so the party was yet another disappointment.

Different kinds of theatrical or music groups have visited Holloway from time-to-time. The most successful were the simple productions, whether it was performing, singing, or just playing. Other production companies do the rounds of prisons and part of their intention is to help women deal with issues in their life. Improvisation forms a large part of performances and the women act out very personal experiences to do with their lives. It can get quite emotional, harrowing even. It often exposes their vulnerabilities, relives past happenings and scrutinises the implications of their actions on members of their family and others. At the stipulated time, the production company clears up and departs leaving the women to cope. They are left, alone, often with scars still showing and unresolved. Depression can result, and other bad feelings. The theatre company writes up its performance notes and others write reviews. Job well done.

CHAPTER 5

Monday

'What you need to do is to start getting really extreme mood swings that will make them think you've got pre-menstrual tension. I'm going to start acting strangely, dressing wrong one minute, going out on exercise in me slippers then being dead smart the next. You know, behaving weird … it's worth the crack innit?! … But if they call up my previous I'm fucked. And I think I might start going to church and ask for my own Bible. I've got an old rosary, some nun gave it to me in Reception, I'll start wearing it. I'll convert and have it put on my parole reports.'

Two nodding heads synchronised and faces chin-wagged conspiratorially. The thought that they might outwit the system animated their Monday morning sloth. Lesley and her mate, reunited from different wings, talked shop. Bernadette marched into the room, liberated at last from the weekend. She bumped into icicles of bubbly curls and flung them away from her face, clumsily fastening the buttons of her fur coat at the same time. The Animal Rights Activist, already organized and ready to work, looked across at Bernadette and reddened with agitation. The thought that some poor creature was bereft of its skin and had died to make that coat provoked an almost uncontrollable tension.

Glasgow born Bernadette paced around the room, expelling words, spitting them out into the cowering space in front of her. She devoured the air, gnawed at it and the words fled from of her mouth in relief. Yanking her coat closer together, the rabbit skins split further than they were before under her arms and a button dropped off and scuttled away under a shelf. 'If I don't get into a single room soon I'll crack up, that dorm's fuckin' mad house … one bitch is on her knees all night long, singin', chantin' and bleedin' praying, that's all she does, then there's another bitch all she ever says is, 'Ere we go ,'ere we go, 'ere we go … all day long. She never stops, not even at night, keeps on like a bleedin' parrot. There's the two lesbians—not that I have anything against them, some of my best friends are lesbians—fuckin' lazy bastards though, always doing the only exercise they can be arsed to do, all the fuckin' time … I can't take much more. And that Susan Five Minutes, I'm going to get her off the wing if it's the last thing I do.'

A few heads, initially indifferent to Bernadette's tirade suddenly accorded her attention. There was comradely support at the recognition of a common enemy. A routine nodding of heads expressed sympathy. 'Listen, if you don't get her I will, Christ she's a right pain that Susan Five Minutes, what's with her … what's her problem? I reckon she does it on purpose you know, ringing and ringing for the officers every five minutes, some crackpots are like that, they like winding you up and that Susan's a right head case. The noise of that ringing, it does my head in … it does the officers' heads in as well. They had a go at her'.

'Too right the noise of that bell goes right through me. Susan Five Minutes is in a single … I'd like a room of my own instead of being banged up with all those nutters! I tell you the more you shout the more you get, there's no justice in prison, she gets what she wants 'cos she's a pain and they want to shut her up.'

Bernadette tore off a piece of paper, pulled it in between chairs and tables and flung it down on her drawing board. She tried to flatten out its bruised and creased surface with more pugilistic handling then threw her fur coat onto the floor. 'Fuck, I can't use this, just look at the state of it … give us another piece of paper Miss.'

I sat down next to her, allowing a smooth piece of imperial cartridge to replace the damaged reject. A new box of rainbow pastels with soft colours lay in readiness for whatever was to come. A smile almost slipped out from her as she looked at the seductive blank sheet of paper and let her head drop to inspect the new equipment, loosening up an enviable mass of black curls. Sympathetic noises emanated from me and with diversionary tactics she was re-routed to the real purpose of her visit to the class. Reaching into her pocket she dropped a couple of balls of paper onto the nearby table. Ironing them out with robust fists, she stabbed drawing pins through the paper fixing it to her easel. She nipped her hair together with a metal paper clip, trapping her crowning glory out of the way, as yet more words exploded from her and went on rampage amidst a multi-coloured cloud of chalk. 'Oh there's another bleedin' thing that fucked me right off … I've got nits … sorry about that Miss.'

The middle-class animal lover knew when to open her mouth and when to keep it closed. It wasn't the time to confront the fur coat. She acknowledged the terms of her imprisonment through its educational opportunities only, mostly through drawing and reading books. Those were her boundaries, otherwise it was complete non co-operation. No-one could call on her to help out with serving meals, or cleaning, or any other prison task. In this way she wasn't recognising the institution, nor accepting the validity of her punishment. Nothing was going to disturb her that morning, she would remain passive throughout.

Geraniums too tight in their ceramic shoes were tugged away from their yellow leaves. Blossoms, not yet quite expired were dragged off their stems. They tottered at the ferocious interest and nearly fell from the window sill. Dorothy the cleaner was finishing her chores. 'I must be feeling insecure, or I'm losing it, maybe it's the menopause. I went to court on Friday on production, came back and put my name on everything, all me bits and bobs. I even put me name on me broom … What a sad cow I am. These want re-potting Miss.' The plants lurched to one side as sharp tugs denuded them of their brown bits and sloshed water out of the pot. Dorothy weeded out the soggy fag butts long ago extinguished on their roots. The Sellotape squealed making everyone jump. Dorothy dragged it off the roll, bit off a good length, grabbed a long paintbrush, shoved it into the pot and lashed the thin stems to it. Grabbing her own, now personalised broom, she clung on as she made her way to the sink. 'This sink's blocked again, it stinks, you'll have to do something about it Miss … look at me ankles. Me blood pressure hit the roof again this weekend and me feet are so swollen I've had to cut my slippers open a bit … what a state to be in.' She shuffled over to her chair, hanging onto the broom for support then fell back into the chair, chin upwards, staring at the ceiling.

'That bleedin' light keeps flickerin' and flickerin'. It'll bring on one of me migraines', twisting the broom around she gave the bulb a punitive whack and it expired. That's better, no more flickerin', you'll have to get that fixed Miss ... I can hardly see now it's so dark. You'll have to get onto Works, they never do anything but walk around and drink tea ... That's men for you ... they're all the same a waste of time ... it's just not good enough. If you say there's some wires dropping down and something is sparking then they'll come quicker. You take me advice: health and safety ... that'll get them over here double quick.'

Another shape entered the room with a thin stringy-type vest that must have been acquired before the lady put on three extra stone. Flesh oozed out of the cotton sieve, stretching all the openings. She grabbed a chair and dragged it along the lino to the nearest radiator. Falling onto it, she basked in the heat, clinging on with fleshy thighs and arms and dropping her face into any space that was left. 'Miss I had three epileptic fits yesterday, look at me 'ead, I've a blindin' headache. They wanted me to stay in my room today but I had to get off that wing.' A huge bruise covered one side of her face. She suffocated the radiator for comfort.

Beryl appeared at the door and hovered in the opening. A big worry in her head made her body quiver. Prematurely aged on the outside, still a child on the inside she hopped from one foot to another, arms rubbing together and stiff fingers muddling themselves up with anxiety. She pulled at the blue acrylic jumper sticking to her body with enough electricity to run a power turbine. Her baggy skirt, too long and too tight, she tugged around at as her body continued to fidget. The dustbin was right in front of her. I pushed it slowly away from the doorway as she screamed, so terrified was she of that black plastic container. Breathing in big gulps of air and with sweat dripping onto her forehead, she glued herself to the wall and followed it round until she reached her favourite chair by the window and claimed her regular weekly spot. Telepathic champions we had become at outwitting the terrors of the black plastic bin. Each session had become less and less traumatic for both of us. I passed her work to her, a picture of a small country cottage—begun a couple of weeks ago.

An immense pastel centaur, holding a gun and with massive, muscular thighs, was emerging through the dust cloud surrounding Bernadette. She stuck on another piece of paper and a voluptuous naked woman with enormous breasts sat on his back. The epicentre of the tornado uplifted the chimera and his concubine. Huge windy blows from deep inside her chest rid her lungs of excess chalk which cascaded onto the floor. It made Bernadette so dizzy that she had to sit down quickly. With her mouth open, she inhaled ferocious squirts from her asthma pump, reached for more pastels to massage onto the bodies in her picture and thundered on with her masterpiece. Hopefully she had eliminated all the current miseries that unsettled her concentration. 'I don't need these fuckin' pictures any more I'm doing my own thing now.' Torn from their pins they got trampled underfoot.

A new student came in and headed straight for the only glass mirror she would have seen since her admission into prison. Beryl watched as the newcomer preened and postured before her reflection. Make-up control was provided in their rooms with square bits of reflective plastic—no glass was allowed. 'I don't like you.' Claudette reluctantly left her reflected image, swaggered up to Beryl, sucked her teeth and then returned to her reflection. 'I don't like you.' Beryl wriggled her backside on the chair and twisted her shoulders back slightly to provoke a reply. She really didn't like this new student so why shouldn't she tell her? Claudette pulled her face from the mirror and pushed it right into Beryl's as she sucked in more air between here eighteen carat gold teeth.

Fists poised for action, Beryl kicked her chair away, and waited for her unlikeable adversary to join in. Who was this woman? She'd never seen her before. First time in the class and here was this bitch running gums. Claudette swung her eyes up and down Beryl's dilapidated torso but decided that this confrontation wasn't worth it. After all, the only enhancement she wanted was her own, so she returned to the mirror to inspect her complexion, her hair and her body. Beryl jogged around menacingly but couldn't psyche up Claudette enough for a fight. Instead she was left with her eyes glowering in Claudette's direction as she painted, hoping to keep things on the boil for later.

Hypnotically, on exercise the previous week, Beryl's wing did a tour of the grounds but were jerked into consciousness when a frenetic frisbee skimmed out of line along the grass, launched itself across the hedges and flung itself at any door blocking the way. Completely demented, Beryl spun around-and-around evading prison officers who were trying to logically predict her next direction. So they too had to run around after her in the same demented fashion: anywhere there was a space, between trees, over benches. Beryl eventually raced towards the wall and tried to climb up. That was her undoing; this couldn't be allowed to go on any longer, so an athletic officer felled her to the floor. It had to rank as an escape attempt however hard they tried to describe it otherwise, so Beryl spent a couple of days down the block. Women don't try and escape very often. One Greek lady did some-how manage to get herself down to Camden Town, hidden in a lorry, but she was soon caught sitting eating tapas in her family's restaurant. In the days when civilian staff could escort women out to galleries or to shop for clothes I went on several such excursions with a ninety-nine per cent suc-cess rate. The exception was when the lady in question waited for me in reception with a new short haircut—odd I thought and felt uneasy right away. All went well to begin with. The Tate Gallery exhibition was appreci-ated and she gave it a lot of attention before asking to go to the toilet. And I never saw her again. I looked in every cubicle, waited around, went back into the exhibition, then gave up and rang the prison. On my return, the officers were sympathetic, and made sure that the vast amount of paper work was completed thoroughly. It didn't help though. I was mortified. She was re-arrested a few months later and came into my class with a big grin, but I didn't reciprocate, though I was polite.

Completely indifferent to the potential confrontation on one side of the classroom the two subversives carried on trying to beat the system. Lesley, expecting her sixth custodial sentence and now fired up with her ideas for a

'The Rain Forest'
Segments from the original
Holloway Mural: see *Chapter 4*

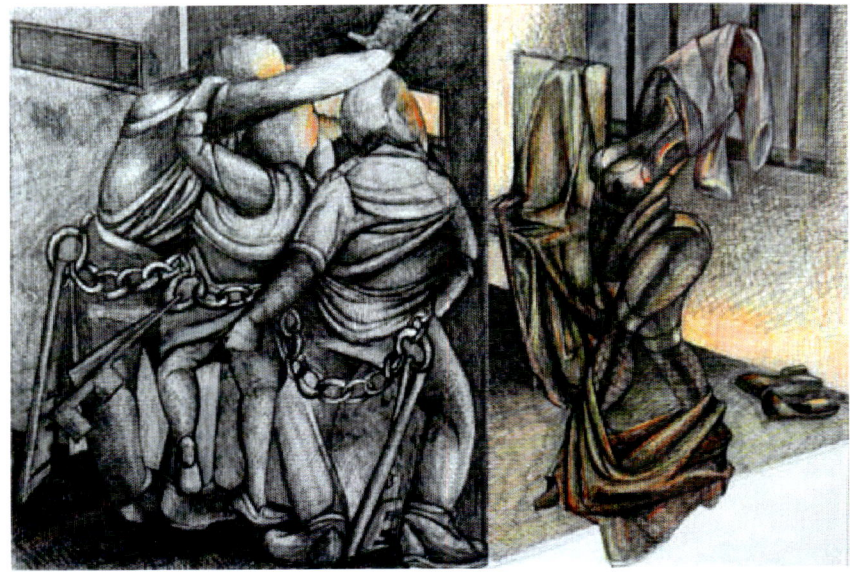

Clockwise from top left
Monday Morning
Case Conference
Conflict
Voyeurism

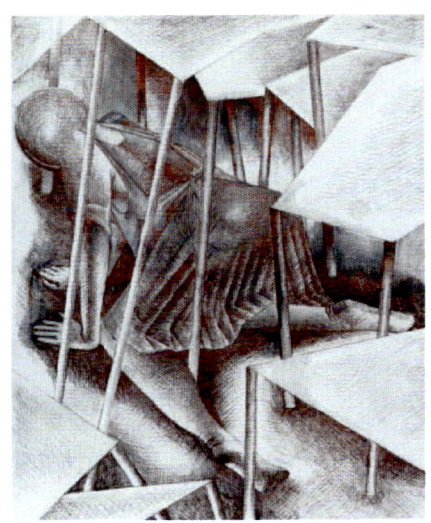

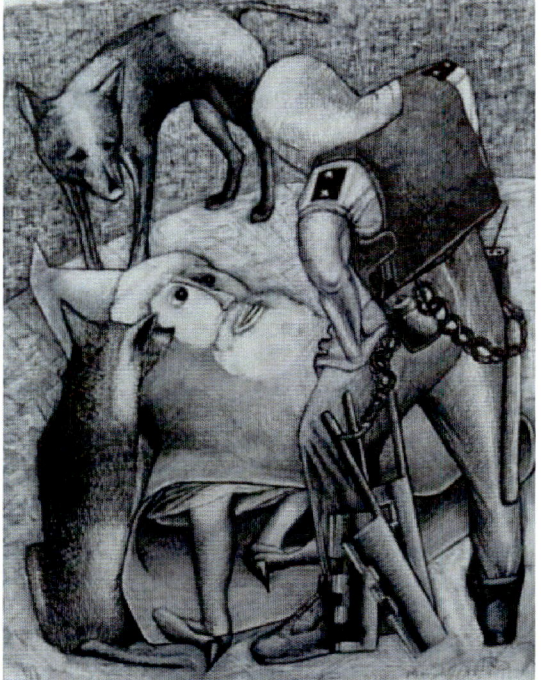

Clockwise
No Further Down to Go
Fran
Father Christmas

The Fight

Clockwise
Imaginary Play
Rope Ladder
Peace

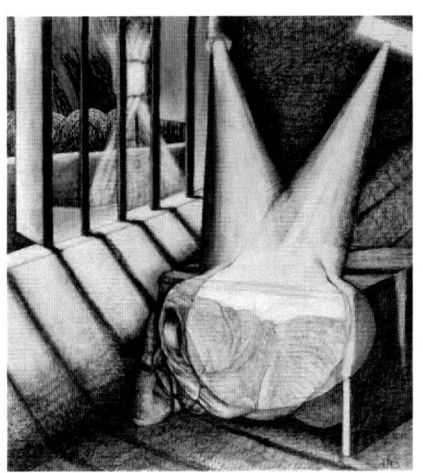

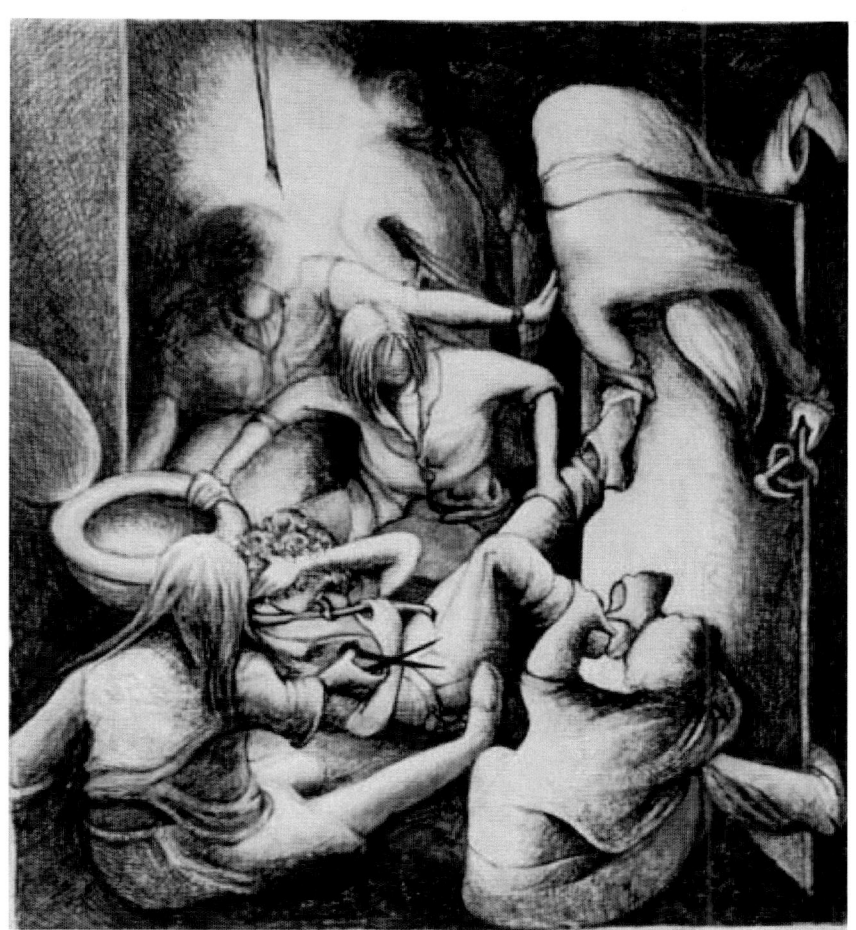

Ligature

Hilary Beauchamp—Self-portrait

quick release, leaned closer onto her mate's side of the desk and lowered her voice. 'This book I have just read ... great it was, honest. This woman got nicked for something real big, went to court and got off ... Yeh, got right off. What a touch ... she reckoned her PMT was that bad.'

Addicted from the womb, Lesley had been in and out of children's homes since she was tiny. Her mother was an intermittent presence and her father could have been any one of several men. Shoplifting from large department stores subsidised her addictions, Kings Cross provided her retail market and she slept where she could. She was a second generation addict, inherited just like her red hair. Spilt-out rather than born, she emerged from the womb with her appetite already well-established. With little to guide her, she couldn't escape the genes, and the dynasty later rolled over into a third generation. Her own daughter had taken up residence in the family's ancestral children's home in north London and awaited adoption.

Drug rehabilitation passed Lesley by—with no 'habilitation' the 're' became meaningless. Holloway was just another children's home for Lesley, another institution. The prison bullies had pounced on her one day, directly after someone had visited her. They thought she'd managed to get some drugs in. Unsupervised and alone in the dorm, they had stripped her with a frenzy known to all deprived druggies, violently explored every orifice of her body. Satisfied that she had nothing crotched, they scraped the inside of her vagina with a green scouring pad just for the hell of it: the vagina whose covert postal service competed favourably with the Royal Mail. It was not just a couple of deliveries a day, but a twenty four hour service, person-to-person, confidential and secure. Casual searches could never interrupt it. Strict rules governed its investigation, so nearly all this privatised mail got through. No monopoly inhibited messages on any level in Holloway. Air mail letters were swung by strings in bags from cell window to cell window, from wing to wing and landing to landing until they reached their final destination. But this was unreliable and too public for anything of value. Outside mail was read and censored, but that was costly and could take days. It was left to that tailor-made, independent personalised service to provide the only viable alternative.

'If I don't get off I'm going for a rehab.' Lesley came down to earth, unsure of her acting skills when confronted by the judge. She accepted all the consequences implicit in her criminal lifestyle. She had put herself on the wrong side of the law and wasn't very good at it. Always living from day-to-day at the bottom of the social ladder, she was just raw—nothing else. She'd never got beyond the effort of sheer survival, never got past that concentrated aim of just getting by, never anything more—all that energy and effort to just keep existing. She lived off her wits and they routinely let her down because they weren't sharp enough, so it was always a struggle with never a break, silence or peace. She was on edge all the time—hustling around for basics or relief: an exhausting way to live. 'But I'm fucked if I'm going to any old rehab', her lungs coughed up a deep rumbling noise that climbed up into her mouth. After that I couldn't watch or listen to what she would do with that mucus so I upped the radio and moved to the opposite side of the room.

The door flung open. 'Anyone got a Rizla?'

'Piss off.'

'I should be so lucky.'

'Ponce.'

'Fuck off.'

'I don't like interruptions.'

Smiling fixedly, without humour, I closed her out of my terrain. The freebie hunter stalked off to track down a more fertile response from someone else. It wasn't just the tenuous quality of some of the students' ability to concentrate that provoked such obsessive guardianship it was also the security issue that always prevented an entirely relaxed session. My shadowboard cupboard was comparatively small compared to, say, that in the Craft Room or the Ceramics Room. There were scissors, a Stanley knife, a steel rule and some lino-cutting tools and my intention was to keep it to such limited items. Despite a strict tally system for each tool issued, inevitably scissors could lie unattended on desks for a short time. Those were the monitored dangers. If anyone had a mind to and was determined enough, then any object could be abused. A plastic fork became a potential weapon. We used them to mix paint.

'Snap!' I heard a noise at the sink and saw a fork being pushed into a pocket. The new student returned to her chair. She had only been in the class two minutes and already she had two sharp pieces of plastic ready for something. I had seen a formidably strong piece of rope made out of plaited toilet paper. Such memories never left my mind and were stored up as a reminder that bad things do happen. Natural requests from other teachers in the prison were never denied. Classes always needed paper, coloured pencils or other equipment, but such interruptions could divert attention. Although I never felt that I worked 'on the edge' or considered myself routinely at risk or under siege, the possibility was always there, even if offences were perpetrated by just a few individuals. My aim was to keep any interruptions to a minimum. It simplified my working life and gave me fewer problems to worry about.

A large proportion of the class had little experience of regular schooling. Others couldn't speak English, still others were so highly medicated and sick that the simplest of educational tasks became difficult. Class protocol had to be taught, sometimes on a quite basic level. Officially we were part of an Adult Education College replicating the values and ethos pertaining to adults. But some of the prisoners had never been to school and could not work independently, and even if they could, the prison constraints pulled on the reins and dragged them back to childhood, demanding such things as toilet passes before women could wander unescorted around the depart-ment. Short attention spans demanded a vigilant presence from the teacher in order to encourage and support the women. With no form of stream-ing, every class presented a whole mixture of abilities, ethnic mixes and age ranges—and most women stayed for unpredictable lengths of time. While some students were able to work out their own space, do their own research and equip themselves with materials, others just sat in their chair waiting for me to wait on them. So it was more complicated than simply imbuing knowledge and skills, it was about accelerating maturity, addressing offending behaviour, creating a positive, safe environment and respecting other people. However much it seemed more appropriate to be referred to by our first name, left-over schooling and the institutional demand that officers be called Mr, Mrs, or Miss carried on into the classroom and in deference to other, more important issues, I let it pass. Flexibility—always flexibility, and balance—always balance.

A scratching noise coming from an empty chair turned everyone's head in puzzlement. The noise guided me over to a window and an empty chair. There was Fran on the floor making a rubbing of the Art Room lino with a 6b pencil as a background to a contorted female figure. The drawing was the second of three such renditions she'd produced in recent weeks. Agonisingly deformed with impossible hairstyles that had become sculptural extensions of the head, the figures sprawled out over three sheets of paper and were constrained only by the extremes of their corners and edges. The body in the current picture was broken up by heavily impressed lead from the softest pieces of graphite, and had then been polished to a leather like quality. The skin took on a shiny sensuous black toughness like armour, as if it was burnished metal. For the background to these female forms Fran rubbed whatever texture she liked—in the Art Room its old, damaged lino, in her room the brickwork of the walls. Given a table on her first visit, Fran chose to work on the floor beneath the desk where it was dark. That's where she stayed from then on because she was more at ease in the dimness; more relaxed when covered up by some table. Her cell, Room 26 on Level c3 was the only one in the entire prison kept in perpetual twilight by fabric draped across the window. Existence would be unbearable spent in the fullness of daylight. Fran needed the gloom. It brought back her upbringing with an appalling nostalgia and everyone made allowances. That's how her mother liked to live—in the dark. That way she could relinquish responsibility for the daily routines of family life and her maternal duties. Her mother had descended into an amorphous timelessness of alcoholism, while Fran nurtured herself as well as the rest of her siblings. She had protected her mother, defended her against an abusive partner and that's why she was in Holloway now. Her West Indian father was somewhere unknown, so she lived with her white mother in a dark flat in London. Alcoholism and violence, that's why Fran was in prison. She was one of the most creative women and one of the most damaged, the most dignified and rational and the most troubled, the most honourable and the most isolated. Considering the nature of Fran's offence and the reason for her incarceration, you would perhaps have expected some maternal response, some outside support while she completed her sentence, but it never came. It should have stirred into action all that love and affection that for years her mother had defaulted on, but it never came.

Michelle had been looking into space ever since the beginning of the lesson. I looked at the sheet of untouched paper in front of her and egged her on to begin. Picking up her pencil she made a few marks then leant forward releasing the pencil. 'I'm shagged out miss ... I can't do any more, get off my case and leave me alone ... Bernadette (she called over to her mate) you know I tried to scam a free trip to Jamaica on the out ... went round to the local nick and told them I was an illegal immigrant and that I wanted to go back home. Bastards found out I was born here in London ... bastards ... could do with a holiday in Jamaica. Miss, I've just got back in prison and me head is not in it yet, leave us a bit and I'll do something, but I'm pissed off, only been out a few months.' Her head lunged onto the table cradled by her two hands.

Bernadette looked up through her usual fog of chalk to catch Dorothy's expression and gave nothing away to infer collusion or dissension with an attempted scam. But there was a look that passed between them, for whatever reason.

'It can't be six thirty Miss, what's up with that clock?' Two hands had got stuck at six and twelve pointed east. Heads revolved to try and figure out the time by the clock above the store room door.

'You've got to get that seen to Miss.'

'I've tried and tried, nobody can fix it, apparently it can't be done ... my watch says it a quarter to ten.'

'God is that all it is,' moaned Lesley who hadn't even started anything yet.

The radio suddenly blasted forth for no reason, maybe it had caught the dis-satisfaction and was complaining too, so I rushed to turn it down just as news item interrupted the music. Prince Charles had cracked a rib playing polo. He would be in intense pain for some weeks the royal spokesperson told us.

'I bet he gets as many painkillers as he wants.'

'I bet he doesn't have to book for his doctor ... he won't have to wait in a queue.'

'Who gives a fuck about Prince Charles,' spat the Celtic dust cloud.

Fran was self-motivated, with good concentration so I could leave her alone under the table. From behind her easel, Bernadette continued to attack her paper. The chalk dust intermittently erupted towards the ceiling and she blew it away like fire-dragon. She wouldn't need any help for a while. The animal rights activist was deep in quiet thought with her back to the murdered fur, making sketches and preparing for some new creation. Beryl was painting her little country cottage with roses around the door, a wavy path, a pond and children on a swing. Dorothy, brazen Dorothy, frightened of nothing, led the scariest of lives on the streets outside the prison. She was prepared to spend weeks down the block and had served numerous sentences in Hol-loway, yet she would wilt with fear at the prospect of having to put the first mark on a pure white sheet of blank paper. Her hand would dither over the surface unsure of its landing field. She would become anxious and agitated, then bang the pencil down and occupy herself with some other diversion.

'Dorothy what are you doing today?'

'I told you I can't draw.'

'Well you can learn.'

'Either you've got it or you haven't, and I haven't.'

'Dorothy … you can learn.'

'Give us some tracing paper and I'll make my grandchildren a card.'

'She won't give tracing paper … not allowed … but she'll issue it if you want to use it on the wings,' Claudette spoke up for me as if reciting a regular refusal. 'If you try with a simple image, I'll help; I'll issue you with tracing paper for the wing, with pencils and all that but not in the class.'

Claudette smiled smugly over towards me at the theft of my punch line.

'OK, OK, OK, don't go on … give us that Disney book and I'll try.'

Lesley and her mate hadn't yet decided what, but they wanted something to decorate their rooms.

'How about a collage?'

'What's one of them?'

'Well you can use any kind of paper, coloured paper newspaper or magazines and cut out pictures or images that you like and create your own composition.' I pointed to examples around the walls.

'We'll use the magazines, let's have some scissors.'

'I want to make my kids a card.'

The string vest flowed onwards to the nearest table. Michelle had started to draw round her hand.

'Well that's a beginning, maybe you could do loads more impressions of both your hands … colour them or make patterns, cut them … '

'No, no, no …. that's all I'm doing, that's enough for today … I'm fucked and can't be arsed … is it near the end? … I mean it, Miss … don't push me anymore, get off me back … anyway I've applied to work in the gardens, I don't want to be here … I never wanted to come, I can't stand art.' The exhausted outline remained untouched for the rest of the lesson, evidence of two and a half hours work.

'You're a lazy bitch you are, stop whingeing and get your arse together.' Bernadette's close friendship allowed such public rebukes.

'Dorothy, I said you couldn't trace.' Between her pencil and *Winnie the Pooh* she'd stuck some greaseproof paper stolen from the kitchens, much safer than drawing freehand! As I approached she tried to hide it under her paper. 'Give it here, come on … I know it's under there.' Standing behind her I waited.

'Dorothy you've got to be a bit quicker than that, anyway I would have known it was traced … come on, let's have it.' Dorothy pushed it into my hand—all huffy and puffy.

I showed her how to measure and square up a drawing, then I started her off. 'Its simple really, anyone can do it'. I threw the greaseproof paper into the bin. She followed the shape and completed the image, and she smiled with pleasure at her completed card. 'Bleedin' hell Miss look what I've done!'

'There you go … it's not that hard is it?' Lesley and her mate had cut out designer accessories, Gucci bags, Prada clothes, Tiffany bracelets, surgically enhanced celebrities and a lot of gold, ready to be stuck onto paper as a reminder of the supposedly finer things that they coveted and which had been the cause of their demise. It had been the cause of their demise. Claudette had got involved and wanted to make her own interior decorations with even bigger and better pieces of gold.

The string vest was next, she'd written, 'I Luv You' on a scruffy bit of card. 'I'll send it to me social worker, so she can post it on to me two kids … can you make me an envelope?'

So it continued with me motivating them into action, encouraging them and keeping students awake long enough to for them to accomplish something.

From the first day of its official opening in 1852, Holloway Prison attracted sightseers. They flocked to observe the opening ceremony and from then on the building and its inhabitants continued to attract the curious. It became a popular Sunday diversion and the locals walked around the walls along a pathway that had been specially built to accommodate prams. Benches were provided at intervals where a limited view over the wall was afforded. Observers trained their field glasses in the direction of the barred windows hoping to see a real live criminal in the flesh. That curiosity has never waned and the prison still attracts interest from all quarters. Nowadays, visits are regulated with a special department providing the sightseeing tour and a guide to explain things. Specialists from all around the world enhance their knowledge of the institution. Some of them press their heads to the windows and even shade their eyes for a better look at the exhibits. 'How are we today, I'm Mr. James so and so (usually some double barrelled name). But you can call me James' Exercising their right to mingle, the top brass with two minders moved freely around in the same space that confined the exhibits, the shiny nametags attached to Her Majesty's politicians met the number plates—the guests of Her Majesty who were in the classroom. The official visitors' mobility confirmed for the women the loss of their own liberty and marked out their essential role: to behave in a suitable way and reply to any questions that might come their way. So the women spoke when they were spoken to, but those more socially adept visitors often asked the wrong questions of the wrong people.

'Wonderful, just had a delightful lunch, pucker tasty dish, but a tad cold and could have done with more seasoning, but excellent all the same. Just picked up my pay packet, too good to be true, five pounds fifty pence. The icing on the cake, life couldn't feel better.'

The West Indian comic abandoned her normal relaxed consonants and raised the tension even more by clipping or elongating words to make them sound posh. The rest of the class didn't feel like calling the man who had volunteered his first name anything, never mind James, so the majority of the women hid behind their drawing boards and hoped he couldn't see them. Totally out-classed, James shuffled off with a smile that meant nothing except to himself because he was just making sure the door was still open for his departure.

It seemed a very simple skill for anyone in public service to acquire: to be able to engage with the very public they represent, so why did they make it look so awkward and difficult?

The group mulched down into a productive growth spurt and I went for some paper from the store cupboard. My purse, usually way down in my bag, was lying near the top fastener. No notes were inside, just small change. Great dread tore downwards into my gut. I closed the door but brought the worry with me. I retraced my movements and the last transactions. I pictured their possible location. I was not always the most organized, but I wasn't mistaken this time. I remembered putting eighty pounds into the purse that very morning, four twenty pound notes. At the earliest break when diligent work allowed for another temporary absence I was free to search again. My fears materialised into concrete fact, my money had gone. Someone had stolen it.

Realising the consequences of such a theft and the inevitable disruption its discovery would cause to everyone, I balked at the idea of making it official. Maybe I should just put it down to experience and forget about it. But I did sums in my head, counted the days to my next pay cheque and realised I just had to try and get it back.

I rang the officers who dealt with my class and waited for the consequences.

'Eighty pounds is missing from my purse.'

'Are you sure it's gone?'

'Absolutely.'

'We'll be over, don't let anyone out of the Art Room.'

Why had I left my bag there? 'I was asking for it', that's what people would say, and they would be right. I shouldn't have left it there. Because of me the whole place would be turned upside down—I should have locked my bag up and kept it in a safer place.

The class responded to the news and prepared for the accusations, searches and lock-ins that would inevitably follow. There was no sympathy or empathy, no will among them to try and recall the circumstances. Perhaps I was mistaken. Money missing, prisoners, prison: they all went together. I told the class about my loss and explained why I had to lock the door. I tried to think who it could be; who had gone into the storeroom—anyone could have done so while I was under the table chatting to Fran, or behind the easel encouraging Bernadette. It could have been taken so easily. Whether or not it was anyone on my register it could have been taken during any interruption. Each student came into my mind for judgement. Unsuccessfully, my suspicions weighed one against the other, but it was a distasteful exercise and one which I couldn't continue with for long. The natural reaction would be of a cynical acceptance of such a theft in a prison, but like everything on the inside it wasn't that simple. Crime was not always about stealing and stealing wasn't the prerogative of prisoners. Fran wouldn't have done it, neither would Bernadette, nor Beryl. My hope was that it was nothing to do with me personally and if it was then it was only money—something replaceable.

Everyone leaving education would have to be searched. The officers came in and made me go over the incident in case I had missed anything.

'I should have locked my bag up; I know I should have done, sorry, I'm really sorry.'

Such a calamity of activity disrupted the whole department and then the whole prison. I was in the middle of it and it was horrible. The officers locked my door, then a bigger door then an even bigger door. Total lockdown. Staff were re-deployed to search, lunch got delayed, and it went on and on. Inmates were individually searched, I was questioned about the how and the when and asked if I could I guess at the whom? The women were talked to, offered a confidential ear in case anyone knew anything. I received some commiserations, but I had increased everyone's workload and that made it all the worse. Nothing came up, no one knew anything. The Security Department wanted a report on the incident. One appointment with Mandy and the afternoon session would begin. Another visit was overdue since my abortive attempt the previous week. Her cell was two levels below ground. I had not gone any further than level one when I was forced to stop. The most unwholesome of smells seeped up from below, making me recoil. Each step further down was less and less tolerable, so I slowed down and was loath to complete the journey. The door to the block was barred by tape and an officer stood in front of me shaking his head.

'No admittance today ducks … nobody's allowed in the block. We're expecting the cleaners in any minute.' Shaking his head again and again, he closed the door in front of me and rearranged the tape. That's all he could manage to do, or say, due to whatever had rendered him speechless. There was no use asking direct questions. It was an operational problem with which I couldn't interfere, so I re-planned my day and left it at that.

'You didn't try and get down the block today did you?'

'Yes, but they wouldn't let me in.'

'Too bloody right love, that new admission did a dirty protest, spread it everywhere, over the walls and floors, covered herself in it … you know what it was don't you?, you know what stuff she spread? … awful it was, would have thought you could have smelt it yourself.'

So I handed in my keys to the Holloway Security Office and left for home. On the forecourt of the prison I saw a huge industrial cleaning van being loaded up with complicated equipment by men covered from head-to-toe in plastic clothing, masks and oversize wellington boots.

As soon as the report was finished and handed in I tried again to visit the Segregation Block. Mandy looked all of sixteen but she was older, about nineteen with frowns and worries that hadn't yet become permanent; reminders of her troubled life. Unblemished and clear, her face could smile and laugh like any other adolescent, but those expressions were less frequent. She was often on a twenty four hour watch because voices in her head ordered her around so forcibly that they rendered officers powerless to intervene—and at those times there was a need for extra vigilance. Depression made Mandy even more of a prisoner than some of the others. Locked inside her black thoughts she'd refuse any social interaction and remain locked up out of choice. Prison officers monitored everything. Every bit of her art and other equipment had to be checked, and it was a very limited supply that she was permitted to have. Paring down risk, she could only have a magazine or two and paper and paper glue in small quantities and only during the day. Sometimes, Mandy didn't want to see me, and why should she always be available? I didn't mind at all.

The prison gossip merchants had reached the block already and the officers muttered consolingly about my loss of money as they opened the hatch in Mandy's door. This time I was welcome. I couldn't go into the room though, just speak to her through the slit. The little figure on the bed uncrossed her legs and rushed towards me with a smile.

'Hello Miss … Look what I've done, it took me a whole night, what do you think?'

She picked up a piece of paper from the floor, and showed me the most wonderful topsy-turvy clown made from bits torn from magazines. It was big and round and fat with a slight twist as if he was in the middle of telling a joke. She lifted the paper to let me have a closer look. Her arms still showed that white, downy hair that only children have, her round face had not yet settled back onto her bones and chubby cheeks pushed her eyes closed as she smiled. My spontaneous appreciation brought an even wider smile and a happy giggle.

'It's beautiful, really jolly ... I wonder what joke he's telling ... it's beautiful!'

'Do you really like it ... do you think its good?'

'Mandy, it's lovely, all the detail, all the colours and his cheeky smile, I like it very much ... and it's really good.'

'I can only use that glue you gave me during the day; they won't let me have it at night, so I saved my porridge. It sticks things together really well, so I can work through the night. I wasn't very well yesterday. I finished it on Saturday. You can have it if you like ... can you leave me some more magazines? ... Would you like it?'

'Are you sure you don't want it?'

'Yes, really, you can have it. I missed you last week, it was awful down here. I was allowed out while some cleaners came in ... the smell was awful, really bad. I could hardly breathe, good job you didn't come down Miss.'

Coming even closer to the door, she pushed her head right up to the hatch and cupped her hands around her mouth to whisper to me. 'It was that new woman, she spread shit everywhere!' She whispered the last few words quietly behind her hand. Her eyes grew larger with the horror of telling me this but her mouth smiled slightly with the mischievousness of believing that she was revealing a huge secret using a rude word.

I explained what had happened, that I had been refused entry to see her and we went on chatting for a while. Any subject interested her. Prison gossip was the best followed by mundane information, which intrigued her, such as what I did for lunch, whether I had a car and what kind was it, what did I do with my evenings, everyday odds and ends.

Her questions stopped when she became interested in the approaching dinner trolley as it rumbled onto the wing. She was too hungry to wait and so I left.

That was the first work she'd ever done. Maybe I could give her more things next time. Maybe she was getting better. Maybe they would let her have some furniture in her room and other items. She'd only got a bed and a cardboard table. Now she seemed responsive and alert and just maybe things were getting easier for her. Whatever had gone so wrong? I shook my head in disbelief along those long dismal corridors like some old fogey whose mind was so full it needed emptying.

I didn't want to see anyone. I didn't want to witness anything else that was going on. I didn't want to have to deal with anything, nor even see anyone. I went to the loo and hid for the rest of the lunch break.

Nobody got locked in, the afternoon session would go ahead as usual. My loss of eighty pounds wouldn't be disrupting prison routines.

Yes Marsha and Lesley could come in for the afternoon session, their normal class had been cancelled—and so could Bernadette.

'I'm on a roll Miss, can't face maths … too wired, besides I want to finish me drawing … could get shipped out any minute.'

Dorothy was always in art. Beryl's name was down for both the morning session and the afternoon session. Five new students—that would make a full class.

Laverne rocked in her chair, a mum chanting to her three month old baby girl. Heavy eyelids rolled up and down, a little pink vest lay becalmed as breathing hushed her to sleep. Lips sucked in and out pursuing her dreams and the pleasure just past. The mothers and babies were now integrated into the main prison, but on a separate Mother and Baby Wing. There was a feeling that the women might be discriminated against just because they had babies, and they might be excluded from education. Because of this it was decided to include them and they could join in just like everybody else. But it was strange having a baby in the classroom.

Staring out of the window from the adjacent table sat Ann, arms folded, lips rigid, just staring ahead at nothing at all. Paper and other materials were put in front of her as Laverne, already occupied, rocked the pram with her foot, hands now freed.

Ann peered at the paper.

'I can't use this, it's filthy.' She was still looking out of the window and never addressed me face-to-face. There was never any direct engagement. Ann was doing the rounds of all the women's prisons. It could be like that if the sentence was a long one. Now she was in her second stint at Holloway and would be staying for a while.'I'll get you another piece.'

'Miss ... come over here, look.' She stared at the wall and waited for me but I saw nothing and told her so.

'Look, look at that black bit, I'm not using this.' A smidgen of dust lay in one corner of the paper.

'That's nothing, really nothing ... if you feel that strongly then you could rub it out.' I passed her an eraser.

'Look at this mucky thing, this is no bloody good.' She was still looking at the wall.

'Who's rattled her cage?' whispered a bowed head to her next door neighbour in the corner.'

Ann, still with her arms crossed stared ahead.

'If you want you can come and get a fresh piece yourself, in fact collect everything new, come on.'

She came towards me still with her arms folded, chest out, head back, eyes looking somewhere else. She took the fresh paper out of its brown wrapper, chose a new eraser, a fresh pencil from the box—everything I gave her was new. Without any acknowledgement and never a glance in my direction she returned to her table.

'What's this red stuff on the table?' She leaned over inspecting the surface. Heads peeped up and down from their work like pecking chickens determined not to miss a bit of the action. A dusty bit of the centaur's thigh had flown over to her table due to one of Bernadette's wild gestures. I put some fresh clean paper over to cover it up.

A mass of curls and an eye flashed out from behind a drawing board, Bernadette peered over quickly then reversed back into oblivion.

'This room is a fuckin' disgrace, I'm not working here.' 'Ann, sit somewhere else if you want to.'

'No this place is crap, it's dirty and filthy … I can't work here, I'll work in my room—I'm off to the library'.

That's the last I saw of her. From then on I got messages from her wing informing me what she wanted. Asked to describe me, I don't think she could, she never looked at me. On reflection, I believe that Ann never had any real intention of joining the class. She just wanted to be on her own in her room and spend her time that way without company until her time came to an end.

Quick as a flash Bernadette's bareback rider rolled over the centaur's back, stretched her legs and prepared herself for more chalk highlights along Ann's vacated table, her chair not yet cold following her withdrawal. Bernadette was able to attack her images with greater intensity now the drawing was in the spotlight under the bright strip lighting. She could see the whole picture, notice the flaws, repair any damage and undertake all the required procedures with this newly acquired overview. She arranged her equipment, tied a plastic apron around her waist and dived in.

'She needs a chill pill Miss, weird or what.'

A strange guttural noise came from the other side of my door. There was the back of a figure pressing hard against it, so I thought someone was trying to get in and went to find out what was going on. Vile, lumpy stuff was splashing onto the floor from a bent shape directly in front of me. Any minute now it would stop, but it didn't yet and the mess got bigger until it sloshed into a moat round my door. The shape pushed past me having rid itself of some noxious substance and fell into the room. The smell of vomit displaced any fresh air that might have resided in that closed and barred prison room.

There was a strict procedure for the disposal of bodily fluids involving the use of a prison spillage pack. Puny equipment inside seemed only to work for drips, squirts and splashes, not an entire lagoon. The poor inmate, now slightly revived, scattered a couple of paper towels over the liquid which floated momentarily due to surface tension then sank under their own weight. Sand, what we needed was sand. It came in a wheelbarrow from the gardens pushed by a man with a wry grimace.

'That's a job and a half.' A whoosh and he was gone somewhere less distasteful, leaving me with a sack of sand. Dorothy, my one ally came over and we both donned the compulsory goggles, gloves and aprons, washed, disinfected and fumigated. Plastic bags stretched at the weight of the sodden sand.

'It was Weetabix Miss … it must have been.'

Aerosol spray purified our hair and shoulders and I pressed the nozzle with greater vigour in response to the implausibility of her explanation.

'Bad gear Miss, she got some bad drugs I bet.' Dorothy sneaked up to me behind the door, nudged me and winked. 'It's everywhere in this place … ease up on that stuff Miss it's getting in me eyes.' No one came near us, fingers pressed against noses, blowing expletives out from mouths, from a safe distance.

'Jesus, what's that fuckin' smell.'

'Pooooo.'

'Mary, Mother and Joseph, that's a bleedin' awful stink.'

'I didn't know art was that bad a class.' There was always a comedian somewhere.

Collecting all the tools up, and noting just one pair of scissors, I locked up the shadow board and the store cupboard. Explaining my temporary absence from the class, I picked up my luggage and made my exit. The mice reassured me they wouldn't play while I was away and poohed me out of the classroom, pressing institutional paper towels into their noses to block out the smell. Everyone standing in my way jumped out of it as I walked through. Officers stayed inside their offices a I passed their doorways and waved me along.

'Yes,' they would check on my students; 'No, I needn't worry.' They held their noses sympathetically, but stayed put.

I dragged myself and two yellow spillage bags through three departments before I safely jettisoned the lot.

'You can't leave that here,' said the man in charge of the skip and so I dragged the sacks away to find somewhere else to dump them.

'Our bins are full,' said the pharmacist.

So I dragged the two fetid loads onwards and knocked on more doors.

The bags stretched dangerously thin and bumped on the floor with the weight of their contents.

'Maybe there's space in that special Refuse Room down the corridor … over there,' a friendly nurse guided me on.

In the Refuse Room I found a half empty bin and abandoned the bags.

The day wasn't quite over yet. Nor was the afternoon session and there were still a couple of students racing to finish. The rest of the class had checked the time before I did and started to make their way out. Dorothy was buying a few favours by handing out drawing-books and pencils to her mates. They scuttled past me with their surprise gifts and winked. Playtime over, the cat had returned.

'Bernice that's a wonderful painting you're doing,' I called over to her while washing my hands repeatedly to get rid of a smell of vomit that didn't seem to want to go away. Rich brown branches weaved in and out of tree trunks and branches which faded into a forest. A network of interwoven twigs grew across the page like a spider's web. In leopard skin sarong with head dress to match, Bernice smiled over her shoulder.

'But where are the leaves?' Still wiping my hands on brown paper towels I peered at her painting.

'Its de Autumn Miss and dey is all dropped off,' she purred her way out of the room. Pity she only came in the afternoons, I thought, she was nice. Laverne was sitting calmly rocking her baby. Bernadette's drawing was now three pages big and a second centaur had been added. Beryl had finished and was sitting on her chair swinging her legs.

A week had passed and I had grown to accept my loss. The eighty pounds would have been exchanged for drugs and could be well out of the prison by now, or hidden far away from the Art Room. Some of the women had approached me with ideas, and other prisoners had contacted different staff and offered other solutions, but my money remained lost.

The administrative corridor had numerous doors and a long clear corridor. It was a prisoner-free zone. Most staff needed to visit it from time-to-time, to see the cashier, visit the post room, things of that kind. The block officer nearly bumped into me at the end of her shift.

'How's things?'

'Fine.'

'Any news about your money ducks?'

'Nothing so far.''Did you hear about Mandy?'

'No … why … what's happened?'

We both stopped racing in opposite directions, her to get out of the prison and me to get to my lesson.

'She was transferred back up to the wing yesterday, normal location, out of the block, set fire to her waste bin and set herself alight, seventy per cent burns, she's in a really bad way … gone to an outside hospital.' That news stifled both our urgent plans, our lateness became of secondary importance. The officer shook her head when telling me and she tried to answer my questions about Mandy's health and her progress as best she could. The shock defeated me temporarily. It took the will out of me, I was no longer in a rush to get to work, and I really didn't care if I was late either.

I'd get permission to visit her—I could go after work.

It smelt like dinnertime, like roast meat, the likelihood that it might be the smell of the Burns Unit and human flesh did not register at first. I waited for permission to enter her room and asked the nurse if I could give her some chocolates. They would not be suitable. Mandy was on liquids only, so there was no point in my leaving them there either. She could have the card, however. I could leave it on a window sill. Mandy was in a side ward on her own, bandaged up to the neck. She lay on a kind of hovercraft. It wasn't like any other hospital room I had ever been in, more like a dental surgery. The only flesh I saw was between bandages, a small face surrounded by the wonders of science. She was completely covered up and lying on a huge airbed which made a humming sound. Huge tubes surrounded her body pumping air to form the bed on which she lay. They protected her body from friction that could exacerbate her burns. She lay on her back just a couple of chubby cheeks and a little round face showing.

'She can drink, but that's all … *This* drink if she needs it,' a nurse whispered to me.

I shouldn't have gone there straight from work, I should have had a break. I was still agitated. I should have given myself time to adjust to this quiet place where calmness forced time to go slower. The prison seemed all the more brutal in comparison when set against civilised, caring procedures. I sat down near Mandy's head and made the slow pace include me. I made myself still and waited a few minutes before I spoke.

'Would you like a drink?'

'Yes please Miss.'

Lifting a straw to her mouth I saw the bandages give way on her neck as she swallowed. Her skin was parched and raw, bright red and yellow. Only her face seemed untouched. She sucked as hard as she could, but it obviously hurt and she soon stopped. She lay back consumed by her agony which wouldn't leave her for one second. She seemed to have no relief, certainly I couldn't ease her pain. I sat watching her face and her damaged body swathed in those bandages. She closed her eyes. The air machine hummed on.

I could have sat there all night in the stillness. Just as it eased Mandy's suffering it allowed me to distance myself from that volatile and brash institution which we had both come from. The chocolates remained in my pocket—they were completely wrong, a thoroughly misjudged and inappropriate present. I hadn't realised she was so very sick, so I'd be better prepared next time. I stayed there for few more minutes and occasionally offered her a drink to alleviate her thirst. She couldn't talk, couldn't even turn her head. Most of the time her eyes were closed until her need for drink forced them open— and then she could follow the straw up to her mouth. I tried to show her the card I'd brought, signed by other members of staff, but her eyes couldn't keep open for long enough. She seemed to be in incredible pain. Her closed eyes were tense and she was frowning even when she tried to sleep.

'The Governor wants to see you.' Nobody would say why, there was just a memo in my pigeon-hole from my head of department. Standing across the other side of an enormous desk he reached into a drawer and produced an envelope which he passed to me. Inside were four curled up twenty pound notes. He'd found my money. An officer apparently put the word about. Someone had tipped her the wink and hey presto there it was in a locker in a vacated room.

'Thanks so much, I'm so pleased to get it back, I'm just so pleased to get it back.' Effusive with appreciation I went on and on. The governor gave me the name of the officer concerned, in case I wanted to thank her too. She was in the office in the middle of the wing.

'I've come to thank you for finding my money, I'm so grateful, never thought I'd ever see it again, thanks so much.'

She interrupted me: 'If I were you I'd get those notes changed at the bank.'

I looked at the role of curly notes, puzzled.

'You know where they've been don't you'.

Holloway's covert mail service had been in use again using tunnels between thighs, where they had been securely hidden, right from my purse to their final recovery point in that locker—and now they lay curled up, but neat in my open hand.

She grinned. I couldn't reciprocate. I tried to find words that weren't there, so I gave up and walked away, trying to prevent my imagination from picturing the journey made by the notes. There was no point in being squeamish over this incident, just as there no point in getting squeamish over any other incident in Holloway, like the vomit or the excrement. As long as I was first on the scene when Bernadette's mighty chalk figures were being created or Fran's morbid nudes were being polished, then such rawness could be tolerated. I remembered my choice to teach in prison and to leave art colleges to themselves. In prison the students just wanted to paint or draw, they were not interested in being artists. It was a good idea to remind myself of that now and again.

Better prepared for my next visit to Mandy, I brought some juice into work instead of chocolates, something she might actually be allowed and enjoy. I could go after work again if I hurried and asked to get off a bit earlier. I told one of my colleagues and showed her my choice of drinks in case she thought they might not be suitable.

'Haven't you heard?'

'Heard what?'

'About Mandy'

'What about Mandy?!'

'She died … She died yesterday.'

Mandy's clown is now on display at Holloway. It was one of the first pictures to become part of a small exhibition in the Bridge Gallery.

CHAPTER 6

One Week

The windscreen wipers were over-exerting themselves that morning, their rubber blades clearing away the rain as best they could. Indistinct features unmasked the building ahead as a prison, not a new office block, nor a hospital. The barriers, the wire netting and the uniformed staff running by the walls with bright chains flickering under their dark coats gave some clues as to the purpose of this sprawling, modern complex. Huge vans driven by dark uniforms ferried passengers to their judgment day down at the Old Bailey. A group of women tentatively climbed out of huge electronic doors that slid open with just enough space for them to step onto the pavement outside. They shaded their eyes from the sudden shock of bright sunlight and looked around at a kind of freedom. Each woman was lugging a black plastic bag and smiles crept across their faces the further they distanced themselves from the building. Black figures pulled sniffing dogs along the perimeter fence. They would recoil backwards as the dogs shook the surplus rainwater from their fur. This was Holloway Prison, the largest women's gaol in Europe.

I moored my car in a reservoir of muddy water at the end of the overflow car park and waited. Staff with coats lifted over their heads dashed into the prison, apparently more eager to work than suffer the downpour. Two fire engines rolled out of the gates and I should have concentrated more to consider their significance. The rain plummeted down leaving massive pools on the uneven path. Unfamiliar officers were manning the doors that morning, so what would have been a quick flash of my prison pass became a deep scrutiny of my identification papers. New officers were on duty, handing out keys and slowing down the routine further. Inexperienced fingers pushed the wrong knobs that opened the wrong sliding doors. The morning shift workers tutted through their teeth and glared impatiently at the novices and their nervous fumblings. I quite enjoyed this leisurely initiation into Monday morning, but it was unusual to have so many faceless personnel working at the same time.

Slightly apprehensive but alerted to something unusual by the irregularity of the arrangements, I climbed the stairs searching for further clues. Looking upwards through the banisters, the clattering sound of sturdy shoes descended. A grand exodus of bats swooped past, sensors locating the light at the entrance to the cave. Navy-blue raincoats flapped in front of my face closing themselves over to prepare for the deluge outside. Sighs of relief followed them down the stairwell and I slowed my ascent due to even more trepidation. At the top of the stairs, staff were grouped together, plotting and planning in earnest. I tried to eavesdrop but it was all incomprehensible.

'Heh, just a minute'. The officer behind the class tapped on it for my attention. 'Don't let Chrissie near any drawing pins in your class, she pressed one into her arm and burst a vein on Saturday, it's really bad. There was blood everywhere, 'Oh and you've got a Mrs. Fernandez joining you as well. She's allergic to all the other types of education or "stuff in the classroom" as she calls it. She's changed her timetable so many times I'm up to here'. She lifted her hand above her head. And I was called in to work on my rest day ... No staff, some dorm barricaded and set fire to—what a weekend ... Don't forget what I said about Chrissie.' Chrissie had tied a ligature around her neck in the toilet of education a couple of weeks ago. A teacher had managed to slip her finger between the makeshift rope and her neck before further help arrived, gaining precious seconds and ensuring her survival. And then there was this Mrs Fernandez, yet to be formally introduced to me.

So that was it. That was the explanation. I waded through a puddle outside the classroom. Rejected drawings tottered on top of the dustbin, ready to join the soggy paper below it with the next gust of air from the door being opened. A splash of water dripped down my forehead. Despite my previous attempts to report a leak to the Works Department, the ceiling was still dripping outside my room. I left another message with that department and shoved a bucket underneath it. The heating hadn't been switched on and the secondary heating didn't work, so I scrambled into third level hidden heating mode and connected up a fan heater. Highly illegal and not in accordance with health and safety regulations, I had to store it in the cupboard, but this air was damp and the day was miserable and shivery and out it came. My other two levels of concealment, known only to me, hid artistic desirables that had to be issued one-at-a-time or they'd leave the classroom tucked down someone's clothing. Institutional behaviour of the worst kind, but as long as I kept it under control my approach seemed justified to me— and common sense.

Quiet corners were arranged for the introverts which cordoned them off from the groupies. And the groupies were right in front of my desk for good visibility unless those who were more fragile needed the space to a greater extent than them. The room was divided into separate sparing partners and different factions and I perpetually adjusted it as I sought a modicum of perfection. But they were always a disharmonious class of unpredictables, however good my scheme was. Talk could be heard, even the whispers that I wasn't supposed to hear and the raucous bawdy repartee that nobody could avoid. All of this would predominate over the scratchings of chalk and pencils. The best times were when the women would chatter themselves to a halt, just for their hands and minds to work better.

Five minutes to go and holding a cup of coffee made with milk that was slightly off, I surveyed my territory—my domain—with a face braced in readiness. As evidence of my age, signs of permanent worry had settled in and stuck. After all the years, the troubled expression was the outcome of my conclusions about life. It even provoked people passing me in the street to remark, 'Cheer up it'll never happen'. Finishing off the coffee with a faintly sick aftertaste, I waited for the next move.

'I can't draw Miss … will you do it for me?'

'Have you any colouring-in books?'

'Do you have any of those painting by number things?'

'Can I cut out and stick in this Bob the Builder picture?'

Equipment was divided between various storage cupboards to reach a balance between what was needed most and things that I could safely leave the room to fetch. Tricky women would run out of something on purpose just to get me out of the way and exploit the situation. When weighing-up a situation, I was taking it to ridiculous lengths. Sometimes I'd deliberately stop being so obsessively careful and I'd be over-generous and give everything away.

A whole dormitory had barricaded itself in over the weekend. The women had propped mattresses against the windows and blocked doors with furniture. Then they had set light to it and caused pandemonium. Fire engines had been called and ambulances stood at the ready. The smoke had caused the most damage, and with it the fear of smoke inhalation, so a whole wing had been evacuated, resulting in inmates now doubling-up in dormitories and with people not of their own choosing. It had been a major disruption. Nobody had been hurt, fortunately, but the threat had been there and it could have been really bad. New staff had been bussed in from other prisons to relieve those who had worked all night. So that's the reason for the differences, the whole prison had been stretched too far and too thin. And the implications of that would now affect every daily procedure.

A couple of bleary-eyed nomads stumbled and groped for their identity badges, numbering and naming themselves without the need for verbal introductions. No more energy left to move on, just more complaints not yet put to rest after the activities of the weekend. In addition, my room was damp and cold, further maintaining the women's dissatisfaction. Worn out already, they sat down in front of the fan heater and closed their eyes. 'Don't you remember me, Miss? I've done really well, I've stayed out a couple of years, was doing really well … I had a little girl. Don't you remember me?' I couldn't remember her, or the fact that she had been pregnant. Sixty per cent of the women stay for less than twenty-eight days, that was why.

Fran glided past me to her favourite table in the corner. Calmly she sat, her eyes looking out of the window to the trees, her arms resting in front of her. Her stillness calmed a small space around her so that people slowed down as they passed and moved more quietly, talked more quietly. Occasionally

she would frown, ever so slightly, and look vaguely at something else beyond
the trees. Dressed in a prison issue Home Office tracksuit she wore a white
elasticated hat casually knotted at the top of her head.

The door slammed open, slapped against the wall and ricocheted back for
another bashing. Why did so many women bully my door? Any grudges,
resentment, miseries initiated somewhere else were all taken out on the fragile
bit of wood that protected the entrance to my room. The new visitor, having
vented her wrath, shuffled her posterior down onto the nearest plastic chair,
which quivered with fragility. Tears fell from her eyes and splashed chaoti-
cally over her face as she blasted her baby's father and his non-appearance.
Cursing his rejection and her humiliation, she vowed vengeance on his future
ability to procreate. The tears ran down her nose and fell into her mouth
distorting her words into one big unintelligible blubber. I passed her some
rough institutional paper towels as the only soaker-uppers, the only make-
do tissues, at hand. If they couldn't sop up the tears then they'd scrape them
off her face. All life seemed wet that morning, all dribbling down from the
sky through the roof into a cold bucket of soggy paper. The fan heater was
turned up to its maximum setting and whined cheap metal.

'I spent an hour and a half down in Cunts Corner on Saturday Miss—I felt a
right idiot. I hate just fuckin' waiting and waiting down in that Visits Room.
Miss, everyone knows when you've been stood up. I felt a right cunt, all
them lies he gave me and all the shit. I keep sending out the visiting orders
and he never fuckin' turns up—and we've been locked in all weekend, no
association or nothing. Some idiots barricaded. I had to sleep with a load
of nut cases … I can't take it'. Dejected and abandoned she tried to ignite
a few strands of Golden Virginia with a lighter that had long lost its spark.

Fran quietly arranged her drawing materials and began work. In front of
her was one of a new series of drawings. Still using heavy graphite she had
made preparatory sketches of several portraits. She'd spent a long time looking through fashion magazines, cutting out images and inventing some
designs of her own. It wasn't the character that interested her, not even
the facial features. What did seem to consume her interest was the overall

shape of the head, made more complex with hair or decorations. No clear characteristics were evident. The head had been drawn as an extension of facial definition. The finished result appeared as a shadow emerging from the paper with intense vitality and energy. Each silhouette had blurred edges implying a thickness and a three dimensional quality completely at odds with the shadowy effect. So they were a bit of a conundrum, a contradiction—yet utterly fascinating. She was drawing something else in her room, it was three pages now apparently and she was rubbing the texture of her floor onto it. 'Soon finished,' she said.

Another guest was knocking, gently and quietly. Nobody knocked on my door so I ignored it. Then someone knocked again, this time even more tentatively. 'I'm sorry about Friday Miss, can I come back in … I must apologise, hhhh'… I was very rude to you'. Her voice was too high, like that of some ventriloquist who had got it badly wrong. Here was this adult before me and she was posturing like a seven-year-old. Her movements were jerky; she swayed erratically, held her body submissively. Like a silent movie actress she exaggerated her gestures, seemingly choreographed by some stage director from the wings. The drips of water had nearly filled the bucket by the side of us. If it went neglected then there would be another flood. If I ignored Mo then she would never go away, so I chose to ignore the bucket and to hell with the flood. But I was getting anxious and fidgety so please hurry up and finish Mo, because I know exactly what you want. Then, after the apologies, the intermittent photographic smile clicked on to keep my interest and I waited for what I knew would be the next page of the script. I knew I would let her back in and she knew I would let her back in. I always let her back in. So I endured this bad acting and recalled the previous Friday—all I'd said was 'How are you?' That really was all I said. I asked how she was. Out came the diatribe. It was none of my business, and would I keep away, not come near her again and so she ranted on and on, menacingly. What business was it of mine? It was nothing to do with me so she told me to go away.

The more I stood beside her, the more she railed on about wanting to be left alone. 'Too many people interfering.' Her arms were crossed in front of her; her eyes followed me to see if I was interfering equally with her fellow prisoners. Best not to be overtly considerate and ask after the welfare of the others, she might find that offensive too, best not to ask after anyone else's health. As a background to any further interaction with the other students her voice could be heard cursing my curiosity as if I represented some secret society collating information that might be used against her. As an accompaniment to verbal abuse, she tore off a large piece of paper and with clumsy arm movements ripped it into shreds. Then she decided to stick it all together again with the help of a large book and a cup full of glue. After that she twisted the flattened paper around and dragged it back to life with more drips of glue and more battering. Above the noise I became, 'they' as though I had acquired fellow members that interrogated and asked questions, so 'they' can find out things that were none of 'their' business. My instinct was to intervene and put a stop this demonstration of a kind of conceptual art with an equal amount of energy to that she was expending, to go over, grab the paper and bring the performance to a speedy end. That wouldn't have worked and thank goodness I'd learnt that much. Instead I indulged my other charges with rather more interest than normal while paying attention to Mo with apparent indifference. That's how the lesson progressed and I dissipated Mo's attention-seeking with the benefit of as much experience and patience as I could tolerate. The more I praised the other students, the more the soundtrack lost strength. When I'd stopped praising the others she restarted, her artistry plumbing ever greater depths. She poured glue over the paper again, squeezed it and reduced it to pulp. Then she sat back on her chair with a large satisfied smile. I'd been killed off.

I never spoke to Mo throughout that session. Only at the end, when everyone was waiting and her shindig had stopped did I question her attitude. What was it all about? Why had she taken against me? It had disrupted everyone else and made the whole lesson more difficult. I talked to a moving object. Further more detailed rebukes would only have been heard if she had stopped striding away from me. She left the chaos on her desk full of my body parts. To try to get her to return would have incurred too much unpleasantness. So I ended the session, cleaned up myself and dealt with my own symbolic destruction.

Some time later, the beautiful circular waterfall edged the bucket and it flowed predictably onto the floor making bigger puddles. 'Hhhh, I'm so sorry Miss, mmmmmy mind sometimes says things … hhhhh … I'm from Balham and hhh … I've been locked in all weekend.' This was going to be a long-winded apology, so she must want something else I thought. 'Hhhh h'I'm a schizophrenic … h'I've been in a Surrey mental home, three mental homes Miss, but h'I'm OK now, but h'I don't know for hhhhow long … They say it's crack psychosis Miss, but h'I don't know'hhhI' was ssssso rude to you.' Stuttering and stammering Mo poured out her regrets. Hopping from one leg to another and smiling primly as her pleas continued. Her left hand appeared to cling to a corner of a wall. Then she drew it towards her body and with it came another hand and a body. A quick pull and out came Tanya, the stage director, or, more appropriately, the script writer, from her hiding place under the stairwell. So this at last was the extra something she wanted. This lady prompt had made her see the error of her ways, egged her on to right the wrong. They were now an 'item' in the prison lingo and inseparable—one didn't come without the other. What kind of alliance it they had formed was none of my business, though it must have started quite recently. Such coupling was frequent, sometimes it consumed both women to the exclusion of everything else and it could be an intense relationship. Tanya was on my register, Mo wasn't now. They hoped that I'd let them both in. Mo couldn't fit in to any other class, she hadn't the concentration, the skills or the motivation—I was the end of the line for her.

'My h'art makes me so h … happy, it makes me feeeeel good Miss.' Mo would have continued her pleas if Tanya hadn't have stopped the flow by squeezing her arm—Mo just didn't know when to stop. Tanya was much more mature—a strange twosome I thought but the oddest of things happened in Holloway Prison. So they stayed in the class and Mo sat with Tanya and they both worked, if they didn't then they'd have to leave. While other women cut out images and stuck them neatly in the middle of the picture, Mo would work from her strange imaginings. While others cut out neat regular shaped hearts or copied from their friends, Mo would paint half a heart at the edge of her paper so that it shook and moved and nearly breathed. Then she would surround it with blackness and stepping-stones and unconnected designs creating a powerful display which was direct, secret and wild, really wild. She carried on with her spontaneous creations with Tanya at her side and it was Tanya who cleared up for her at the end of the session—just to make sure that they would be welcome in future. It was Tanya who listened to her ramblings and kept her stable, a symbiotic relationship, for however long it lasted.

Chrissie entered and sat down waiting for service as though it was a restaurant and I was the waitress. She always did that, waited for me—she couldn't initiate any action to do with work unless it came from me. So I served her once more and even told her when to begin. Clumps of tangled women fell into the room making up my full complement of learners. One of them seemed to have rolled off her bed and landed on a chair without knowing quite how. One side of her head had been cane rowed neatly into an intricate pattern of plaits, the other flowed freely in lush black curls. An enormous Afro-comb was stuck in her parting, bookmarking the break in style. Half of her was still in the bedroom in furry pink slippers, the other in a badly fastened duffel coat, evidence of the speed of her eviction from her room into the outside world. Four of the women were sitting across from each other looking vacantly into space, waiting for something to happen.

Whenever I had to confront such apathy I recalled a smart little number and her two mates, all lodging on the same wing in the old prison when passivity was much more prolific. They'd decided to do an experiment, a social survey. They chose a gap in the prison routine when nothing particular was going on. The idea was to line up against a wall, one behind the other close to a door. The affect of this on the rest of the wing population was just what they expected, only they needed to prove their theory. Other women started to stand behind them until a queue formed. When the queue was long enough to justify a conclusion the three women moved away to the surprise of the other prisoners who then became confused as to why they had chosen to line up in the first place. That was the result they needed. The conclusion was clear: institutionalisation makes automatons out of everyone. I celebrated the fact that such apathy was much rarer now.

Hoarse, throaty coughs recalled the previous weekend's events, the smoke and the noise. The irritable insomniacs cursed the light show from the fire engines and the ambulances, and the fact that they had been forced to share their room with a couple of 'Muppets'. 'Is this art?' My door creaked open tentatively. There was a pale little face in the gap whose fragility was made even more striking by her diminutive stature. Wispy grey hair was tied up loosely on top of her head and huge circular spectacles magnified her eyes like those of a bush baby. She strained her neck towards me and I bent right over to shorten the gap. Several white hairs popped out of her chin and black curly ones stuck out from her top lip. It was the bag of bones from Madrid, Mrs Fernandez. In she came, right into the centre of the room and sniffed the air, then ferreted around the equipment.

'I 'ave this sickness you know … I'ave very severe allergies, so maybe I can't stay 'ere'. She twitched her nose amongst the bottles and powders wrinkling up her whiskers. You could have folded-up those neat little limbs into a parcel. 'Is this all there is in here?' I pointed her over to the store cupboard and observed her inspection defensively for, despite that apparently feeble frame, there was a voice of a bear. She found the fixing spray and grimaced, pulling her head away to distance her senses. Then looked around a bit more with those huge eyes and declared that she would stay. There was nothing else in the room that might aggravate her allergies, they were very simple pigments and she should be okay. If anything bothered her then I asked her to please let me know and I would do something about it. Mrs Fernadez worked with total commitment. She worried and struggled and persevered until it stopped being so difficult for her and became enjoyable. At every class she showed me still life studies accomplished in her room. She'd draw anything, shoes, boxes, doors, windows, all completed in heavy charcoal. Nobody bothered her. She was small, weak, eccentric and foreign and nobody in my classroom bothered her. They didn't understand why her work was good, I could tell, because they never commented when I displayed it or when I explained its merits. She started to change her timetable, stayed and added more art lessons. I know staff on the wing were fed up with her for some reason, just the mention of her name provoked moans and headaches. I couldn't see anything wrong with her except that she seemed a bit eccentric. Life on the wing however reveals sides of everybody's nature not apparent when they are 'away from home'. Domestic existence brings out characteristics which teachers never witness. The reverse is equally true.

'Why have you got such a reputation?' I asked, then, 'What have you done?' I leant over her drawing and waited for a reply. 'I've been down the block and I was very happy to be there ... I disobeyed an order' Mrs Fernandez' voice was determined and hugely impressive. That shocked me, this little old lady down in the bowels of Holloway. 'And you know why? ... If people are nice to me then I am nice back, if people are nasty, then I am nasty ... and when those officers abuse their power then I call them shiiit!, and I will always call them shiiit if they do that, and that is why I don't mind going down the block.'

Those big bulbous eyes opened even wider and the force of her voice nearly dislodged the spectacles from her nose. Her hands gave them a violent push back to their rightful place and then she settled down again. Over in the corner she seemed glad to join us and had chosen art to the exclusion of all other classes. Occasionally she'd redden and strip off a couple of layers so we could see that small, boney frame close up. Then when the hot flush had paled, on went her clothes again and she would fold herself back up into the drawing position. My face indicated my sympathies but before I started to say something she beat me too it, 'And don't tell me I can take something for them, I don't want anything, I can get through this on my own, besides I'm probably allergic.'

The class filled up that morning to full capacity. Everybody wanted to leave home and get off the wing. They were all fed up with the way the barricade had affected them. They competed to see who had suffered the most. Something was wrong with Chrissie. She was drawing awkwardly despite her facility. She could draw in a slick kind of way, all highlights in chalk and a bit of thumb-rubbing for the effect, like they tell you to do in popular art instruction books. These things impressed her peer group; they envied her them, but they didn't notice she was stuck somewhere years ago and she was just repeating herself. I had tried to give her more challenging projects but she only had one kind of drawing and couldn't handle anything else. The rut had been dug so deep and too long ago. It was too comfortable to climb out. She enjoyed being stuck in it and intended to stay stuck.

'What's in your hand?'

'Nothing.'

'Let me have a look.'

'No.'

'Give it to me please.'

'No.'

'Please.'

She unbent her fingers and a piece of sharp plastic fell to the floor. I picked it up and threw it in the bin. Her arm showed several old scars from self-abuse—superficial scratchings, nothing too bad, but enough to act as a warning.

An enormous bluebottle bumped into the windows and whizzed around keeping out of the rain. It must have fled into the room from a black plastic bag. Women leant away, jerkily following it around the room in disgust. Then one woman opened a window to allow it the freedom they didn't have. But it wanted to keep in the dry, or it had no sense of direction. Dot slowly peered over her book and followed the fly with the eyes of a bounty hunter within spitting distance of her prize. Pushing her table away from her she rose in slow motion. The chair creaked and she slowly rolled up a stiff piece of cardboard and held it high in her hand. She chased that big fat fly regardless of where it led her. Over the tables and around the chairs, into each corner of the room she chased it. Buzzing past her nose it pulled her behind it like she was on elastic. Dot's anger distorted her face and she panted for lack of breath, spinning together. It was hard to tell who was following whom.

'I hate bloody flies, they're disgusting, and I just want to kill the lot ... ugh ... Ugly filthy things'. Beside herself with hatred she went after that fly with a demonic stare whirling the tube of cardboard like a deadly weapon, single-mindedly pursuing her enemy the fly. We all had to stop and watch. This was a revenge killing and a very public assassination. She looped the loop, so did the fly and the cardboard tube. It buzzing round the room. Then, flinging the tube down with a great thuds, bashing onto tables and windows she struck like someone possessed. Over chairs she leapt after it, never letting it out of her sight, never letting it land. She just panicked it into flying in ever tighter circles. Then they caught each other up, the bounty hunter and the outlaw in mid-flight and her target fell down, knocked senseless. Even then she didn't give up, she beat it and beat it till it disintegrated and there was no trace of it left, only a dirty smudge on the tube. Sweating with relief and contentment she smiled all satisfied with herself, sat down and opened her book again. A few of the students gaped at each other like they were just about to comment on that impressive pursuit but decided to clamp their jaws safely shut because they'd never seen that side of her before and weren't sure if her aggression had been satiated.

My watch showed that only fifteen minutes had gone by. Frankie came into the class and headed over to see her friend Sara, co-defendants on the same drugs charge. 'Two minutes, then please leave ... I don't like interruptions.' They chatted for a couple of minutes then Frankie disappeared back to the computer class.

'I reckon the Alsatians must have eaten the Shih Tzus ... if they only found a bundle of fur and a bit of blood, then that's what must have happened'. Worried about her six Alsatians and two toy dogs, the police had been summoned to investigate her home after Sheila's arrest. That's all she had talked about in the police station, the fact that her pets were on their own and might starve or fret. 'I keep the Alsatians separate from the Shih Tzus with a door on the stairs ... the door was down and there was no sign of the little dogs, only the Alsatians.' Sheila didn't even stop work, she was talking down to what she was doing. Her new friend Sara looked up from her book and watched her speaking. As the lurid tale led to the disclosure of further grim details her arms dropped the book and her eyes rolled upwards to examine the strip lighting, as if that would stop the fantasist testing her gullibility. She folded her arms tight and waited for the story to come to end. She stayed like that until she saw that my head had popped up to listen. Some wisecrack would finish that saga, surely it wasn't real. Sara turned her head away and I could see her shoulders shaking with giggles. It was inappropriate that I should even smile because Sheila carried on worrying about her dogs and their possible destruction. This was no fable, there was no joke, she wasn't making it up. I turned away from Sara and tried not to listen.

'You are joking aren't you, you mad cow!' Completely unmoved by her reaction Sheila totally ignored Sara's response, in fact Sheila didn't even look up from doing some intricate shading. 'Well they were either dead or hiding somewhere in the house. I wanted to phone my neighbour to ask her to pop in and have a search, but we had total lock-in all weekend and I couldn't even make a 'phone call because of that barricade. Maybe I won't phone her, she was so jealous of me and fancied my husband … the slut, always trying to come between me and my husband … You know she stalked him, always flaunting herself at him, and watched us all the time with her binoculars, that's what got me in here in the first place.'

Sheila's thick Australian accent was still evident after twenty years in England. Middle-aged, slightly plump, greying and a bit scruffy-looking, she slobbed along into her habitual place for every session. Painting was strictly a nine-to-five job for her, this art education—and she never bothered about any other class because she was in this for the money, that's all. No visitors ever helped her out, she ran her own business inside, and was completely self-sufficient. Her octogenarian common law husband had left home for some reason and never visited Sheila. He fitted into her life in some corner that was never really made clear. Sara laughed out loud at her bizarre story, calling Sheila a 'Mad, fucking bitch' but causing no offence. They got on well. Sheila's flat manner took everything in its stride; she was bright and knowledgeable. I think her flat way of talking was something to do with the number of cigarettes she smoked. She'd tried to raise and lower her tone, in laughing or in anger, but it always ended up with here coughing and going red in the face, spluttering for air, so she didn't try any more and unlike many Australians just spoke in a monotone, completely without expression.

Sheila had an appointment concerning her psychiatric reports which would be presented at court. They should have taken three hours but it hadn't worked out like that. The psychiatrist had come late and could only give her three-quarters of an hour's attention. Reaching down into a home-made knitted bag she brought forth a thick clump of papers and started to unfold them. So often read and re-read the paper was worn and limp. She read to Sara from the final report, her cigarette dropping grey ash intermittently which she flicked off the paper. It said—and she was not concerned who listened-in—that she wore no make-up and was dishevelled. Sheila was annoyed, because she thought this was sexist and, anyway, appearances should not be so influential and her own should be of no consequence. Though maybe it would be a disadvantage in court, she reflected—her scruffiness might work against her. Sara volunteered to instruct her in the art of 'facial aggrandisement'. She lent her some make-up, gave her advice and even painted up her features to bring out her hidden femininity, but it looked wrong and freakish, though it must have had some beneficial affect because she later came back from court with three of her charges dropped.

'May I have some more pencils please … I need a 3B'. Fran gestured into the store cupboard and helped herself'. She wafted back to her place making no sound, winding in and out of the chairs and tables. She touched nothing, just glided along until she reached her chair and sat down where she continued to draw. Annie came into the class late, with a pale face, red eyes and slow despondent tears. She was thoroughly dejected. She had signed away her child for adoption and with this had gone her happiness. The father, with no paternal attachment, was living out his own incarceration in Pentonville Prison and her mother, disabled in a wheelchair could offer her little support. It all tumbled out in tears and she gulped noisily, heaved and even shook. A photograph was pulled out of her back pocket. On the back were remnants of the toothpaste that she had used to stick it to her cell wall. On the front was a blurred image of a baby wrapped up in a blanket. At the sight of her child she gave in to it all, hid her face completely with her hands and wept. By the end of the lesson an awkwardly drawn card got completed as a present to her offspring, though how she finished it without it being waterlogged with tears was a miracle.

Chrissie beckoned me over. 'My boyfriend died last year Miss, I really loved him. He used to inhale everything, glue, solvents, the lot. One day he inhaled some gas or other and lit up a cigarette, and his chest burst, he blew himself up.' She had something in her mouth that she was moving around.

'What's that in your mouth?'

'Nothing.'

'Let me have it please.'

'No.'

'Give it to me.' I held my hand underneath her chin.

'No.'

'I'll have to get an officer then.'

'If you get an officer I'll swallow it.'

'Please give it to me.'

'No.'

The internal telephone extension inside my store cupboard had been installed for just such an emergency. Never susceptible to such threats, I didn't hesitate, but phoned for help. Sometimes I benefitted from my isolated position, completely blocked off from the rest of the classrooms; it prevented random intruders with the excuse that they were just passing by on their way to somewhere else. There was nowhere beyond the Art Room, only the

stairs leading to the craft shop at the top of the building. That was only visited by the serious craft specialists, so there were no loiterers. Chrissie sat
waiting, belligerently, still chewing at whatever was in her mouth. Despite
the officers' attempts, her mouth wouldn't open and reveal its contents. So
used to such an event were some of the women that they barely looked up,
just continued working. It could also have been the brutalising affect of the
institution that caused this lack of interest. Chrissie refused to empty her
mouth despite further requests from both me and the officers, so she was
escorted off the wing to the medical department.

'I swallowed glass once, when I was dead young, felt depressed or something,
first time in the nick, thought I was going to die, never tried it twice, God
it was painful.'

'Who's the mad cow then … you or me?' Sheila got her own back on her
Sara's youthful nostalgia. Betty with her broken arm in a sling moaned that
none of her trees looked straight. They weren't, they all bent over to one side
because she had to lean to re-educate her other arm to draw. It worried her
enough to think of destroying her drawing. 'What if it was a windy day?'
I suggested, 'if it was really blowy then it wouldn't matter if the trees bent,
would it?' Such an idea hadn't occurred to this woman who wouldn't think
twice about breaking social rules outside and looking for quick fixes for her
own convenience. Here in the Art Room, it only took a sheet of cartridge
paper to frighten this fearless recidivist.

'Can I do that then? Can I really do that Miss?'

'You can do what you like.'

'Yeah, Miss, yeah, I'll make it into a storm …. Yeah, great Miss, I'll make it
into a storm.' This was the same woman who had been terrified of making
the first mark on her blank sheet of white paper and now she had become
even more anxious at the idea that she might be doing something that was
not allowed. Lola brought over her card for me to see. Her daughter had just
made her a grandmother and it warranted some acknowledgement from her.

Excited and proud she had added a flower and glitter but no writing. 'Can you write, best wishes love gran?'

'Miss, can I help you today? I don't feel like doing anything like work, but I'll help you sort things out or anything you want … I'll do anything you need me to do.' Angela offered her services. Her heavy medication slowed her speech and dried up any moisture in her mouth, but it also activated her legs so that they were in perpetual motion. It was as if they were climbing stairs. One came up then went down, then the other came up and went down, but the main part of her body never moved. She couldn't keep still—her feet climbed those imaginary stairs as her shoulders swayed from side-to-side. I gave her the broom and off she went, climbing along that flat lino trying to brush the floor clean.

'My husband won't talk to me Miss, I've tried and tried to phone but he won't answer. He's divorcing me … if I try and change Miss do you think he'll come back to me?' I heard sobbing, someone was trying to be strong, but she just wept.

'Men are all fucking bastards.'

'I'm taking the wrap because of my bloke and he hasn't even sent me in any money, or come to see me, they're all crap. I just love my husband and I want him back … Do you think he'll come back to me? … Fuck men … I don't givum nothing for free. They have to pay for everything. I just take the money and don't give out, just leg it … stupid bastards all of them.'

Then out came all the male hatred and everyone joined in with their experiences. It was always like that, bad stories about bad men whether it was partners, lovers or fathers. That's until a male of the species came into the room, or passed by the window, then they would whistle provocatively—just to give it another go. And in a men's prison, there were equal amounts of hatred of women, like that of Ted in Pentonville. I had worked there for a while and this student needed a few more extra assignments and me to organize his exam before I left the job. The final preparations went well, though I was always uneasy, because he seemed to look that little too long in places that didn't require such attention. And he smiled at me a lot. Maybe it was my determination not to talk about anything but the exam and his work—and I must have seemed intense and serious. He was in prison for committing violence and had served a few sentences, always for the same kind of offence. But it would only be the exam now; one-to-one and then my work would be over. Whereas other male inmates hadn't bothered me—teaching there had been straightforward and simple—with Ted things got complicated. I was glad when the hour was over. Ted didn't ever relax—ever, so I watched everything I said and the way I said it and how long I said it for, and how I looked. I didn't relax either. I was less experienced then and much more youthful.

The classroom for the exam had glass half way down the wall on one side. That was good I thought because I didn't want to be isolated during the invigilation period. I could see the heads of people passing backwards and forwards. It was reassuring. I organized the still life as per instructions with the chalks and the paper, and then I noted the time and allowed him to begin. He wore glasses and worked and smiled at me above them intermittently. When he did that I avoided his stare and remained looking serious, writing something that looked important enough to consume me to the exclusion of all else. Then he started drawing and talking as well and making assumptions about my life away from the prison, asking what car I drove and where I lived. He boasted that he could find out the whereabouts of anyone if he wanted to. He could find out any details about anyone. I never said a word but I concentrated less and less on that supposedly important document under my nose. In the end I just listened to him with my eyes muddling up all the letters and words.

He was in the middle of the exam and had got his hands dirty with the chalk. He asked if he could have something to wipe them with. I looked around for something but there was no sink in the room, nor any cloths. So I just shrugged and apologised. After a while, he stopped working with an over-exaggerated, dramatic flourish. He was making the whole drawing dirty with his hands and ruining it as if there was no point in trying anymore and he would have to give up. 'If you rested your drawing hand on a piece of clean paper that would protect it.' Hopefully, my compromise would put an end to his tantrum, but of course it didn't. He approached my table and told me he had a hanky in his pocket—Yes the front pocket of his trousers. Without clean hands he would not be able to work any further and would fail the exam, with the tissue he would carry on. 'Can you reach in and get it for me?'

'No.' Then the tension started; the pitiful smiles as he tried to persuade me to put my hand into his pocket and extract the tissue. Why was I making such a big deal out of such a simple request? What was my problem? Why was I being so unhelpful? Didn't I want him to pass the exam? I looked up out of the windows for passing heads, just one would do.

The pressure increased and Ted's composure started to disappear. He came in closer demanding that I take the tissue in his pocket and anger started to accompany his initial politeness. Why wouldn't I put my hand into his pocket? What was all the fuss about? Then started the humiliation and the put downs. I must think he really fancied me or 'Who do you think you are?' kind of talk, so that I felt stupid resisting what might have been just an innocent request. His two arms stiffened and his hands grasped my table. If I was to reply, I would need to look upwards, a long way upwards towards his face, so I stood up without looking and moved away from my table. He applied more and more pressure and became increasingly impatient. I no longer spoke, just stood there and did nothing. If I hadn't known about his record I would have been less intimidated. If we hadn't been in a prison then I could have asserted myself more. That's what I thought afterwards, it was the whole situation that disabled me. His persuasive tactics would have outwitted any of my verbal skills, he was too much of an expert. His stature would have overpowered any of my feeble defences, so all I could do was to wait and resist in silence as long as he persisted. That was my instinctive decision and I hoped that I was right.

Then at last I saw a figure walking past the classroom. With that extra presence and confident of imminent support I walked further way from my desk and opened the door. Ted went towards the objects he was drawing and kicked the table so that they would all dislodge and fall. He wasn't going to finish the exam because I was a useless teacher. I was unprofessional with no ability. I stood there silently and so did the officer until Ted's ranting subsided. 'Take you back to the wing then, eh.' With no comment from me, just an expressionless nod past Ted's anger, the officer left the classroom with his charge obediently leading the way, kicking on a few invisible obstacles as he strode on.

Whether he did that because he felt that the exam was beyond him, I don't know. But he was led away three quarters of an hour before the exam should have ended. So I retold the incident, in its smallness and hoped that I would be understood. So I was, and when he was routinely searched on returning to the wing no tissue was found in that pocket. Even then I thought I may have exaggerated my reaction, maybe misinterpreted the whole incident, and I guess that was partly his intention. It wouldn't have taken much more for him to get a really good grade, but it didn't happen. He did pass, but only just—which was a waste given his potential.

The rain still streamed down from a full, dark sky, showing that there was more to come and I remembered the bucket outside my room. It was full now, with water flowing over the sides making further puddles on the floor. Dragging it over to the sink I poured the water away and replaced the bucket under the dripping ceiling. A cry from one student working near the window alerted the rest of her 'groupies' who clambered over and pushed their faces against the glass. About half of the women in the class, those easily distracted and the most institutionalised pushed themselves as near as they could to the glass and stared outside. A prison van had stopped opposite the window, near to the Segregation Block. A tabloid remand prisoner alleged to have mistreated children was being held there and her presence provoked controversy in the prison population. She was on trial now for murder and newspapers ranted on, page after page. The details of her alleged crimes were torn out and passed from hand-to-hand to spread the news from cell-to-cell and wing-to-wing. Everyone wanted to catch some sight of her. Four or five women flattened their faces up against the window and they banged on it, winding themselves up into a state of hysteria. I stood up and looked at the lynch mob. The rest of the class including Mrs Fernandez shook their heads in disapproval and continued working, but it was hard to concentrate.

'I haven't taken the register yet ... I must mark you all off'. I spoke to everyone else. All I needed was one member of the rabble to hear. No response, they persisted in making their feelings known, just in case that inmate emerged from the van. Threats as to what they would do to her if they caught her made their grotesque behaviour seem even worse.

'If I don't get the register right none of you will get paid.'

'Fuck that Miss, I'm out of tobacco, right out.'

'No register, no pay.'

One woman turned and moved away from the window. Then the others followed the sheep trail back to their places. Not until they were all seated did I mark them off as present. They remained seated but were kept in touch with outside activities by those seated nearest to the windows. It was a nasty spectacle.

'Would anyone like to speak to me about anything at all?' On her chest was a badge saying IMB which stands for Independent Monitoring Board, the new name for members of Boards of Visitors. 'Would anyone like to speak to the IMB ... anyone got any complaints?' Hands went up and students shouted about the rough weekend, the barricade, the cold, the bad food, they all rushed to join the queue. To minimise the disturbance, the IMB lady gestured to them all to congregate outside the class and come to her one at a time. The volunteers who formed the IMB were impartial watchdogs and had a good reputation for vigilance and care, but after that weekend most inmates queuing up to moan had few expectations.

'Nothing will bloody change, nobody listens in this place.' Angela stopped sweeping and went into the store cupboard, impelled there by some invisible urge that was out of her control. I looked through the crack in the door, and there she was trying to ring her husband on my internal phone. She was desperate at the lack of access allowed to her during total lock-in over the weekend and the 'phone might reassure her of her bloke's renewed attention.

'Angela, you know you can't do that … come on.'

'Do you think he will come back to me, Miss … I need to phone him, I couldn't call him yesterday, nor the day before, they wouldn't let me.'

'Angela I just don't know, I really don't know, but you can't use this phone, you know you can't. Besides it's only an internal one, you can't get an outside line … its impossible.'

'Fucking forget him, you don't need him'. The class expert proffered her advice.

'But I love him Miss, I really love him'. Angela leant on the broom and snivelled. 'Why don't you just go for a walk, just for some fresh air Angela, maybe it will make you feel better.' She complied with my suggestion after she'd been further consoled with a roll-up from some soul sister.

'Where's that magnifying glass. I can't see a friggin' thing, the waiting time for opticians is three months … that's no good to me'. I passed it to a regular who squinted all the time and complained of headaches. 'What do you think of these?' The Australian rummaged around somewhere under her clothes and produced a home made pack of cards. They were beautifully made and she showed them to Sara.

'Fuckin' great, give us them.'

'Bugger off.'

'Well do us a pack.'

'It'll cost you half an ounce of baccy and a pack of Rizlas.'

'Fuck that … you're 'aving a laugh aren't you.'

'No, that's my price.'

'Just give us them.'

'Bugger off, what about these … what do you reckon?' And there was a pack of home made dominoes.

'I'll have them then.'

'Bugger off.'

'Mean tight-arsed bitch.'

Sara wasn't as creative as Sheila, but Sara was the more unscrupulous of the two, so Sheila pulled at the neck of her shapeless T-shirt and quickly dropped both items down into her bra away from Sara's acquisitive hands. Another face appeared at the door and pressed against it. Sara caught sight of her friend Frankie and sped out of the room, returning a few minutes later with an extra bit of spring in her step. Colleen flung open the door and headed over to Sheila.

'That's great, thanks'. She took a pencil drawing copied from a photo of her kids and gave Sheila a wadge of tobacco in exchange. The portraits were of poor quality but Colleen thought they were great, a good business deal. Down went the tobacco into Sheila's bra. The elastic was overstretched now; with all that extra porterage, it sagged. After a few minutes, Sheila wriggled with discomfort and peered down at her lumpy front, a real giveaway for any vigilant officer. She slid both of her big fat hands along her T-shirt and rolled, pushed and prodded the objects further and further down next to her breasts, tipped them all over her nipples and laid them to rest in the cavernous overhang beneath. Contented now and with her smooth outline restored, all that was left was to complete another commission to supplement her meagre earnings and keep her life's small luxuries. 'I'll get you this one finished for tomorrow … okay? … Same deal'.

It was a Victorian costume drama now, all elegant ladies in long dresses with parasols like those on chocolate boxes and trays that used to be made for basket-weaving kits in occupational therapy, years ago. Sheila rocked back in her chair smugly, with her hands over her head. But this new position was too much for her body to tolerate. It must have been the expansion of her lungs, but there was no space left for them to stretch out. She squinted with one eye to avoid the smoke as she rocked backwards. Her ciggie clung to one side of her mouth and dropped ash over her chin which she wiped off of it with fat, clumsy fingers. A crackling sound could be heard between her ribs from the burning cinders which kept igniting in her lungs. Her chest heaved noticeably, every breath forcing the oxygen down to keep the flames fanned. Normally a hoarse tenor, Sheila's lungs whistled like a first soprano, getting higher and higher. Sara bashed her on the back shocking the lungs back to normal. Sheila sipped water out of her paint pot to extinguish the fire in her throat. 'Jesus you're disgusting you are, really disgusting.'

Sara tried to re-engage Sheila with her Picasso book. She lacked Sheila's talent so tended to spend a large percentage of class time reading about different artists. Her concentration was difficult to harness. She stood up and gave a twirl.

'What do you think of my new jacket then?'

'Fuckin' awful.' Sheila shook her head in disapproval. Actually it was vile, in a kind of shocking pink it was a crochet number with frills, tassels and twinkling bits of silver. It was made up of squares badly sewn together and there was a hat to match. Not Sara's style at all. 'I know, I fuckin' hate it myself … My old lady sent it in, I'll just wear it inside but I wouldn't be seen dead in it outside.' Sara was consumed with giggling at the hideousness of her mother's taste. 'I've never had such big tits, my old man's going to love them, and I've put two stone on since I got in here.' She pulled the outfit over her bosom, making it even bigger.

The warm smell of freshly cooked food from the home economics class over-powered us all. 'Go and get a drink of water from that new water fountain they have in the cookery class and then you can nick some food.' Sara and Sheila sent orders over to Angela who'd reappeared with her broom. 'It's some sort of pie I think, I've just had a look in.' 'I could do with some pie; go on Angela go get some' and off Angela climbed in search of that fresh smell. Sara reminded herself that it was Passover soon and she slapped her lips at the thought of all that Jewish food. Too much for Sheila, she flung her brushes down and told her to shut the fuck up. Sheila had married a Jewish man, her first husband and kept his name. As her second husband wasn't fussed about it, she never changed it. But she wasn't Jewish, unlike Sara so she'd never practised the faith. Religion wasn't her thing. 'Teach me some Yiddish, then I can get the Jewish diet too … after all I've got a Jewish name, they'll never know.' Sara feigned shock at the chutzpah, thought for a moment, paused and then agreed, giggling more and more at the thought of this profanity. 'It'll have to be quick I'm on the shipout list … I could go any minute'. And so began the first of many lessons to improve Sheila's diet.

Angela reappeared and climbed lopsidedly back into the room carrying a plastic cup of water. Sheila and Sara leapt up to meet her, smiling with welcome but only for the chance of whatever food she might have stolen. Underestimating the power of Angela's medication they had to wait for the slow motion lady to rehydrate her saliva glands with the last drop of water.

'Did you get anything?' Still climbing up and down, Angela reached under her jumper for some greaseproof paper. She opened it and inside was a portion of pineapple upside-down-cake. Sheila grabbed at it and devoured some. Sara bashed into Sheila for her bit of cake and shoved it down her throat. Angela was left with the smallest bit, but her medication had sup-pressed her fighting impulse so she smiled benignly and chewed the last crumbs—very slowly.

'There's a puddle here near the sink … I'll mop it up Miss'. Chewing and climbing Angela replaced her broom with a mop and started pushing it into the dampness, hypnotically staring into the middle-distance. The water looked as if it was leaking from the radiator so I rang the Works Department once more. There were holes in the ceiling outside the door, a hole in the ceiling in the Art Room itself (that hadn't started to leak as yet) and now a hole in the radiator. There was also a permanently blocked sink. The list just grew and grew.

Sara and her husband were chronic heroin addicts, both recidivists and both now being held in custody. Sentenced to four years for possessing drugs, her days were numbered in Holloway. She'd be up the motorway to a more permanent residency. Sheila was in for a civil offence to do with her neighbours. The snack over with, they lost interest in Angela and carried on where they had left off.

'Anyway where're you been the last week, why haven't you bin down in the class?'

'I've bin down the block,' Sheila replied like it was nothing to fuss about.

'What the fuck for?' Sheila wasn't the type to cause problems so Sara was intrigued.

'I refused a piss test. I said to the officer "Have you run out of drug addicts?", So they put me down the block.'

'Shit what a bummer!'

'So I'm still on basic pay. I want to get on to standard pay. I asked an officer why I was still on basic, you know what she said? … that I had an attitude problem … me! I never leave me room. All I do all day is paint. I'm no bother, I never mix with anyone else, I'm no drug addict … I just have a problems with my neighbours.' She tried to laugh but it came out as a heaving of her chest followed by a splutter. 'I think I'll write one of my famous appeals, one of those that takes up fifty pages, that'll piss them off … Christ it's good to get off that wing, first a couple of days down the block, then locked in all weekend.'

'Miss can you sharpen this for me.' It was eyeliner that needed crafting to a point. No sharpeners on the wing, so requests got saved up for the Education Department. 'Can you mend this Miss, I'm in court tomorrow and I've only got this pair.' Part of her shoe had come unstuck so I got the glue gun, stuck it up and clamped it together in the printing press. 'It will be ready at the end of the lesson.'

'I haven't seen you for a while, have you been sick?'

'No … I've had visits from my brief every day for about a week now.'

'Do you have confidence in him?'

'Yes … I think he's good, but he brings it all back.'

'Have you got a date yet?'

'Yes it's in three weeks, on the tenth at the Old Bailey. I have to go over it and over it in every detail, every time he comes. And I can't come down to education afterwards, so I just stay on the wing, and think about it all the time.'

'Have you got enough materials?'

'No, I'd really like some more paper and some glue, but I'm not allowed it am I? I'm working on this drawing on three big pieces of paper and I can't stick them together and I don't want to use toothpaste.'

'I'll give you some stick glue, you can have as much paper as you like. I wrote a short note to validate Fran's extra equipment so that she could show it to security. On my way out of the prison that day, I passed a group of women returning to their wings Ahead of them was a cluster of hands and feet in a twisted knot of many ends—some black over-active spider with a couple of legs missing—it lurched unbalanced and askew. There was grey hair that bobbed around and the muffled sound of physical exertion. As I got nearer, the image separated itself into four officers carrying a squirming thing. The squirming thing was Mrs. Fernandez, swearing oaths that spat out of her wriggling body, now all scrunched up like a piece of waste paper ready for the bin. I couldn't see her face and I'm pretty sure she couldn't see anything except blue lino and miles of floor along the corridor. Her captors were struggling to keep hold of her. She wriggled so much, despite being so puny. Maybe the officers were wary to put pressure on her because she was such a weakling. Off she was going down in the direction of the block again. But the next day I was surprised to see her standing first in the queue for my class.

'What on earth was happening with you yesterday?'

'I spent the night down the block.'

'What for?'

'Disobeying an order.' She started to cry and out it all came. 'Well … I am so upset, so very upset. I'm cold and my room is cold. Yesterday someone threw some water over my bed and it went all over my sheets and mattress and everybody laughed. And I had to sleep on it. My room is the one on the corner and there are big gaps in the windows so the wind blows in and I have no heating. So I was cold and really upset. On my way over to education yesterday with the other women I saw a door which said 'Chaplain' on it, so I stopped and knocked. I wanted to see him because I was so upset. She started to hiccough with the effort of weeping and her nose started to run. The officers told me not to stop and to keep up with the other women, but I wanted to see the chaplain so I kept knocking. The officers got angry, then the chaplain answered the door and I asked to see him. Then he saw what was happening and waved me on, said that he couldn't see me, just waved me away like I was a nobody and disappeared back into his room. So I stood in front of his door and yelled.'

'What did you yell?'

'Well fuck you and fuck the officers and fuck the prison … and I started to knock again. The officers asked me to move on and keep up but I refused.

So they told me I was disobeying an order and I would have to go down the block. I told them that I would not walk down the block because I didn't see why I had to … I just told them all to fuck off and … fuck everything … I was so upset.' Tears were falling in lines down her blotchy face and her nose dribbled too. 'They picked me up and carried me down … Anyway it's warmer and drier down the block, I didn't mind. But I was so upset … I have only one set of clothes and now those are wet through'.

'You have only one set of clothes?'

'Yes, and now they are all wet, so I wear this tracksuit, but I have nothing else underneath, I am so cold.' She sat down near the radiator and started her work after she had dried herself up a bit and wiped her glasses. I gave her a project to do but everything was upside down and back to front and she tried to start again and again. She couldn't improve it despite my compliments, so she lost faith in herself. They were nice drawings and it fascinated me how she saw things. Her recent miseries had diminished her confidence, overpowered her creative spirit.

We talked quietly and she stopped being quite so upset. She didn't have any visits, because she had nobody. She had one child a long time ago, but it died at six months. She got pregnant a second time ten years afterwards, but had a miscarriage. She shrugged, as if she had accepted it a long time ago. Over in one of my levels of hiding there was a black plastic bag which had been donated to me ages ago. I'd completely forgotten that it was there. Inside were some decent quality second-hand clothes, all ironed and washed. I remembered them as a gift from some visitor.

'Mi ..i.ss, can I have another pair of scissors, these are fucked?'

'Just a minute, I'll be out soon.'

'We've only a few minutes left Miss and I need to finish this card and these scissors are buggered.'

'Does this look okay now Miss, I've finished it?'

'Hang on … just wait please.'

'She's losing her rag now.' I heard a giggle behind my back.

'Maybe she didn't get any last night.' Another giggle.

'How do you make an envelope?'

'I meant it, just wait.'

'Oooh Miss you need a joint, calm it Miss don't get out of your tree.'

'About bloody time too … how do you make an envelope?'

I emerged from the storeroom to a heap of insulted women baying for my attention and aggrieved that I had deserted them for a few minutes. This week was going on forever. Was it Tuesday or Wednesday? The exam student hadn't arrived. 'Where's Petra? … She's usually in here on time … it's not like her to miss a lesson. Where she is?' 'She won't be down today, she's had to have some stitches in her ear … She got her head stuck between the bars yesterday having a chat with her neighbour out of the window.' Poor Poor Petra, she was a floating mass of blond vagueness from California complete with a West Coast drawl. I always thought 'poor Petra' because she never seemed to be where everyone else was. She was a trusted inmate who took her job very seriously and was deeply conscientious. It was her responsibility to free the corridors of fluff and muck from the travellers who forever walked up and down. She was the first inmate I saw every morning and always apologised for her lateness and she was so sorry that she was late finishing. Forever wanting to please, she would enter a room with an apology and vacate a room saying, 'Sorry'. That's why I always thought poor Petra.

The storyteller began a more protracted explanation. Petra was having her chat with 'this other bird' and getting all involved with the chitchat. They were like two old friends, with their heads outside the bars in the fresh air, talking together like neighbours with a fence between them. When the conversation was at an end Petra couldn't withdraw her head. She had felt a kind of suction that stopped her head from re-entering her room. Anyway, she had tried again but her head remained stuck. Several lame efforts and a low panic started to grip her. She thought her head was starting to expand and her panic developed into a suppressed hysteria. Answering her urgent calls, her neighbour reappeared out of her own window and tried to calm Petra down. It didn't work despite her great exhortations and patient, soft encouragement. Petra was breathing with difficulty now and her face was red and she was shaking. So the neighbour rang the emergency bell and pleaded for help. The officer came and the officer called the nurse.

Both went out into the grounds and with heads craned upwards tried to talk Petra back inside. But it wasn't working and poor Petra was simply gibbering. Then a couple of officers and a nurse appeared behind Petra and rubbed her head and ears with Vaseline. She tried again to release her head, but it still didn't work because Petra was convinced it had grown bigger. With desperation in her voice, she begged everyone to leave her alone. She was sorry and grateful, 'Thank you very much,' but could she be left alone please. She was so sorry for being such a nuisance. So the staff left from both inside and outside. Petra knew she needed to calm herself down before her head burst. That is what she thought was going to happen. Several times she tried to withdraw it from the bars, but her ears were lying in the wrong direction and got in the way. She couldn't budge. Petra held herself calm until she felt like she could try again. Then she just breathed gently and pulled herself inwards and inwards, ignoring the pain and noise and hurt and a suction kind of popping noise which she couldn't quite explain. And she managed it, but at the expense of a cut ear, which needed four stitches, and a scratched face.

Fran's drawing was complete. She laid it out over two tables. It was drawn with a graphite stick. A woman, four pages long, prone, with exaggerated, elongated features. She was glad it was finished, glad it was out of her room. Though it was too soon to talk about it, it symbolised some trauma that she needed time to recover from. Its completion provided the only positive response, a sigh of relief that the burden was over and she could put it aside and do something else. She spent the rest of the time in class idly looking out of the window and flicking through books. She needed a break, just to do nothing at all. Yes, I could have the drawing for the competition, that was fine. I could give it any title I wished to, Fran didn't care, she was glad it was no longer part of her life, that it no longer lived in her room.

'Can you take an extra one this afternoon, the computers are down and there is no-one to take her back to the wing?' That was the Art Room, the class everyone could slot into, that could expand to fit any emergency or contingency—and the computers were down. That excuse seemed to hide all kinds of discrepancies, all kinds of delays, had become the modern—day explanation that nobody could argue with. Anne was introduced and sat down. Her hair was pushed up and held by a frayed ribbon, tied in a bow on each side of her face. Her drab dress was bursting its buttons and she wore stockings, rolled down near her ankles with slippers, old and worn. She was difficult last time I remembered, but it was a long while ago, so I couldn't quite recall how difficult. Every time I approached her she involved me in a conversation about the number of black staff in the prison. I tried to limit the conversation to her work and nothing else. She drew stick people, a bit like L S Lowry, but without the charm.

Last year, she had lost a baby, now she was carrying twins. We talked on about her pregnancy and its progress. The twins were due the following year, which meant that she was barely one month gone, but she said it was four months. Pregnant women lived on a special wing but this lady was on normal location. She disliked the black doctors, that's why she refused the Mother and Baby Wing. She didn't want to live where they worked—that was her explanation.

'Who would shag *her*?' I heard the whisper from some hard-nosed eaves-dropper, but couldn't be certain of the source, so I had to let the remark pass. Maybe Fran heard Anne's remarks, I wasn't sure, maybe others in the class had heard too. I rang up the wing to find out if she was really pregnant.

'No she isn't pregnant. She was lying'. Noticing that Anne had opted for my class the next day, I waited to confront her in the office. In she came with a complaint about bullying on the wing.

'The officer on your wing tells me that you're not pregnant.'

'Well I wasn't tested in Holloway ... I don't trust the officers.'

'Who is bullying you?'

'The whole of the wing.'

'That's about forty women ... have you got any names?'

'No ... but there's a lot of black people'.

'Do you think your attitude might be one reason for that?'

'Well where I come from there are no black people, I'm not used to them.'

'Where's that?'

'America.'

'But there are lots of black people in America.'

'Not in North Carolina.'

'There are many black people in North Carolina.'

'I didn't mean North Carolina ... I meant Norfolk.'

I related this conversation to her wing officer for the record. The next day she came to the class excitedly, telling me her waters had broken the previous evening. The rest of the class didn't seem to notice. I rang the wing again from the telephone in my room.

'Are you sure she's not lying about being pregnant?'

'No she isn't pregnant … definitely not. No her waters haven't broken … but she is being transferred to a special hospital tomorrow, she'd been assessed and that's where she is being allocated for treatment, she has mental health issues.'

So that was that. I gave her work to do, told her to take care of herself and that I hoped the pregnancy would go well. She in return, thanked me kindly, told me she would name one of the babies after me, and I never saw her again.

'I'd like to issue these to Mrs. Fernandez … she' got no clothes.'

'Are you sure she hasn't got any?'

'Yes … I don't think she'd lie.'

'Huh … You'd better check with Reception.'

'I'll go and check … Is this going to be a regular thing?'

'No … just a one off.'

'Bloody hell you're right, she's got nothing, absolutely nothing … write down all the clothes you're giving her on her property list then you can take them to her.'

'How are your legal visits going?'

'Same as ever. Over and over we talked, but then I suppose we have to, to be ready for court'.

'Have you got any support outside?'

'No not really.'

'How about your Mum?'

'She can't … only my sister can come up … they're all to do with it. My mum is back on the pills and the drink … she's not good on her own. He was awful to her Miss, beat her up and beat her again, he never stopped. All I can remember is seeing him dead on the floor, so I ran away … I knew they would catch me because of my card and my phone … It's the first time I've been sober for years. Not long now Miss and I'll know what I've got to take.' Fran's enthusiasm for drawing was diminishing into small sketches in a drawing book, doodles mostly, just textures and lines.

The last session of the week and I eyed up all my regulars. In the corner was Mrs. Fernandez with a new red jumper, a cardigan, fresh socks and shoes. I'd cut through the red tape and managed to get the clothes to her myself. Sara and Sheila were swearing at each other for some unknown reason. There was Mo, waving her brush around then bringing it down with a splatter of colour for Tanya, her loving other half to clear up at the end of the lesson. Angela was there making her husband a card all red hearts and tears and 'Luv'ya' and Petra with her damaged ear who was rushing to finish a painting that should have been completed sooner and so was apologising for that even though she had been in hospital. Chrissie with her different medication had no new scars on her arms and seemed disinclined to swallow anything. And there was Fran sketching. Frankie joined us for the afternoon, 'Just popping in this once to do a card'. Finally there was a group of newcomers who all sat together weighing each other up, surveying the Art Room and assessing me.

'There … Here, here they come.' Sara saw the pee testers approaching the Education Department. Two officers in charge of testing urine were heading straight for the Art Room. Sara saw them approach. I wouldn't have known them, but she recognised them immediately. The rest of the class barely moved, but the officers had rattled Sara's composure. Behind her desk, hidden from sight, she took something out of her shoe and wrapped it in a piece of paper towel, then placed it casually next to another screwed up bit of paper on her table. It looked just like any other discarded tissue. Nothing happened until we heard keys, the unlocking of doors and the sound of footsteps getting nearer. Nobody else reacted, the rest of the class carried on with what they were doing. Sara moved the piece of paper over to the radiator and placed it on top of the pipes.

The two officers came into the room and took Sara out, nobody else. Some while back she had been caught receiving drugs from one of her visitors and had been put on closed visits, now she was being subjected to regular urine tests. No sooner was the door closed than Frankie volunteered to clean up Sara's space. I thought this was unusual, she was normally lazy and her actually volunteering surprised me. But I didn't think that Frankie had seen Sara's last minute adjustments to her shoe. So I went over to Sara's space, and as I picked up her drawing board I also shoved Sara's crunched up paper down behind the radiator concealing it altogether. The over-enthusiastic cleaner began clearing Sara's space and took all the used equipment over to the dustbin. What she did with it didn't concern me, I was only interested in my part of the detective story.

The class ended with the paper still behind the radiator. I put the light off and with the classroom gloomy and dark ran upstairs for another teacher. I needed a witness. We both re entered my room, retrieved the paper and took it to the corner of the room so that we could not be observed. We sniffed it. It smelt vile, acrid and unpleasant. Should we inform ourselves of its contents? Should we know what was inside? That information might implicate us as being knowingly concerned. At the moment it was just a piece of debris, gathering dust behind from the radiator. If we opened it then maybe we would be conspirators, which would be worse. Ignorance was the best option; any other decision would embroil us in events best avoided. We both agreed the best thing to do was to throw it away as a bit of debris and leave it as unspecified rubbish cluttering up the Art Room. So I wrapped the paper in more paper, put it into a black plastic bag and slung it into a skip along with other items from that day.

Sara had a positive pee test and was immediately shipped out. Why didn't I report it? Well I didn't and it was for the best. Some people will think I should have, but the process was underway and it didn't need my contribution. Evidence of drugs had already been found in Frankie's urine. Illegal substances had been found, whatever they were. Whatever had been in that tissue was irrelevant to what happened next.

Mrs Fernandez and Petra successfully passed their exam. Fran's drawings won great acclaim in the Koestler inter-prison art competition and one of Sheila's paintings was highly commended. Fran was convicted and received a long sentence. I remember the description of her mother's first visit to her after months of ignored invitations. 'I was waiting and waiting in the Visits Room and I thought that she would never turn up, then I smelt a whoosh of alcohol from behind and I knew it was her.'

CHAPTER 7

Sickness

The first prisoners with the HIV-AIDS virus were delivered to the gate of Holloway and moved straightaway to an isolation cell in a special dormitory on the Hospital Wing where they were to be kept. They could be visited, but they didn't visit others. The news of their presence preceded their arrival making the current media sound-bite a reality.

'AIDS IS EVERYONE'S BUSINESS'

Every week, similar captions stoked an epidemic of fear, with theories about a 'new virus' and how it could be contracted. What kind of contagious disease was it that seemed to destroy the immune system, that apparently had no cure—and how was it being passed on? A muddle of misinformation, inaccuracies and contradictions fuelled anxiety. Amidst the speculation and rumour, the fact that there seemed to be no evidence to suggest that transmission was airborne was about the only constant fact. Other than that, silence allowed the public to fill the void in information with wild imaginings. When it was thought that the disease could spread through bodily fluids, blood or mucus, the public stigmatised certain groups of people, inflicting more suffering on the vulnerable. Other groups became even more fearful and panicked, spreading the misery onto those most in need of comfort.

'HAEMOPHILIAC BANNED FROM SCHOOL'

'GAY PLAGUE'

'FIREMEN BAN KISS OF LIFE'

Could AIDS be caught in swimming pools? Could hairdressers pass it on with infected combs? Communion wine, was that a possible source of contagion? Until science found its tongue then this apparent hysteria would continue to dominate the headlines. It was at this stage of understanding, that two particular new arrivals were admitted to Holloway.

My delivery of creative material to them was initiated by a request from a member of the medical team on the Hospital Wing. A week or two must have passed since they first entered the prison and by then their routine was established and what other people could do was recognised. My slots were in-between their solicitor's visits, their social visits, their medical appointments and canteen days. There was nothing to say that my entry into their room was forbidden, but I did feel that I was doing something that I could get out of if I wanted to. It would be understood if I refused to see them and just dropped off equipment for the two prisoners concerned. My visiting them was no casual event therefore, but a purposeful statement of some significance. Images from the media of terminally ill patients accompanied my descent down the stairs, making me worried, nervous and apprehensive. Incurably ill and in prison: this double punishment was the clincher with regard to any timidity on my part.

My eyes took a while to distinguish anyone at all. They were slow to register the dull light of the dormitory as against the bright electricity of the adjacent corridor. Rooms below ground level didn't get a fair share of the mid-day sun and the heavy plastic windows hindered the light flow. Shadowed in monochromatic shades of grey that seemed like one of Henry Moore's drawings of underground shelters, the reclining figure wrapped tightly in a blanket could so easily have come from one of his sketch books. Six beds were arranged around the walls. Four were without blankets, just bare mattresses, and a crumpled bed lay abandoned. The room seemed larger than a regular dormitory, an immense space of drab coldness just for sleeping-in and nothing else, no bedside cupboards or wardrobes as I remember, just objects to lie on.

Lillian was standing tall against a wall, silhouetted near the window, hands trapped behind her body with only small details of her features showing. The powdery light gave her the abstract quality of a stone sculpture. Christine lay with her head covered and wrapped in prison sheets, all scrunched up with just a flash of hair visible on a pillow. There seemed to be no relationship, no familiarity between these two women who had somehow found themselves sharing so much. Therefore my appearance didn't break up any communication between this detached pair, only the general atmosphere. A heavy, languid feeling united the listlessness in front of me. It was a still life, silent and immobile which I had suddenly disturbed. The possibility that I was imposing my own response to their illness on the scene before me might have been true but it was a desperately miserable room nonetheless. Christine shifted her head towards me, Lillian looked across and I smiled inanely between both, prattling on about the pencils and drawing books that I had brought for them. That's what I was offering, six coloured pencils and two grey drawing books. Expecting no response to my puny contribution to the quality of their life, I dropped the equipment onto a vacant bed and closed the door on two almost inaudible thank yous.

The weeks passed and little by little things eased. Lillian and Christine were allowed to venture out and enter some of the more positive parts of the prison. The situation gradually normalised and they became numbers, just like other women within the prison population. Christine was discharged from prison and Lillian started to attend classes. But her medical history was public knowledge and nothing could change that now. From cat-walking around the fashion houses of Europe, she still looked the part. Her elegant profile stood out from the rest and she moved easily taking long strides and looking straight ahead. She'd been well-loved in her middle-class family, well-supported and well-educated. Designer clothes and designer drugs, Lillian had it all. Stares now picked her out as the AIDS patient. Immune to the groundswell of twitching stares, nudgings and whisperings, she remained on the catwalk, never distracted, never reacting. That serenity changed only when someone in uniform irritated her. Then I saw the attitude of defiance deform that usually calm disposition. She admitted to me that the institution had a bad effect on her, brought out the worst in her, uncivilised her. We never discussed her illness. Those new red marks on her legs were something to do with it, she'd noticed them, but they got little attention, a fleeting inspection now and again that's all. She kept to her timetable attending the creative lessons. A self-portrait built up of harsh quivering lines revealed a little of what was going on behind her calmness. The irony of her poems also conveyed much.

Most of the women in Holloway Prison seemed to be sick and on some form of medication. Epileptic fits were a frequent event and still are, as are asthma attacks. Ailments aggravated by years of drug or alcohol abuse put pressure on the human system. To even start some form of recovery can take years of sifting through the layers of whys and hows. The whole staff structure had to get involved and pool their skills: doctors, psychologists, governors, probation officers. Lack of resources stretched them further and further. Hepatitis, in all its manifestations, liver damage, abscesses that had left bruised craters on the skin, some new under bandages, trackmarks and cold, swollen, vein free hands were all evidence of unhealthy living. But it went further. Dentists dealt with missing or unfilled teeth, long ago dissolved by bad diets and drug-induced psychosis meant more medication and closer observation. Sometimes a finger or toe was missing, or other digits were blackened by gangrene. With the New Age drugs came the New Age sicknesses, heroin became crack, hypodermics became pipes, crystal meth, cocaine, ketamin and endless scientific inventions emerged to create a buzz, for kicks, for women to 'get out of it', ' turned on' or to 'chill out'.

The first female prisoners in the old-style Holloway were required to wear uniforms. A few examples were left in stock for the poorer inmates to use if clothing became scarce. They were blue dresses with flowers on them and the towelling bath robes were blue too. My first resources were left for me in an old toilet; just piles of sugar paper and bottles of ink and pens. The glass bottles had become a potential danger and the inks were causing a problem. There was so much tattooing in a desire to form a contrast to the impersonal uniforms. If a woman's instinct to decorate herself was suppressed, the only way left to express her individuality was to have a tattoo. Then someone said that uniforms were dehumanising and so the uniforms stopped. And to make life easier the pens and inks were banned to stop the amateur tattooing, the makeshift unsterilised needles and the cross-infection. A grey tracksuit replaced the blue flowery dresses for inmates with few resources, which was at least modern and practical.

Silver paper had long ago been outlawed because of its heat resistant quality which allowed it to be used to burn illegal substances. Even the Kit-Kats were confiscated from the prison canteen. There were (and are) always new directives; new things to look out for — with staff running to keep up with the designer gear and similar shifts. New operational directives were passed on to educationalists: no more tinsel on the Christmas cards and so on. Piccadilly was the place most talked about then, the central London meeting place for those who were drug dependent to stock up. Then it became the crack houses, and toilets of night clubs or pubs. These could be anywhere: vocabulary changed to suit new addictions and the physical and mental illnesses that accompanied them.

Excited conversations in class involved women comparing notes on their medications. Women who couldn't spell 'birthday' could write the name of every item on their prescription. Four and five syllable medication terms rolled off their tongues. Women who had difficulty adding or subtracting the simplest maths could work out kilos and grams of some kind of dope or other—they could show me how much so many grams looked like and what space it could fit into. This specialised knowledge, albeit limited in its own way, sometimes indicated that their genes were linked up into one big dysfunctional family. It united a section of the class and bonded them and concentrated their minds in a way drawing or painting could not. The drug addicts were the majority shareholders in the class and decades had not changed their obsessions.

'I love my speed I do—I never stop when I'm on the out.' Fizz had only been in Holloway a couple of weeks and she was still whirring away leaping from one activity to another, changing her mind every ten seconds—a now you see her now you don't kind of presence, short attention span and so on. Pills were still dissolving in her system and affecting her metabolism, making her hyper-active and driving her out of control. 'Amphetamines, they're the business.'

The women would go on and on all day relating drug-induced experiences and talking about what they were 'into', how long they'd spent addicted, what they'd snorted, sniffed and smoked, the men in their life, who knew which guys on the street, whose babies might have a common father—in a way they too were just one big happy family, all cosy-wosy in my class. Then they'd go on about the medication they had been prescribed in the prison and how they were trying to get some more out of the 'sweet shop' which was their name for the prison chemists. They'd rub their eyes red raw to impress the doctor that they were nearly at breaking point just to extract an extra pill or two. Out-of-hours shoppers traded, whilst dealers and sharks bartered their pills, medication and loans with desperate addicts in dark corners.

'I love my glue I do, I'm going straight back on it when I'm out.' Another recidivist in the making. 'I can't do anything today Miss, I'm still clucking.' Eventually she would stop feeling like a chicken flapping around the yard as her particular addiction wore off. It sounded to me like a lot of nervous energy that was going nowhere: like too much exertion inside your belly with no door to let it out, so it just whizzed round the system until it ran out of steam. It was a complicated process coming off drugs.

Noreen flung down her pencil and swore. There was no point in her trying to draw, she couldn't see anything, anyway she couldn't draw, so what was the point. I thought a bit of intervention might encourage a response, so I initiated the start of a leaf, slowly and simply—just to start her off. 'Christ look at all them lovely veins Cheryl.' A cold clammy finger prodded around my hand and the two of them admired with envy the long blue lines just under my skin. 'What I'd do for a hit of them Miss—I've got no bleedin' veins left, they've all collapsed on me.' 'Mine too; I have to get a hit in my groin or me neck now, all my veins have disappeared.' Couldn't she book to see the opticians? 'No Miss, there was no point in getting glasses it wouldn't make any difference.' Her reply was the same for all my suggestions, all of them were pointless. After two shaky leaves and a couple of thick stems and blossoms too difficult to even attempt, her life story unravelled across the near empty page. Lemon and vinegar: those apparently harmless fluids had caused her poor eyesight. Oh, and the bad gear that she mixed it with. In the worst times she had cut her heroin with urine. No medical intervention could change the fact that her eyes were getting weaker by the day, she was sure of that.

Bonded together by the sisterhood of illegal substances, the women's kicks were now relived in sentimental memories stirred up by enforced drying out. Whipping themselves up to stimulate those drug-induced moments could destroy the minority's efforts to deal with their imprisonment constructively. Yet a direct admonishment would be ineffective against the strength of the addiction and addiction is what seemed to motivate their whole lifestyle. Besides, confrontation was their speciality, their coping strategy and they were masters at it, reducing me to the role of a loser if I once accepted their terms of engagement and joined the debate. Heedful therefore of my own limitations I turned up the volume on the radio, instantly killing unwholesome conversations. I always played a mellow kind of music, a middle of the road sort of sound, despite repeated requests to change the station.

'Good on ya, Miss—nice sounds.' How long this new amiability would last depended as much on my apparent indulgence as whether their goodwill was reciprocated through creative industry. 'Don't come out of that storeroom heavier than you went in.' Maggie reappeared flicking a new paintbrush to prove her innocence. 'That's all I want, that's all, I need a really thin brush—you're too up front Miss, getting too cheeky.' But as she bent over her painting that bulky pocket weighing about a couple of ounces established her guilt. Should I confront her? Whatever it was could be sacrificed for the greater good of that beautiful painting she was doing. Non-intervention was a realistic compromise. Theft didn't much bother me in moderation. Only inactivity was bothersome—well except activity that was destructive, or contagiously destructive, that was the very worst kind. Mostly the materials that disappeared were used creatively as they should be, they were not abused even if charcoal and other powders and potions could be also be utilised to glamorise eyes and cheeks, but that was about all.

'You really are good you know.' I was talking encouragingly to Olive who had surprised me with her talent. She was an unexpected find and she needed to know just how good she was. But from the first time I saw her I thought there would be difficulties. Her entry into the class made us all jump. There was a banging of doors against chairs, a cursing, and a clumsy lunge into the nearest chair. Her hair fell forward over her eyes and was repeatedly flung backwards with clumsy hands. I had to teach Olive without her knowing it, offer advice without her realising it—because she was institutionally defiant and uncooperative. I don't think she ever agreed with anything I said, for that would have implied a shared understanding, a fellow feeling. She wasn't much of a talker either. Her head moved upwards; she'd flick her hair away, look over and then invariably decide against talk. When she did reply, the words jerked out in blasts of sounds as if she was flinging them at you. But from the start of the lesson until the end she worked with absolute concentration and made the most beautiful drawings which she left discarded on her table at the end of each class.

I sat down beside her and congratulated her on her talent and ability to draw, but her expression never altered. I hadn't pleased her like I thought I would. Her daughter was good at art at school. That's about all I heard her say. Desperation must have showed on my face, or maybe I just over-did it in amongst the communal apathy. The less the prisoners responded, the more I felt the need to compensate with over exuberance—usually on a rainy day when the heating should have come on in the room and it hadn't (or the day before payday when the women had run out of tobacco). However much I praised Olive she remained impassive. I took it as some kind of perverse modesty that denied her any pleasure from my encouragement. Perhaps she'd had enough of me.

'Actually Miss, I'm not interested much in the lesson, I only come here because it passes the time. I prefer Tennents, I love me drink and I don't care anything about this.' At that she shoved her drawing away and folded her arms tightly shut. 'And I'll be getting right back into me drink as soon as I step out next week.' Personalised files, alphabetically upright had been launched as a new initiative a few weeks ago, to be implemented immediately. Each student would have her own diary with aims and objectives, lesson plans and targets and it would be inspected by a corporate consultant every so often. With the high turnover of women, my files had advanced along to a second, third and fourth column along a table. New stationery stood in readiness for a fifth column. With all this information, my ability as a teacher could be demonstrated. Every prisoner's attendance would be monitored under the appropriate headings for some statistician to analyse in the erroneous belief that it would empty the prisons. This statistician, inspector, analyst never arrived, nor were those files ever examined. But they certainly made it look as if things were under control, like I'd found the solution, solved the puzzle. This glut of information created on the instructions of some unknown expert even had *me* conned sometimes. They looked impressive. But it was a sham, as much a mirage as a drug addicts' hallucinations.

In Olive's file, under the heading 'TARGETS', I wrote: 'To develop new skills'. Under the heading 'INDIVIDUAL LEARNING PLAN', I wrote: 'Explore new media'. Fudging the books seemed to be an acceptable practice with regard to this cynical exercise in misrepresentation. Some documentation, some record-keeping would be invaluable but information was always on bits of paper that slotted into more bits of paper that lay in stagnant files that just piled up on top of more stagnant files. On rare occasions a member of staff would inquire about some student's progress. So it felt as if our contribution counted enough to be of value, was noted somewhere in the records, but nobody looked in our files. My feeling was that such intensive documentation was suitable in a prison for convicted women who stayed for a sufficient length of time, but not in Holloway with its high turnover of remand and other short-term residents. I would have liked to have written in Olive's designated cardboard box: 'Olive has exceptional talent but intends to renew her old addictions. Her target is to buy some Tennents as soon as she is released and she plans to forget about Holloway and her experience here as quickly as possible.'

But to write that would have marked me out as troublesome, so I sacrificed precision for the greater good of future talent that was too cockeyed for rectangular boxes. At least that would be an accurate representation—you could build on that. Unfortunately the forms didn't fit this unique teaching situation; they were just forms that queued up next to more forms created for other educational establishments. More such forms were created by new education providers who were bought into the privatised Education Department of Holloway every four years. Previous bits of paper were swept under the carpet and new employers would organize workshops instructing the teachers how to fill in new forms. And so it went on. One morning, in need of more space I recycled the columns of cardboard and threw all the files away. Olive was readmitted a few weeks down the line with more charges to add to her collection and more cans of Tennents to reminisce about.

The noisy majority started up again, this time it was the drug addict's obituary column. The litany of the dead souls of yesteryear was tallied up. 'So and so overdosed last week, did you know? And remember so and so?' She's been found in the Dilly. Brown bread, she was … right under the statue of that guy Nelson … Haven't seen so and so recently, I hear she copped it too.' Today's variant was about who'd been dead for how long before they were found. A name came up that I recognised. She had become a favourite in the Education Department. Completely cuckoo, she was not only off with the fairies but the goblins gnomes and all the other mythical folk you can think of. She was bright as a button and continuously philosophising, backed up with formulae written on the mass of paper that she conned us out of. Sheaves of theories stuck out of her folders and her drawings were written on, intensively, explained. All this would be laid out in front of anyone who happened to pause in transit. She would make mosaic crucifixes and funeral urns, then get a huge white piece of paper and fill it up with someone's last Will and Testament, or she'd paint wildly and scratch words into the paint that only made sense to her. She'd died of a drug overdose somewhere under the Notting Hill Gate flyover. I rummaged about and found one of her old paintings. I decided to pin it to the wall in her memory as a mark of respect. Impressive comments warmed the audience up to smile at her eccentricities reflected on that paper. Used to a certain amount of drugs at her reception into Holloway, she had imbibed the same amount on exit, over-estimated her tolerance level and fatally overdosed. Maybe it was the thought that it could have been their own death we were talking about which focussed the women's efforts on work for a further few minutes, but they all seemed to shrug off the news as the inevitable result of that prisoner's lifestyle.

Ellen liked being in the class. She didn't stay long but spent most of her time under medication on the Hospital Wing. Her head was a mass of scabs, so that most of the other women kept clear of her. She was the reason her neighbours got little or no sleep with her relentless head-banging. She was the reason an art therapist allegedly had fled the building never to return. 'Express yourself, just express yourself, just feel free.' She'd picked up the biggest brush she could find and covered it with blue paint. Wiping her forehead lavishly with that colour she brought her whole head down on the paper and started banging bright blue impressions all over the white surface. Nothing the therapist could do would stop her; Ellen just banged her blue forehead, her movements getting more and more frantic. The emergency bell had to be pushed. Ellen was forcibly restrained. And the therapist? She was never seen again.

'I can't start yet Miss, I've just had my injection and my bum is so sore.' She grimaced and tried to twist her body off the chair so that only one cheek made contact with prison metal. From the age of four, schizophrenia had been diagnosed. If Irene didn't get her injection then something awful would happen to someone and it had—on the outside—and Irene was now paying the price. The thick papier-mâché paste dripped quicker than the artist's slow-motion style of application. Soon it would evolve into a complex shape, a simple three dimensional sculpture made by moulding the material over other shapes and peeling them off, creating other forms. But progress was slow because her visitors needed her attention. Joan couldn't get rid of those persistent presences her head. They talked to her wherever she was, they intruded into her isolation and encroached without invitation. She took the same medication prescribed to many other women and it shut the door on those intruders, but it slowed her up, sucked out the moisture from her body, leaving a compulsion to drink and drink. It slowed speech, slowed hands and caused her to shuffle along instead of walking normally. Each day Ellen was expecting to go to court, each day she expected to be told to pack up her bags for home.

Her one son was all she had on the outside and she was desperate to continue her maternal care of him at home as soon as possible. Chances were that she would do so, because it looked likely that the charges against her would be dropped. That's what her solicitor had said. Such good news provoked Joan to start refusing her medication. She'd had enough of being treated like an invalid with no brains; she wanted to liven herself up a bit. After all she coped well enough outside on her own. 'I didn't get in touch with the Social Services for a couple of years after my baby was born, I supported myself and him, and we did okay … after all I got myself pregnant, Social Services didn't put the bun into the oven!'

What worried me was that other inmates latched onto Joan, and seemed to take advantage of her. One woman in particular, with eight kids and who lived in Birmingham, was forever inviting Joan to come and stay with her. She even gave her directions to her flat, and made all kinds of promises of a good time. As Joan's last day neared I asked her if she would be moving in with that particular lady. She burst out laughing with her newly restored, medication-free reflexes. 'God no … If I'm hearing voices now what state will I be in surrounded by eight kids?!'

I'd seen Sally down the Hospital Wing. The staff there had tried to talk to her and they would continue to help, but last time during the session with her no conversation had been possible. Wisdom had decided that the Hospital Wing provided the 24-hour care that was needed. She'd become introspective, distracted and remote, distancing herself from everyone, regressing to some place that hurt. She'd reactivate the pain with burns from cigarette ends stubbed out on her arms, then she'd rock herself backwards and forwards because no one else was around to comfort her. 'Somebody just brought me down here Miss, but I don't mind, I really don't … I feel better down here.' Before that she'd been up in the Art Room.

'Now the drugs have worn off Miss, I'm remembering things and I want to talk to someone about the things that keep coming into my head. They just won't go away, I can't sleep or anything. Before that, as a newcomer to the class she had been so loud, always bragging about her sexual experiences, painting pictures for her boyfriend. One picture was of some half-naked woman offering a line of cocaine to her boyfriend. Another was of them sharing a crack pipe. By what she was saying to anyone who would listen, she had done just about everything, with hundreds of men and all by the tender age of seventeen. A crowd always pushed to sit next to her. She was pretty, brash and talked big about everything. Other inmates were impressed and became hangers-on. They wanted to be associated with her charisma, they wanted it to rub off on them and they wanted her paintings as well. But it all changed within a month. From being an exhibitionist and the most desired member of the groupies she became a quiet talker, silent worker and finally self-harmer rocking to and fro in the Hospital Wing in the bowels of the prison.

Hyacinth with sickle cell anaemia had just recovered from another painful episode in that relentless illness. Always stoical, she was glad to be about again after spending a day in bed. A psychologist had referred a woman to me in the hope she would get peace in my class. She had a degenerative disease that King George IV had suffered from and was constantly medicated for her pain. I went over to check on her progress and to make sure that some tranquillity could be harnessed for her in a quiet corner. She was wearing a lowish-necked jumper and all around that neck were reddish weals getting bigger and bigger, watered by sweat, that reddened her skin and which quickened her breathing. Twenty minutes her stay lasted, that's all. 'Yes,' she wanted to go back to the wing. 'No,' she'd tried to work but couldn't concentrate, she'd really tried, she really had. So we left the class and started that slow journey back to her wing. Ever so gradually we made our way to the main door of the Education Department for others to escort her the rest of the way to her room. Strictly forbidden that was, I shouldn't have performed that small favour because I shouldn't have left my own room, though my 'phone call for assistance hadn't been answered.

As I returned, I made the inevitable comparisons. The maths students were all sitting behind their desks and the computer students' eyes were fixed on their screens in their carpeted room. I heard the noise of the Art Room before I saw it. The radio was throbbing against the walls, pumping out music and causing them to vibrate. All those colours, the paper, the paint, the dancing, the backing group. Olive couldn't care less, she just worked on. The young offenders were resting their feet on the tables throwing pencils at each other. Cheryl and Noreen were banging on the windows at their mates in the gardens. Someone was trying to scratch off some paint from her jumper at the sink with the water just below the flood line. Joan was edgy at the lack of control and was worried enough to think of leaving. Music thumped bottoms and breasts into gyrating their stuff. The whole class made a meagre effort to revert to educational mode as I re-entered the room.

My main concern was that they were sliding rather than banging on with 'The Universe', the current painting commission for the ceiling of the prison dentists. Patients would be able to gape open-mouthed at the planetary system above their heads while they worked away filling gaps in or extracting bad or damaged teeth. We had been evicted from the Mural Room a long time ago: office space had taken precedence. Michelangelos we weren't and the dentists wasn't the Sistine Chapel. Painting in situ was therefore out of the question. With no other place to go, the Art Room had to be used for a twelve foot by five foot map painted on plyboard. Because the ceiling at the dentists was full of lights and fixtures to hold scientific equipment, the board had to be split up into bits making the job even more difficult. All the planets were drawn to scale, so it was correct in that respect, though artistic licence had blasted the universe into a mass of astral forces, black holes, explosive stars and cosmic energies in wildly exaggerated colours that hopefully would distract the patient from the dentist's drill and educate her at the same time. When a full capacity class made painting impossible then the picture had to be laid on the floor and protected with paper. It could only be worked on with low student numbers and when the chosen artists were available. The last phase was the varnishing and then the huge picture would be complete.

My re-entry into the art room was not noticed by Maggie. Madame Apothecary was hunched over the palettes peering at the powder paints and mixing colours with one pokey finger of her right hand onto a piece of paper held in her left. During the next few minutes she tweaked a bit of this with a bit of that, dropped it onto the paper, stirred it around with a plastic spoon, then brushed the colour onto her skin. I watched intrigued by this dedicated colourist.

'What *are* you doing Maggie?'

'Aaah, ummmms.' Unperturbed by my question, her colour exercises continued with more mixing of pigments, more testers on her skin and another couple of 'aaaas' and 'ummmms.' Again I repeated the question and again she ignored me.

'You're mixing make-up aren't you Maggie?'

'Aaaaaa, Aaaaaa.'

'Yes you are, you're making blusher.'

'That colour is too orangey.'

'Yes, you need a bit of cold pink, that'll do better.' I started to tweak a bit too, with a bit of this and a bit of that until finally we came upon the hue that toned with her skin.

'What about eye shadow, we could mix some to match.'

'Put them in an envelope then the powder won't fall out.' Non-toxic powder cosmetics, harmless and free.

'You know Maggie; if you'd have asked I would have helped just the same.'

'Well, I'm on basic pay and can't afford to buy.'

'Okay, okay, well why didn't you say? … What colour are you looking for?' Non-toxic powder paint, suitable for small children couldn't do much harm. Just a small amount would be fine. The rest of the class was still settling down after my absence and were oblivious to the interchange.

Maggie's appearance took immediate priority whenever she was newly admitted to prison. Her comfort came a close second. First she'd stake out each class for any new desirables, she kept to the creative classes but wasn't averse to the occasional academic subject if her needs warranted specialist equipment. There was probably a list somewhere prepared especially for the education supermarket. A bag was the first requisite and a folder. The bag was made in the craft class and the folder one issued free from the office. After that she was all systems go. Exotic fabrics vanished onto Maggie's head all tied up in a flamboyant twist. Cottons, beads, buttons and wool disappeared only when Maggie's name was on the register in the Craft Class. I would ask her what she was taking out of the classroom, and there was always something that she hadn't been issued with. Pencils, scouring pads, dishcloths, drawing books escaped into her folder. Curtains and covers, cushions and rugs upgraded her residence. She had become the universal provider in her corner shop of a bedroom. Only dedicated twenty four hour surveillance could have prevented the exodus of equipment. It wasn't as if I couldn't do something, but I just didn't want to spend all my time watching Maggie, always waiting for what she might pick up, looking and following her around. I would invariably have happily given her bits and bobs if she had only asked. It was all about balance, so as to temper her entrepreneurial skills and her trading in Holloway memorabilia. If I put her on report then she'd be banned and wouldn't be able to paint. Besides I never put people on report, everyone knew that. So I balanced the damage and chose not to see: this occasional temporary blindness would balance out the pros and cons. It was a real dilemma for the teachers because she was the ideal student, cooperative, clever and creative. Nobody wanted to ban her, so a strategy was formulated in an attempt to curb her kleptomania.

'I don't want to ban you Maggie, you're too good and I know you don't abuse the materials because you are inventive. You're great in the class, you work, you inspire other students, clear up, co-operate and you are so clever. If you ask like any other adult would then I will gladly supply you with anything … within reason. I just don't want to ban you. Why didn't you ask me for the paper, or whatever it was, pencils crayons, cards? Because you could have had it, Maggie. I hate this checking up on you, that's not my job. This is further education, not school. We're women not kids, can't you just ask? I hate having to search your folder and your bag. If you want extra materials, just ask.'

I gave Maggie as much as I could in encouragement and compliments. I tried to discuss the matter as between colleagues with a common enthusiasm for the creative arts. My hope was that she would, in one fell swoop, realise how adults could consolidate their interests and maximise their potential to grow as human beings. She sat next to my desk and listened, contemplating her reply. 'Yes', she'd really try because she liked the classes and she asked if she really was that good. She said, 'Okay, no problem … I will ask in future, I really will'.

It was worth the effort to achieve a better rapport, a sound teacher-student relationship, to get away from the cat and mouse suspicions of the previous days. While our mutual smiles were still evident a quick hand movement slipped across right in front of me and a pad of yellow post-it labels flew into the air from my desk and landed right in Maggie's back pocket.

Ethel in her wheelchair was trying to tear out a picture from one of the best art books. Her hands were under the table pulling away at the page. 'Ethel if you really want to work from that picture I'll get it photocopied for you … please don't tear out the pages from my books.' Cool as you like she looked over her crooked glasses and thanked me with simpering servility. She hadn't realised there was such a facility or she wouldn't have dreamt of tearing out the picture! One day she would tell me that she was wheelchair bound because her career in the SAS had been cut short. Abseiling down some skyscraper, she'd fallen, never to walk again. Another day, it had been that accident on the stairs at home, or a car crash. The story changed to suit the audience and how it could be exploited to her advantage. Some people said they'd seen her rise out of her chair and walk, but rumours were only rumours. When her way was barred, tears would fall and she'd suck her thumb.

That morning before my work had even started; I'd heard that Lillian had died of an AIDS-related illness. Waiting for my keys, I'd been pulled aside by a governor who had given me the news. Lillian had finished her self-portrait that day and lingered so as not to be part of the rowdy mass that pushed to get off the wing for lunch. The cleaner, Lillian and myself had sat huddled together in a little island of good humour. We were in a light-hearted mood for some reason; maybe it was a bit of hysteria left over from one of those familiar frantic, frenzied kind of classes. The cleaner opted out and started washing-up, leaving Lillian and me to collect the palettes for her. It was my turn to parry a remark, a brief pause as she registered the joke and then she turned her head and gave me a swift bite to the upper arm. Panic and ignorance moved events on in a way that could not and would not happen today.

'Look at her arm Lillian … you've gone right through her denim blouse.' I looked at the damage and saw a blood blister of a bite at the top of my arm. 'Look at it.' The cleaner got some water and doused my arm .We both looked up at Lillian from the sink and saw her disappear out of the room, all humour gone, with just a frail look to her features, still staring straight ahead. The cleaner had to follow; the officers needed both inmates to rectify the count before the general exodus. I pulled down my sleeve and walked up the nearest stairs to the top of the block. I walked up and down, every step moving me into some kind of panic. I saw disinfectant on a draining board and let if flow over the bite. As the wing quietened I descended to the office and with a feeble voice related the incident. A few phone calls were made and I was ushered to a seat. Nobody mentioned the a-word—nobody mentioned the illness—and I never heard it referred to in any one of the phone calls. Another member of staff was to escort me to the Hospital Wing. Still nobody articulated anything like the term HIV, there was just an instruction for 'a test'. We walked along those endless corridors, with me just sheep-like, seeing nothing, registering nothing in the knowledge that this walk would end somewhere with a doctor.

'Well at least you know you are really healthy and strong, so you will last longer.' That believe it or not was meant as words of comfort from my escort, who hadn't even seen my arm. The doctor was waiting and I rolled up my arm for him to see the bite, the small blood blister. Maybe he said something, I cannot remember. What I do recall is that a nurse helped me onto a table; I don't remember her face though. The doctor wore glasses, that's all. There was no discussion, nobody asked any questions. He simply got the needle and took my blood, telling me the results would come through that evening. I was put on a couch and someone put a blanket over me. I stayed there and slept; though before I lost consciousness I heard mumblings from the next room and someone shushing someone else up and another voice that fell into a whisper. A door opened and slowly closed. I slept. Nobody had mentioned the word AIDS. It was implied in all the remarks, the looks and the test but still no-one mentioned it.

My hazy recollection is that I think someone drove me home after I had woken up. I didn't like how nice everyone was being to me; in my unstable state of mind I twisted it into their smug relief that they were not me at that moment in time. Nobody wanted to be me, that is why they could smile; they put their head on one side and sympathised. But in reality it was a relief that it had not happened to them. Later on that evening. a 'phone call arrived. 'No', I wasn't infected but I should get tested again in six months. I needed a second test for them to be sure. That weekend I pictured my death. It was there in everything I did and especially during times of inactivity. At night, my dying moments kept me awake. My fertile imagination, always useful as a resource for liberating the creative mind, descended overnight into a hostile force that weakened the spirit. Symptoms started to indicate a deterioration in health, the inevitable spread of the virus, marks I'd never been aware of grabbed my attention and I felt ill. Inside of me somewhere, starting from that blister, things (whatever I imagined them to be) started to move around my body: into my other arm and my head, they invaded my whole system. I could trace their route, feel them travelling around destroy-ing my immunity. I started to act like an invalid. Only essential activities kept me on the right side of sanity and reason, but it was a struggle to hang on. I arranged my funeral, counted the mourners and hoped there would be more than that. What would it feel like to be inside a coffin and what songs would be sung? Who would cry and who wouldn't? Normally, seeking to escape dull chores, I found relief in menial tasks that under-dramatised the event and dulled the effect of fearful images: There were hospital beds with tubes and sickness, endless dark corridors with no doors. At no point during that weekend did I tell anyone what had happened. I never discussed it and avoided the subject in any conversations. I disowned the events, denied their existence and just lived in my own Cloud Cuckoo Land of fear.

Lillian had refused to come out of her room. She had insisted on eating on her own. She wouldn't leave it all weekend, however hard people tried to entice her. I knew I would have to go and see her. But I didn't want to ever see her again. It wasn't because I was angry, but I just didn't want to have to deal with her feelings. I resented having to endure such matters, just because she had had a moment's forgetfulness. But I knew that I would see her. I tried to convince myself that here was no malice in her action.

Then there was nobody to talk to sensibly about AIDS. I doubt if a test would have even been recommended if it had happened today. It was a blood blister, not directly inflicted. There was no blood as such, just a nipped bruise under my skin through the sleeve of my denim blouse. Nowadays there are systems set up with experts giving accurate details of the disease and explaining how it is spread. Sane, knowledgeable medical practitioners advise of the risks and prospects. Science has caught up and literature is available, backed by hard facts. In those days there was nothing but hearsay and ignorance. Safety regulations now protect staff, information warns them of the risks, and science keeps a sense of proportion. This applies to everyone at Holloway Prison, whether they have a number or are wearing a staff nametag. Experts are employed to give advice, talks and sound information is readily available. Leaflets are displayed in the prison's reception area and wherever inmates might congregate. Help and advice are everywhere. But Lillian's day someone in the prison even came up to me shaking his head and murmuring, 'Thank God for denim.' What was that supposed to mean, what was I supposed to make of that statement?!

It was Wednesday before I could be prevailed upon to see Lillian. The success of the visit would depend more on what wasn't said, what could be avoided. That I instinctively felt would apply not just to me but to Lillian. The event was the most important; it was a reassurance that there had been nothing actively malevolent, no residue of ill-will, and no real bitterness. Inept phrases best left silent might expose deep anxieties. That was the safest ground to keep within. Lillian was sitting on her bed vacantly looking at nowhere in particular. She offered me a chair and asked how I was. I asked her the same question, but didn't and couldn't elaborate. Then we asked each other again in a different way. That's all really, that was it in amongst a lot of silences. So a kind of peace was made and I left. Good care and love from an attentive, caring partner had prolonged Lillian's life. She'd volunteered to work for an AIDS charity to help other sufferers. Then I had heard nothing more till that morning. Another death to remind me of the rawness of Holloway that had temporarily confined two very different women. That period of remembrance lasted until Madame Apothecary called me over.

'Come look at this, I reckon it's finished now.' A whole hour had passed without Maggie moving from her work. She had changed the painting so much that up to six earlier paintings lay beneath the final composition. Exotic background imagery had been replaced by simple lines and decorative forms that accentuated two figures, an elegant odalisque and her male counterpart in deep purples, emerald greens and silver.

'Got any gold paint Miss?'

'On the desk … That's beautiful Maggie … Let's have a look at what all of you are doing then.'

The teenage group of offenders flopped back on their chairs and looked up at me. The scraping chairs revealed a bit of planet Earth underneath the wooden legs. Truculently they lifted up their behinds while I pushed more paper over the mural to safeguard it against the pummelling chairs. Well there was the heart on a card, that wasn't unusual, nor was that eye full of heavy mascara, dropping a huge tear from its corner. I'd got drawers full of them. And those cuddly puppies, with huge eyes, looking up all helpless. They filled other drawers—whilst I'd seen quite a number of pit bull terriers like the one drawn by the inmate with the spider's-web tattoo covering half her face. Other drawers contained mass-produced sunsets and crude, badly drawn naked women, accompanied by poems intended to seduce a lover, or two.

> Roses are red
> Weed is green
> I love your legs
> And that bit in between.

Bubble writing was always in demand and there it was on every card, with 'Love' spelt 'Luv'. One of that gang was the expert. She attracted admiration from her mates and bubble wrote for the rest of the class. And I could have filled a store cupboard with hands clinging on to bars with sad foreheads and 'Freedom' written somewhere in a speech cloud.

'I couldn't get me 'ead round it today Miss. I can't come this afternoon, I've got to stay on the wing for me methadone script, but if you let me in tomorrow morning I'll really do something'. Three months pregnant and still so thin. Two other young offenders returned after a toilet visit smelling of fresh tobacco. The introduction of a cigarette ban had increased the demand for comfort breaks which now extended into social gatherings along the corridors linking the classrooms. The two young women with their tobacco addiction now fed slid indifferently into their chairs. I went over to them and asked where their work was. With only thirty minutes left, I asked them to get on with something—for the umpteenth time. I wasn't particularly on the ball. I started to nag about the noise, which I hated myself for, because normally I could employ more effective ways to motivate. My voice started to screech and climb up the scale. The young offenders were getting on everyone else's nerves and disrupting the class. Other students, with all their problems, had a right to a peaceful working space away from the hullabaloo of the wings. The quiet ones were being neglected in my efforts to contain those teenagers. And that happened too much in this institution; the gobbiest got all the attention.

I renewed my round of the classroom. Eight new students mingled with a few regulars. That was the daily register, no terms, no holidays, and no new annual starts, just relentless numbers shipped into prison and shipped out of it. The two young offenders still sat with empty paper in front of them. Between the times that I left my desk to view this absence of activity, the two had backed themselves together, leant over and scribbled something for me to see. Leaning back with brazen smugness they presented their achievements with a dramatic gesture of their hands. One of them had drawn a tree, all of two seconds' work. The other had drawn a man, all of half a second's work. 'What do you think of it, Miss?' I looked down at the stick man, formulating a reply befitting my position as artistic critic and creative adviser; someone with technical prowess and an expert in interpersonal relationships. 'That's crap,' I said, allowing my tolerance threshold to show. I threw it into the bin together with my understanding, tact and everything else I had learnt over the years. The other one took her picture of the tree and they sat belligerently shuffling shoulders and downing pencils.

'Tools in are they?' The officer popped her head around the door.

'I went to check the shadowboard and there was a pair of scissors missing. I'll find them, come back in a few minutes, or I'll phone you in the office.'

No scissors, they were nowhere to be seen. I searched the shadowboard and the space around it, checked my desk and recalled which students who had used them. They also searched but came up with nothing. No amount of visualising those scissors disappearing as ashes up a chimney could move me forward to forget this loss. This disappearance was a major security issue, therefore nobody could move anywhere until they were found. Security searches had become a regular occurrence. Even the staff were searched on occasions but when the search was in response to a loss then everything became more purposeful and serious. I gathered up all my wits and ordered class members to pay attention. They moaned and groaned and searched around, looking under papers and in boxes, but nothing was to be found. I rang the officers and gave them the bad news. Other staff having locked up their classrooms came over to help. They joined in, peering under the chaos of paper, poking into vast tubs of powder paint and upturning a black dustbin to inspect its contents.

One student ran out of the room, rushing towards the toilet. She had just started her period and was flooding—she just had to go. More likely that at the imminent possibility of a body search she was going to make sure she'd emptied herself of any illegal substances. No embarrassment, just desperate to avoid discovery. Maggie swaggered out of the room raging about not being in for violence and that she wasn't a nutter either, so there was no point in her hanging around. She hadn't got the scissors, what would she use them for. Her protestations persevered outside and down the corridor. Then both women reappeared together, forced back into the classroom by a search party of prison officers. Personal pronouns and prepositions were the only recognisable examples of the Queen's English amongst the expletives, obscenities, profanities and lesser swear words that burst out of Maggie as she defended her offended ego. The other student reappeared and grumbled on and on about her menstrual cycle and the rights of a woman, her human rights and her bodily needs. Despite all their efforts to avoid the imminent search, they both sat together and waited their turn in full view of the officers.

Doors were all locked, minor chores were placed on hold. The world turned black and white as uniformed officers filled the doorway reminding us all where the real power lay in this institution. I continued to search apologetically. 'Yes,' I had left the room but I'd locked the tool cabinet before I did so, I was sure of that. Harassed staff already stretched thin were stretched thinner. I could hear the complaints.

'I'm bloody starving … I can do without this.' 'For fuck's sake just get on with it and let's get back to the wing'. A women flung her hands up over her head, pushed herself in front of an officer and offered herself up to be searched, or whatever else was on offer. A roll of sticky labels was found inside Maggie's turban. Down her front was a bottle of fluorescent gold paint. Down the back of her tracksuit bottoms was a pack of coloured pencils. Held secure with the elastic bottoms, one trouser leg held a roll of tissue paper and in the other leg there was a stick of glue. In her pocket was a bottle of glitter glue. Maggie's little weakness had tipped over—but still no scissors were to be found. Queues formed, women were taken aside and the search continued as yet more objects were confiscated—but still no scissors. I was frantically rummaging through the chaos that had become characteristic of my room. 'Is it always like this?' An officer with an appalled look at the prospect of trying to find anything amongst the clutter shook his head and began searching through my books. 'Who had the scissors last? Can you remember?' Questions and questions and I answered as best as I could.

The search was nearly at an end and the thought of the inevitable total lock-in appalled us all. I was feeling guilty at the thought of the effect this event would have on all of Holloway, its prisoners and staff. The drama continued and more officers were redeployed to join in the search. They searched the garden space just outside the windows, and my room was ransacked. Every book in my library was flipped open in case the scissors dropped out of one of them. Toilets were unenthusiastically prodded around by staff wearing rubber gloves and with their nostrils squeezed in. Women waited to be searched and surreptitiously dropped more unofficially obtained items onto the floor between their legs, then moved on disowning any knowledge of them. They lifted their arms and made provocative suggestions to male and female staff as a distraction while they were patted up and patted down as part of the search. Dinner was delayed and the scissors stayed lost. Everyone tried to remain patient and sympathised, but I'd caused this havoc. They were my scissors, my responsibility and the guilt lay with me.

'I've found them, I've got them.' The missing scissors were placed on my table by a pair of white plastic gloves. Everybody stopped, and registered their gratitude. Normal routine resumed, lucky inmates slithered passed the officers as searching stopped and everyone left. 'Ethel, that one in the wheel chair, she had them, the bugger. She was sitting on them , cheek of it, sitting on them, I'll have to ban her and put her on report … Well at least they're back, I suppose that's something … thanks.' Everyone suddenly deserted the grounded ship for other problems and other obligations like dinner and cups of tea. The scissors were found, job done, incident over. Not for me though as I had to right the upturned bin, clear up the paints, organize the papers and labour on with suitable contrition. There was still enough time for everyone to have a decent lunch break; it could have been worse. I'd got a half hour before the afternoon session and the kettle had just boiled.

'Someone has put in a formal complaint about your teaching … they have put in a paper criticising your methods.' The Head of the Department called me over. 'You better get down to the wing and sort it out quick' It was getting worse. 'Something about your teaching methods—you've upset some young offender, she's put in a statement against you, and you're wanted on the wing to explain yourself.' Maybe she would actually go through with this complaint and I could get the sack, then sue for unfair dismissal and never have to work at Holloway again. I talked over this possible scenario in my head, then discussed it further with my imaginary inquisitors who apologised before awarding me colossal compensation. I cleaned up and grovelled in the bin for the stick man who was surely involved in this somehow. On the other hand my brain cells could provide an open house for sitting tenants, extremely vocal residents forcing me into medical retirement—that would be another possibility.

I had every intention of making this a quick visit. But it had to be endured, someone had started a procedure and even if I myself had thought it a mere blip, I was being forced to give it my time and attention. This caused irritation and resentment and it all seemed such a waste of energy and I was missing-out on my lunch hour. Fumbling to find my keys I shook them in my annoyance. The chain got tangled up so I had to stand on tip toe to open the door, otherwise I would have hung myself from the waist and dangled, swinging to-and-fro. The trolley route stretched ahead, it seemed miles to the Young Offenders Wing.

A hospital nurse could be seen coming towards me from the far end of that long corridor, like a milkmaid, evenly balancing metal cans to either side of her. Just a black silhouette in the sunlight until she sped closer and became three-dimensional. Her hands yanked the metal cans to behave. They swayed precariously, sploshing the liquid specimens onwards towards the gate in time for the second stage carrier to deliver those bodily secretions to the local hospital for testing. Nobody stood in her way, or expected her to do anything but to get that 'mail' through. I held the door for her, as did others and she headed past, just a tight mouth compelling her to the exit. All part of Holloway's routine punctuating the daily calendar of events—the medical department's specimen collection.

Quite a formal group made up the awaiting tribunal, standing together in the office on the Young Offenders Wing. The official complaint was on the table. The inmate was called and then there was me. The first officer spoke.

'Apparently you called this young woman's work "crap" this morning and threw it in the bin … is that right?'

'Is that what this is about then, that's the reason I'm here?'

Staring insolently from behind the officer, the student folded her arms firmly establishing which side she was on.

'There's been a complaint so we have to take it seriously.' With righteous insincerity the student nodded in agreement. 'What's this?' I held up the stick man drawing and pleaded guilty, having been told that witnesses could be called. It was for the tribunal to reach a fair and unbiased verdict. The evidence in the form of the stick man was peered at and passed around, avoiding the prosecutor.

'It's crap.' Said the first member to see it.

'Yes, that's definitely crap,' the second agreed.

'It really is crap,' said the third. A unanimous decision acquitted me. The prosecutor was asked for her opinion. She sniggered and not wanting to back a lost cause admitted that it was crap and withdrew the charge. I retold the whole story to my judges and waited with as much patience as a complete waste of time could muster. 'Well, my friend said you called her tree—shit.' The young offender decided to play the institution further and manipulate procedures established to benefit those without a voice. She wanted to amuse herself a bit more and get something out of all the fuss she had instigated and stick up for her rights. She was enjoying the attention. Her sidekick appeared in the doorway and tried to look offended and hurt until she caught her friend's giggles. Turning to the officers I told them that I had not called her tree 'shit'—of that charge I was completely innocent, witnesses could be called if required.

'Okay, okay, you didn't … You didn't call my tree "shit"'. We all looked up to the ceiling as if that would rescue us whilst the two women ran away arm-in-arm, relieved of pursuing their grievance. They laughed out loud unashamedly all along the corridor and into the dining room. Gone with them were my dreams of an escape plan to get me out of Holloway. The complaint was demolished and dropped in the bin, chased by the stick man down amongst the rest of the garbage.

Maybe a new day would mean a new beginning of good results and a professional feeling of wellbeing at the end of the day; until that is, I saw evidence of the cleaner mopping the floor and a man-type person sitting in the classroom reading a magazine. The figure had wide shoulders and a male physique. I rounded the corner of his body and smiled at the beard and Adams apple pushing out from underneath it. He must have been at the end of his treatment, but he would cause extra problems for me if he attended my class. He must have just come up from the Hospital Wing. This must be the completed product, his jumper was flat, and he had no breasts. He certainly had the muscle tone of a man rather than a woman. 'What's your name please?' I glanced at my register and waited. He was obviously new, and keen, the first in and already sitting down. I was eager to give him work to do to settle him in.

'My name is Greg Walker, I'm the psychologist, and I've come for your cleaner, Liz.' There was that deep voice. It was at that point I could have gone over the edge of institutionalisation into a different dimension, never to return. Maybe I already had with my first impressions, so I had to re-examine the person in front of me. It was not a woman in transition to a man, here was a real live male person. I had to sort him out all over again in my thoughts, in my head and before my eyes. So I looked again as he stood up and offered me his hand. On reflection, maybe my initial reaction was a good sign. I had been troubled by such things before. Charlie came into prison hardly having the confidence to speak, nor the confidence to look at me. Forever turning away and seeming to give her answers to the wall, she came into the class only intermittently. How was I to know about here treatment?

I'd talk about her work and for some reason she'd never return for weeks until she needed something or another member of her supervisory group wanted information. So we didn't have much rapport. If she could have attended my class but remained invisible, I think that would have been perfect. She tried to hide herself against walls and arrange her space in the darkest corner. Even her voice hid from me as she spoke. I had to listen hard for those weak sounds as they were sent in directions other than towards me and her eyes cowered. Trousers, tops and jackets hung off her and were always too big and too long. Hats were worn low down, hiding as much skin as was possible whatever the weather, hot or cold. Her hands popped out from too long cuffs, that's all I saw, apart from her fingers which hung down aimlessly. Then she started the treatment and it all changed.

So my mind was still very much open to the unexpected, but my response to Greg Walker had nevertheless been positive, supportive and I had taken him in my stride. But I had seen him as if he had been constructed medically and that worried me. Thank goodness I wasn't on his case file to be assessed in preparation for *my* trial. I did my best to extricate myself from the embarrassment with enough apologies to make him smile. It was a weak smile though. I think I had offended his masculinity to an irretrievable extent.

As Charlie's treatment progressed her face began to smile occasionally, and her voice spoke to me in strong sounds and we started to have conversations and jokes. Her work improved because she started to understand the criticism and work on assignments. As the treatment continued, so confidence developed and stronger work of greater intensity was possible. Then Charlie the man emerged and that's how it was to be from then on. It was 'his' confidence that impressed me, and it had seemed so simple to acquire it, just a few male hormones, that's all that made up the difference. 'There's no moon, did you know that, you forgot the moon. That picture on the ceiling, at the dentists, you know Miss, that new one, me mate painted Jupiter and some stars. That picture that was being done in the Art Room on the floor … just put up in the dentist's surgery, there's no moon in it … I looked and looked, it's just not there, don't misunderstand me Miss, it's fantastic it really is pucker, but there's no moon.'

Well how Charlie must have searched around the universe, the stars, the planets studying the mural and finding that omission. The absence of the moon was a complete surprise to me, but well spotted by that particular student—good for him. He'd obviously searched, knew about its presence in relation to our planet and couldn't find it. Like the change of gender it rankled a bit, why hadn't I noticed?

'You know why there's no moon?' I said. 'There's no moon because there was a total eclipse, and I think that must be the explanation. That's why there's no moon.' 'Touchy Miss … who's being touchy then.'

I had promised to see Janet before she was shipped out to another institution. Such wing visits had become rarer because outreach workers were now employed to deal with prisoners who were confined to their rooms. I glanced into her hatch window in case she was asleep or busy with something. Black plastic bags lay ready for packing but Janet had decided to delay that chore, take a break and start a game. A solitary chair had been turned upside down so that the legs were facing upwards. On a table were hollow slices of bread with just the crusts left, in a square shape. Tight in the far corner Janet aimed the 'bread hoops' and tried to get them over the legs of the chair. A few rounds of bread had already landed successfully but she continued to play and to try and improve her accuracy.

'Just thought I'd pop in before you leave … anything you need?'

'Come on in and have a game … and don't forget to leave me something to do. I'm bored out of my brain at night. Make sure I can take it with me … You never know what other places allow.' A round of bread hit the door and broke into crumbs. 'Bugger it.' Janet wasn't allowed out but I was given permission to visit. She was another peripatetic prisoner who would soon be admitted to a special hospital and possibly spend the rest of her life hibernating permanently, away from society.

The sound of banging and shouting next door provoked a threat. 'If she doesn't shut the fuck up, I'll shut her up. She chucked her piss pot over the officer this morning, straight through the hatch. Must have been waiting for her.' Ferociously loyal to the staff, it was the other inmates that provoked Janet's temper. She looked like she'd spent her whole life away from all direct sunlight deep down below the ground. She was pale with brown pigmentation around her eyes, and her skin was dull and white. We talked about football for a while then she decided to show me her paintings before they were packed up for transit. One self-portrait, a drawing on white paper documented her self-harm lacerations; her scars and what she had pushed into her body or swallowed. She had pinioned herself onto that piece of cartridge like a creature ready for dissection. The drawing was built up of absolutely straight and strong lines showing passageways. They toured her body along her arms, down her chest into her stomach. Other tunnelled veins crossed over into her hands and ran across her fingers. They bulged with needles, drawing pins, pieces of glass, nails and arrows, like a scientific diagram which explained points of entry and exit. Now and again scribbles of red paint broke their journey and stitches roughly re-attached them. Holding up the drawing, Janet pushed her finger along the contours, verbally detailing her damaged body to make sure I understood, like a teacher preparing me for an anatomy exam. I felt no threat as she talked about them, nor did she demonstrate any emotion.

That over, she showed me some landscapes of stark buildings against a sunset. These she liked because they were a lucrative source of income and she replicated them relentlessly to meet the demands of staff and inmates who commissioned her more and more. She even made some into cards and had gone into mass production. I liked the paintings which she would keep for herself, abstract colours of minimal definition, with gloomy, dark areas worked in chalk like thick textured carpets—a bit like Mark Rothko but without the scale. Intermingled throughout our conversation, this attentive hostess in her London apartment would offer delicacies to all her guests. A choice of fizzy beverages and snacks would appear as well as biscuits and sweets. For the most prestigious visitors she would produce the à la carte menu of posh coffee, cigarettes (not roll-ups) After Eight mints and chocolate éclairs. I wasn't in that bracket. For me she offered the in-house nibbles bought in the Holloway canteen. I was given the penny chews that broke your teeth and the pear drops and boiled sweets that took the skin off the roof of your mouth better that any industrial sander. But when you were on the road, trekking from wing to wing then that quick rush of sugar made sure you'd arrive. She hated the woman who had thrown pee. No staff had anything to fear from Janet. It was the other women that made Janet's blood curdle and that's why she was isolated from other inmates. Janet liked that poor member of staff and at night time she shouted threats to the pee-pusher just to warn her to keep out of her way.

Institutional life suited Janet and she had adapted to her incarceration and its constraints. And she was now finally being allocated to a secure unit in a hospital, where she would spend the rest of her life. I liked her, it was nice to visit and see how she had organized her life and her activities. She knew she would never be released—it was a wise decision she thought.

CHAPTER EIGHT

Violence

Each new student was asked to produce two drawings on a coloured paper of their own choice. On one paper they were asked to draw a woman, on the other a man, both full figure representations. Together, on the same pages, they were asked to draw two objects which they felt related favourably or adversely to each figure. I imagined that the two pictures together with the objects would personalise the nature of gender in a way that a solitary figure would not. The women might have chosen to draw any symbol, any popular icon without much thought, but including the objects meant bringing the images closer to their experience—that was the idea behind this. Imaginative drawings were a difficult proposition for an inexperienced student. To reduce their fears, each finished painting was displayed on a washing line using pegs, right in the middle of the room. The drawings thus became as ordinary as their name or number. Nobody's efforts were of greater value than those of any other student—preciousness was taken away along with the anxiety. Spontaneous comments provoked a casual discourse amongst those contemplating this haphazard rogues' gallery.

Some women produced self-portraits, consciously or unconsciously, and the added images became a kind of guessing game for the audience which stimulated further interest. People of different nationalities produced their own styles provoking more discussion. This was no deep sociological survey, just a bit of visual fun to encourage spontaneity and thought. Such projects also provided a common bond which united the class. Resistance weakened when the students realised that everyone was taking part. The use of coloured paper wasn't just for decoration, it was intended to complicate the task. Mixing colour on coloured paper is a very different thing from mixing colour on pure white paper; more difficult for a start. Curiously, most students instinctively refused the coloured paper, which normally attracted them, as they thought that there might be a catch, or that a coloured base would cause problems, so they chose the pure white cartridge—they didn't fall for my ploy.

My sales pitch emphasised choice of media, style, interpretation and the time that should be spent on realisation of the pictures. Choice within the prison context always grabbed attention. Instructions were almost carelessly to promote the exercise, there was no pressure. This seemingly casual approach defrosted newcomers who were often more terrified of an empty piece of paper than their committal to Holloway Prison. Formalised lesson plans as practised in mainstream education often made little sense in the prison environment and replicating any mainstream-type curriculum was impossible. There were also too many invasive commitments which took priority in the prison system, making regular attendance at classes impossible. The primary function of the prison system is to fulfil the needs of the courts and education is only one part of this aim. Medical visits, legal visits, family visits—these all took precedence. The quick turnover of students was in some ways a blessing because we were forced to invent our own work plan. It had to be flexible enough for such a complex regime. The needs of the institution had to come first so that individual and flexible teaching plans worked, whereas rigid, long-term formulae didn't.

Many artists have been influenced by studying other painters, and other works of art. For that reason my library of books was an important resource. For those with language difficulties, pictures and illustrations are particularly useful introductions to art, and a quick way to motivate beginners. But this very resource was often used as an easy option. I recognised that danger and veered clear of the rut as soon as I saw it ahead. In a way it was kneejerk teaching in an unpredictable institution whose priority was not educational. It also involved teaching students for indeterminate lengths of time and some whose attendance was unreliable, often adults with little school experience. Always there were conflicting expectations. No wonder the Art Room looked like it was on the move. It had caught that same sense of impermanence, or was it my inability to organize for so many eventualities?

Finally and perhaps of most consequence was 'attitude'. Students in prison are reluctant participants—they all want to be somewhere else. Nobody really wants to be in prison or in a prison classroom. The result is often uncommitted art students, anxious not to expose their fragilities in a tough environment. Most of them challenge any prescribed project on whatever grounds they can muster. The nature of Holloway's inmate population, now standing at around five hundred, includes all racial mixes and ethnic groups with consequent language difficulties. And many of these women return to Holloway when least expected.

It helped in this unstoppable rotation to invent a focus that would create its own beginning and end. This suited the character of Holloway's population, over which we had absolutely no control. The gender project was just one small example of our artistic promotions. Those organized events, planned and produced within the Education Department, were proofs of success which perked everyone up. Energy consumed in positive and creative activities drained away criticisms, which were an unwelcome interference and wore everyone down. Most important was the fact that such projects were related specifically to the prison experience and not imposed by outside or mainstream criteria, and they were liberated from irrelevant targets that would have made cynics out of us all.

Students were encouraged to work towards competitions. They painted murals and regular exhibitions were organized as a means of publicising their achievements. Exhibitions raised awareness of the positive side to the prison, outside audiences opened up the institution and demystified it, enlightening and informing a general public that might have preconceived ideas about the prison community. The whole institution gradually became involved as staff put in requests for murals to brighten up dull rooms and bare walls. We had become an integrated department called upon to adorn places of visual poverty.

So that's why we devised a new project, 'Perceptions of Gender'. This took a light-hearted look at the students' ideas of womanhood and manhood. An hour or longer could be spent on the task, depending on personal interpretation and the extent to which the inmate concerned wanted to get involved. Holloway's multi-cultural population, its age range and the mixed status of the prisoners added diversity to this enterprise.

The last public exhibition of works from Holloway took place almost a decade ago. We were in the first stages of planning another and looking for a suitable theme to unite all the disciplines we hoped to represent. The subject would need to be good enough, wide enough, and flexible enough to adapt to each department and every creative skill, or so I thought. It would 'test the waters' and tease out what the response would be. A group project representing many women which could be installed as one unit was ideal.

It was a generally accepted fact that many students chose to attend art classes because they thought it was a soft option. Art was easy, not too demanding. That's if they traced, copied or stuck things on paper. The soft option came with ready-made images or drawing kits which the women imagined that I would provide. I did give out tracing paper but only on request, for in-cell activities. In the Art Room more demanding exercises had to be accomplished in situ. Whereas other students accepted that they could learn about computers, maths, or most other subjects, they believed that creative activity could *not* be taught. You either had it or you didn't. 'I can't draw,' so often those were the first words uttered by new students, as if it was a universal truth that talent in art was acquired only at birth. I was so fed up with this response that I had borrowed words from Dr. Betty Edwards and wrote them on the wall: 'Drawing is a learnable teachable skill'. And that's how I replied to questions. I just pointed, at the notice, read it out and got on with the class. Virtually without exception those students professing no artistic ability realised that Betty Edwards was right. I'm not saying that everyone undergoing art training could come out the other end an accomplished artist, obviously it was more complicated than that, and talent gave anyone possessing it a head start. But to a certain standard, art could be taught. Why was I employed to teach it? Nobody could ever answer that one.

Slowly arising from the prison torpor and with a lot of encouragement, the exercise caught the imagination of the students. They completed their project pictures with varying degrees of skill. Some spent days on their women, others rushed to complete them. Few rejected the subject until the empty paper was put in front of them and a representation of a man was required. This second stage met with a less cooperative response. Two women out of one class of eight looked at the paper and waited. One picked up her pencil then let it fall and dropped out of that part of the project saying that she didn't want to do it, and couldn't do it. Then she swore about some man who had come into her mind. She apologised but asked, 'Can I do it later?'

Another student suffered more openly. 'No way Miss ... you know Miss, I can't do it and I don't want to, maybe another time, not now,' then a few hardly coherent memories mixed her forehead up into various frowns about fights, hate and betrayal. She shook her head from side-to-side as if amazed that she had lived through such painful misery, never mind survived it. She chose the long empty view over the gardens to settle her eyes on and to help her regain her composure. She then asked if she could do something else. The project was still in the early stages and such an intense, troubled reaction was unexpected. But if they didn't want to complete the exercise that was okay. That was a good enough reason I thought.

Those women who did take part, painted their men in business suits and tracksuits, with water bottles, iPods, briefcases, computers, mobile phones and other electronic toys. One man had been separated from his manhood and stared impassively at its limp ineffectuality inside a dustbin. The first draft of that picture showed the man fully equipped—large as life. Then the woman asked for the scissors, castrated him and bashed the offending appendage down inside the bin with a dollop of PVA glue. 'He's a bastard Miss, but he always waits for me on the out. I love him, I really do and he always visits me ... but he's a bastard.' Their perception of women? Nearly all carried handbags, whilst some drew children, pets, money, gold, vodka and flowers—but mostly handbags.

A small corridor led from the trolley route to the kitchen. It was an empty space, somewhere of no interest that was a lodging place for bins and an odd assortment of radiators and notices that nobody ever read. It was valueless as a space, a kind of in-between area that nobody owned up to. Just the kind of visual emptiness that brought the Art Room expertise to mind. I measured the walls between the institutional plumbing, waste bins, air vents and Home Office warning notices and took on the new commission from the governor who was responsible for the Catering Department. This was another outlet for the creative energies of the students; another possibility for women to work together in a joint venture. It was a compliment to be asked to decorate that part of the establishment, a real privilege, so our response was immediate and research was soon underway. Such ambitious enterprises could only be completed in one way, certainly not by a defined group that would start the mural and finish it within a given space of time. On the spot analysis of a student's abilities on their debut lesson would give me a clue, then a barrage of questions wheedled out more information. Their consent usually finalised the contract and an eight foot by four foot piece of blockboard would be theirs. That was how two giant crustaceans came into existence. How the woman in question coped, did credit to her fortitude. She rose to the occasion without one objection and a small but solid bit of painting was produced in the first half hour of her induction lesson. She thought she'd be in prison for about three weeks and wanted to stay in the lesson. Her daughter was attending Art College and she agreed to the commission. All criteria adhered to, the information about her daughter clinched it, and it transpired she must have inherited the talent from her mother.

A collection of mushrooms and a huge red pepper were completed by an extraordinarily self-sufficient young woman. Our initial rapport was slightly abrasive because she so resented her new home that at first her work was carried out reluctantly. She was obviously a bright button because of the way she related to the other prisoners. There was strength of character and a strong survival instinct, so nobody took advantage of her, but there was also attitude, lots of it. Something changed as encouragement convinced her to continue with her studies. My tentative invitation to contribute to the mural confirmed for her a confidence that she had maybe never before found. What she produced staggered us all. Her paintings were expertly crafted and if her stay had been longer she would have completed the lot, I'm sure. She achieved highly in other subjects as well. Everybody wanted to teach her because she was so good. She even made her grey prison issue tracksuit look stylish. Without exception each day she would appear immaculately dressed with not a mark or a crease in sight. At the end of her painting session she would present herself in perfect order. Not obsessively though, she always reached for an apron and tied it ever so neatly behind her back. Her white trainers always looked new although they were worn daily, brilliant white with not a scuff or stain—and in the Art Room too. Somehow, she customised her off-the-peg tracksuit until it looked like designer gear. She'd roll up the legs, wear them inside out, and interchange her tops, transforming her clothing yet again. And she'd alter her hair to match. Everything was coordinated. At the end of her stay she had passed all her exams at quite an advanced level, and completed three massive paintings. She had made phenomenal progress. 'I don't know what I'll do now my sentence is over, maybe I'll start something else, do something new, there's not much future in pole-dancing.' I wished her well. Another young woman left a beautiful pineapple behind as evidence of her presence in the Art Room. She smiled all the time and never complained. I think she'd served some apprenticeship prior to her imprisonment that had guaranteed her a job after her brief stay inside. In a way, I wish she could have extended her lessons, but after completing the pineapple she moved on.

I only pressed the emergency bell once; or rather I got someone else to press it for me because I was too far away from it. So I only felt threatened enough once to seek help. The panic button had been installed at the furthest corner of my room, well away from my desk and the store cupboard. Its position was badly thought out, access was difficult and it was hard to see. It was in the dimmest, darkest corner which late-comers were forced to occupy or which subversive students opted for. Most students preferred to be near the windows or the paints, or around my desk where they felt safe. I'd thought about pressing the button a few times, but a prompt phone call from the extension in my store cupboard alerted the officers and this was usually sufficient to douse any impending catastrophe. Always reliable if they weren't patrolling the rest of Education Department, the officers would immediately respond and provide whatever support was needed.

Tango's name reappeared on my register. A regular prisoner she was overdue her visit and there was her name once more—she having chosen art against all the other options. She must have been over forty by this time and it was two decades since her first stay at Holloway. 'You don't want to go in there, Miss.' That was the first thing she ever said to me.

'I am just trying to find a student, I think she's in this dormitory.'

'You don't want to go in there Miss … you really don't.' Tango looked more intensely at me, protecting the doorway, keeping vigil in case of unwelcome visitors. She spread out her arms and straightened her legs to brace herself in case I was a do-gooding busy-body. An officer in uniform would have seen a different attitude, but this eager beaver, just a teacher and just the art teacher at that, easy-peasy! You could take liberties with her! 'But I think that's the dorm I want; her name says she's in here … look.' I pointed to the name on the card outside the door, right next to Tango's ear.

'No! Now listen, listen very carefully … you don't want to go in there, I'm telling you Miss you don't want to go in there … You really don't want to go in there.' I couldn't have been in the job for very long, too short a time to imagine such a confrontation. All I was doing was finding a student who had shown a lot of talent that same morning. Such skill should be nurtured and encouraged, that's all I was doing, encouraging and nurturing—doing my job.

'What's that you've got there? Is that for her?'

'Yes, I want to issue them to her.'

'Give'em to me I'll make sure she gets them.' And with that the items were gone out of my hands, straight into hers.

'But the say I should only give them to her, nobody else.'

'Really Miss? Well bugger the rules and now you bugger off.'

That was my first experience of Tango. Unprepared for this encounter and not knowing how to respond, I lurched erratically onwards in my efforts to cope. The rest of the small team of teachers were in the same boat. We felt ourselves to be pioneers and our wisdom grew painfully. Only our support for each other and a strong belief in what we were doing determined our optimistic commitment as educators. At the beginning we fumbled and sometimes fell in our attempts to make sense of things, function appropriately and exercise proper judgement. I found the constraints of prison life particularly difficult to adapt to.

Only another smoker could ignore the prim smugness of the nicotine-free to donate life-saving strands of tobacco to those similarly addicted. I smoked ten a day, which increased to over twenty in times of stress. Even now I lie and underestimate the true extent of my dependency. Twitching with despair over an empty packet of cigarettes or a surfeit of lonely Rizla papers, it was the duty of those similarly afflicted to give generously. Nothing could revitalise smoke deprived organs more than a blast of nicotine. Surreptitiously, I placed a dollop of tobacco on the lap of a student too poor to buy any more that week. Two chairs in front of her, I plopped another handful of Golden Virginia under the drawing paper of her mate who was similarly poverty stricken. The class of ten temporarily housed in the dining-room suddenly painted away with great enthusiasm. This was in the old prison, when education classes were just beginning. Making my rounds, advising and offering advice to each student, it became apparent that nearly the whole class somehow had 'loss of spends'. Naturally, it affected their performance. I understood that, life was hard.

The following week the class increased to fifteen hard working prisoners who aided by more tobacco inducements and with yet greater affability re-engaged their creative skills and produced paintings. My reputation for success was slowly spreading along the wing, so much so a line of twenty inmates waited impatiently outside the dining-room door the following week for their share of art tuition. Again I secretly distributed to each student some tobacco to inspire their creations. Then the next week even more students queued up, over thirty had applied for my class; nearly the whole wing. With my arms laden with art materials and my pockets bulging with tobacco, I was beginning to doubt the wisdom of my incentive scheme. It was getting too public, maybe someone had been indiscreet and informed on me.

'You've been supplying your class with tobacco haven't you?' The wing governor sitting across the desk from the education officer waited for my reply, with a pen and paper containing a statement in front of her. 'Yes, how did you find out?'

'Thirty students waiting for your class … Come on, something was going on, everyone knew it. I'm going to view this lightly, because you've only been here for such a short length of time. It's not allowed you know, that kind of thing is absolutely forbidden … can't do that sort of thing, people were bound to find out … too good a thing to keep secret, and couldn't you see it was getting out of hand. How long were you going to keep it up?'

'I just don't know. I was getting myself into a real mess. The women were so nice and they honestly hadn't any tobacco, but you know if it had carried on I would have been working for a loss, I suppose. I would probably have had to resign by then, I just couldn't have afforded to come to work.'

'Well I'm going to put a statement in about it. You mustn't do it again, you really mustn't, but that's all I'm going to do … just don't do it again.'

Thank goodness it had all stopped. I had started to dread the classes, dreaded seeing those long queues of prisoners. What had started as misguided kindness had become a complete drain on my resources. Thank goodness it was now all over because future classes in the dining room would have been even harder. One inmate had intimated that she wasn't being fed enough and asked 'Can you bring in some chicken and chips please?'

Between the decades, Tango's presence had always made me apprehensive because of her reputation as a bully. Stories abounded about her influence on the less strong and more vulnerable prisoners. Her criminal activity revolved around drugs—whatever offences had caused her incarceration drugs always featured somewhere along the line. Because of her recidivism this lady wasn't about to change her ways either. Even inside prison she continued dabbling in something subversive. It was the way she conducted her social life, her contacts, and the how and why of the women she related to. The signs were that whatever she wheeled and dealt on the outside she wheeled and dealt just the same on the inside.

I'd seen her temper on a couple of occasions, at a safe distance. She could rip out a toilet from its plumbing, throw beds, tables and go several rounds with the strongest male officer. Her time was mostly spent down in the Segregation Block, but even that wasn't safe from her rages. She could rip the radiator off the wall, flood cells, drag sinks away from their plumbing and smash them to bits. Being in the wrong place at the wrong time, I witnessed her at the height of one of her storms. Water was flooding from underneath her cell down into the block, and there were enormous breaking noises and loud thuds which indicated more destruction from inside her home. It was chaos and officers could only wait and watch and soak up as much water as they could from outside her cell. As I passed quickly through the wing, her face suddenly pushed itself against her plastic hatch and she stared right at me, froth bubbling out of her mouth. That was a long time ago but I saw that image every time she reappeared in my class. Most of the inmates not involved with her conspiracies and not wanting to join her gang would keep their eyes down and walk past her quickly. She was a powerful woman and any form of interaction with her needed to be purposeful, deliberate, not casual, throwaway or in jest.

Amongst the rickety women sitting in the rickety chairs deep inside the Occupational Therapy Unit of the old prison, Tango sat rigidly painting. Her friends offered cigarettes and praised her skill—trying to please her. The officers monitored her closely and Tango knew she was getting all the attention that day, from everyone. She smiled around a lot affecting a happy, couldn't care less indifference, which her fans reinforced and her gaolers noticed, but pretended not to see. No one would ever find out where that extra medication had come from. Too bad it had been found on her though, but usually the officers could watch all they liked, and her friends, well they could flatter her all they liked, but they wouldn't find out anything either. Further close supervision was needed thought the officers—a spell in the block might rock her complacency and it might even loosen her tongue. A surprise was planned to catch her and her personal minders off guard when being escorted down the block. It would happen any minute now. I was on edge as I gave Tango equipment to draw with, always animals, cuddly koalas, pandas eating bamboo, elephants, she just loved animals, especially cuddly ones—the kind you see on sugary birthday cards and popular calenders. This anti-Establishment woman, leading the most chaotic of lives shocking the natural order with her lifestyle of breaking rules sought as subject matter the most comfortable of images, all gentle and sweet. Whereas outside the walls budding artists rising up the prescribed ladders of success in art colleges produce work that attempted to destabilise, cause offence and destroy convention, Tango was more conventional.

She was unaware of the official conspiracy concerning her impending relocation, unaware that she was about to be moved downstairs. Making out that nothing was amiss, all staff carried on regardless, but all the time keeping one eye on the door and the other on Tango. It wouldn't be just one officer that would be called to carry out her removal. No, with Tango it would be a full 'guard of dishonour'. We all carried on working, though in the superficial way that folk do when more momentous events are looming. I performed as best I could, but I was nervous and hoped that it wasn't apparent. I knew Miss Lanzarote was on duty that day. I'd met her coming into the prison with her brand new tan and healthy appearance. She was feeling refreshed thank you, had just flown back yesterday, had a great time. The metallic grating of a key turning in the lock was followed by the door being opened to reveal five officers. Heading the group was Miss Lanzarote herself, newly invigorated by her time in the sun. She led the group towards Tango as her colleagues, overdue for their own holiday breaks, advanced with a weaker spirit and less conviction. The path was clear for their progress towards Tango. Staff already present in the room stopped working and prepared themselves to help out if necessary. I walked towards the art cupboard and locked the door on all movables. Tango had seen them coming before their keys even hit the door and her eyes fixed on them as they walked towards her. She stopped work and stood up behind her chair.

'Tango, we've come to take you down the block for adjudication.' 'I'm not bloody coming down that hole, you'll have to take me,' she bellowed, her reply making us all flinch as she braced herself against the nearest wall and waited. One leg she secured behind a radiator, then she grabbed her chair to use as a shield. Backed against the wall and wedged in by the radiator she stiffened into pure muscle. The officers came closer and the radio was turned off. Some of the inmates who were sewing or knitting just carried on, others stopped and watched nonchalantly at an event regularly observed in prison. That response surprised me at the time but as such procedures became more routine, I too became just as acclimatised. Those fans sitting at Tango's table shuffled uncomfortably but continued with whatever they were doing, though sniggering in a way that they hoped Tango would inter-pret as support. Other more fragile souls shuffled their chairs away or moved towards the front in the shadow of protective staff. 'Tango, you know you'll have to come with us, one way or the other.'

Nothing happened, nobody moved. Tango installed herself closer to the wall and wedged herself securely up against the radiator. Miss Lanzarote broke ranks, patted a stray curl back into place behind her ear and chewed carelessly. She seemed so laid back after her holiday that she could still have been on that white beach under the palm trees looking up at the sun. 'What's that you've got in your mouth?' Tango bellowed forth her demand, throwing up a chin towards that tanned brunette and managing to look contemptuously across at the officer. That was new, that kind of thing didn't usually happen, it wasn't her place to question.

'It's a bonbon,' Miss Lanzarote chewed on with the insolence of one still on a package tour. Nobody quite knew how to react to this conversation, it was best to just stay put and not stare too much. 'A what!' Further bellow-ing and the tension caused a few folk to move away in a huddle towards the blue uniforms now in the office.

'A bonbon' Miss Lanzarote squeezed out her response from a mouth that refused to stop chewing or savouring the sweet juices. 'Give us a bonbon then.' Gruffly, Tango chanced her arm and held out her hand. Miss Lanzarote didn't react for what seemed like an age, the sweet just kept on revolving round in her mouth accompanied by satisfying sucking noises. She didn't move her head away from Tango nor her eyes away from Tango's stare. Then with absolutely no change of expression she opened her mouth, rested the remnants of bonbon somewhere inside her cheek and gave Tango what she wanted—in musical terms!

'Bonbon de bonbon,' she started off her song, 'Bonbon di bon, bon, bon.' Upping the beat she got right into the rhythm, 'Bonbon de bon, bon, ohhh-hhh! Bon, bon, bon—Ohhhh! Bonbon di di di di bon.' Her arms joined in, she clicked her fingers and swayed her hips. She bon-bonned on until completely carried away with her aria, comprising a classical-cum-jazz melange. A paint brush microphone joined in the second verse, with much the same lyrics—just more exhibitionism and more wailing bon-bons from the sun kissed prima donna. Tango listened to the singing with her head on one side, though with a look of not quite hearing it properly until a break in the singing for breath triggered off a huge roar. As the wailing bon-bon rose higher so Tango's response, intensified into a warlike wail that erupted from her lungs, like some precursor to a martial arts move—a deep baritone wail as of someone psyching themselves up for a fight to the death. For a minute I thought the solo performance would develop into a duet, that some common language might be discovered that would unfold Tango's arms, letting the chair drop, disentangling her legs from behind the radiator and causing her to lean against the wall laughing hysterically.

The officers behind Miss Lanzarote were not quite prepared for a change of tension, so they hung on to their watchfulness, taking nothing for granted. Anyway it didn't seem befitting to lunge forward while their prey was in the middle of such hilarity, so they stayed alert and held their fire. Miss Lanzarote came to the end of her song with a finale so loud and off key, and with hands so high up in the air and a smile so ready to receive any applause that it was clear the performance was at an end. Tango clapped like thunder, immense gestures from outstretched hands that thumped together. She stood away from the wall and walked right through the gang of five without any more inducement, applauding all the way to the exit. Making a ninety degree turn all the officers, not quite believing the ease of their task, scurried after Tango who led the parade straight down to the block.

Nothing seemed to change Tango's bullying or her criminal predilections. She was a worry when she was being nice but was also a worry when she was being fierce. Our familiarity hadn't brought me any favours, maybe on a superficial level, but that was all. She'd introduced me once to another inmate as 'Hilary's the art teacher. She's sound, we go back a long way.' What did that mean I thought I nervously. Now, there she was again in front of me again greeting me like she'd never been away. Why she came to art I will never know and I wished so many times that she would find another interest. She sought out the same creatures that she'd painted hundreds of times before, wasn't receptive to new ideas and was disinclined to experiment. With a lot of help she could make an attempt to put the animals into a background as long as she could still receive her visitors from other classes, as long as they could still whisper together secretly plotting some deal. She'd keep an eye on the door as she worked, then suddenly she'd vacate the class as a head appeared and a finger beckoned over to her from my doorway. She just did enough, no more—just what was required to sustain her social life, her business transactions and retain her place in the art class.

'Hi Miss, have you got that picture I did last time? You remember I got shipped out before I could finish it?' 'Tango! ... No, it's been ages, I just don't store paintings for that long.' 'Ah well I've still got the one I did before, them elephants, got it framed on my wall at home—it's wicked, and the koala bears, the pandas, all framed, the lions are the best, everyone thinks they're great especially 'cos I got them all framed ... any pictures I can look at?'

This time there did seem to be a difference. She walked less stridently, nobody popped in to see her. She was cooperative, concentrated for the whole lesson, demanded less. She even cleaned up. Other younger prisoners appeared more prominent now, she seemed diminished somehow. Maybe it was something to do with age, but she was less confident, less pushy, quieter and not so much involved with the prison culture. Other prisoners didn't seek her out; she seemed more isolated and more self-contained. During that afternoon session she was already half way through a picture of some polar bears and was quietly working. The rest of the class, a real mixture of new and old faces took their places and work was distributed. Some started on the new project; others sought out images and practised drawing from a prearranged model of still life.

A trio of Chinese prisoners were held on the remand wing: painting and drawing seemed to be an unknown activity for them and they squirmed as if in pain when I showed them paint and other materials. Instead they folded paper into exquisite objects, based on one basic form which was replicated by one student who then passed it to her co-defendant who slotted all these forms together to make a flower, a swan, a bowl, or a vase. The final worker at the end of the line stuck all the pieces together. I supplied the paper, which they had chosen jointly on their first visit to my classroom. Inside the store cupboard they clustered together smoothing over cartridge paper then testing the thickness of other samples. Chattering together in Chinese in a tight, earnest way they caressed, stroked, frowned, rejected and then agreed on the right kind of paper. All of this was carried out incomprehensibly while I showed, unwrapped and rewrapped every kind of paper that was available. They needed a special thickness, specific colours and I waited like a shop assistant for their decision, not knowing quite why they were so picky. These origami objects became their currency because so many other inmates coveted them. They developed their own enterprising business, of which I purposely made myself ignorant. Each lesson they became an origami conveyor belt, cutting, folding, sticking and completing the most beautifully artistic objects. At the end of each lesson they packed up their finished merchandise ready for distribution. Not much progress was made with the English language though, despite the valiant efforts of the English for foreigners teacher trying to extricate them from the art class. On their departure, which was due either to deportation or reallocation, I remember two thank you gifts which they left for me—a beautiful bunch of delicate origami flowers and a tube of fungicidal cream wrapped up in my finest tissue paper.

Reeta was always the last to take her place, her predictable place, with her back to us all and her face to the wall, near the window. Her paintings varied in quality. At their best they were wonderful figurative compositions of families or friends, folk holidaying or people sitting in idyllic landscapes; all with a background of somewhere hot. The black figures were decorated in exotic clothes with beaded hairstyles, huddled together in primitive friendliness. She would often decorate her own hair and plait it, or adorn it with scarves in the same style as her paper heroines. Her calmness concentrated her efforts enough to produce work of a high standard and all in that naïve style. On other days her unkempt appearance signalled a different kind of working day. The way she dressed dictated her mood and I learnt to read her before we'd spoken. Most times she didn't need conversations with other people, she'd reply to her own questions, her own thoughts and memories—and she'd plan her next argument with herself and plot her next quarrel. Little bursts of half words burst out along with sighs and a nod of the head. Then there would be a question and a reply in the same spurt of sound. She'd shut up for while but start up again with further chit chat. Paint would pile up on her desk in vast quantities of cakes and puddings, which she would reject as being the wrong colour. 'Not exactly what I want,' she would say. Then she would spoon more paint into bowls slurping the powder all over the table and onto the floor. The entire unwanted colour would then be tipped down the sink, blocking up the drain as if it were a gallon of cholesterol. And no actual painting would get done, just more mixing and throwing away. Her moods moved up the scale and she would shout in shorter bursts making us all feel uneasy. Each week, assessments and reports from the medical department took her away from art and until they were complete, she would be remaining in Holloway. She was tall and strong with a booming voice; extravagant movements that would fill sinks as she cleaned a plate or threw dust up above your head as she swept a few bits of paper towards the dustbin. Her poor blunt pencil would be pushed senseless into the electric pencil sharpener and shredded to death, causing the blades to screech before it was released as half the pencil it was before being inserted. Conversations innocently started could often erupt into a maelstrom of misunderstandings. Compliments would have the reverse effect and make her angry; jovial banter would trigger a memory of some deeply held grudge and it would surface, silencing all other conversations.

Somebody pushed in front of her. She had been queuing up outside the Education Department and someone had hustled their way to the front. One continuous swearword constructed from the dictionary of oaths blasted the wall in front of her. Those Africans, those rude Africans, she turned towards me as if to include me in her criticism and flattened down her paper onto the table. Perpetually, I advised her that folding her paper or rolling it would cause damage to it, telling her that she should keep her work flat. I had offered to keep her paintings safe in a drawer but she refused that as well and carried the lot around with her, scrunched up under her arm. Already drawn upon, she unrolled her paper and held it down with a couple of books preventing it flicking back into the curls it had grown used to. Over her shoulder I tried to calm her down. 'Everyone scrabbled to get into education, nothing to do with race, everyone does it.' Words like that were spoken softly so she wouldn't feel criticised, or demeaned or put down. I asked her to get on with her work, forget about the incident, she was in the Art Room now, 'No harm done, forget about it, just forget about it.' But she didn't listen or didn't want to listen and rambled on cursing people from around the globe. 'I hope you're not being racist.' Tango leapt from her chair looked over her drawing board and screamed at Reeta's back, 'Where do you think you come from any way … you're from Africa you are … so cut the crap.'

Refusing to turn round at whoever it was, Reeta continued to recount the incident and tell of how she had been forced down the line of prisoners by an African inmate. Then rising up from her chair as the allegations intensified she turned round to identify the opposition. The three Chinese ladies all sitting in a row sat tighter together. They looked over towards me with alarm. They wanted to watch in case it started to involve them, though if they didn't watch it might all go away. That's as far as I noticed anyone else. This was the best thing in such situations unless others became embroiled in the scuffle or were affected by it. Only afterwards did I pay attention to the others. To me there seemed to be only two people in the class. The rest just floated away into invisibility.

'Listen, you, I'm born in this country so don't tell me where I come from.'

'Listen you I'm fucking half Turkish so don't get racist with me.'

Both women started to leave their spaces to join up with each other. They didn't walk around obstacles. They just pushed the chairs away with their arms and hips tipping them over as they advanced towards each other. These rough gestures gave each of them an inkling of their each other's strength and conviction as to the looming confrontation. Reeta's chin went up and Tango's head went back and there was more aggressive body language. Sensing the impending battle I went inside the store cupboard and rang for an officer. 'Just pop in. No it wasn't a panic button situation; but I think a uniformed presence would be advantageous.'

I very nearly decided to push the emergency bell, but resisted: the situation was still containable. Reeta was becoming more agitated and she continued ranting, and jerking her eyes and her head which rolled clumsily. She stared at Tango, then at me, then at nobody in particular, just at the wall or a table. Tango condemned Reeta's prejudice and screamed further invectives about how bad it was and what a hypocrite Reeta was. Why was she going on about one race? Her interrogation of Reeta's allegedly flawed judgement interrupted Reeta's insults, so it seemed as if there was just one enormous rage that would explode when the two women bumped into one another. Whereas there at least seemed to be some logic to Tango's arguments, Reeta's behaviour was getting more and more unpredictable. She was becoming less coherent and wilder. She didn't expect such opposition, never mind someone who made her doubt her own arguments. Her hatred spread to the whole world, against all men and all women. The two were nearly face-to-face, only my presence blocked the way like a sandwich filling waiting to be squashed flat. The worst thing you can do if a fight ensues, is to get in the middle of it. I'd read that somewhere in a self help pamphlet issued by the Home Office. I should have read it further, or had some expert on managing stressful situations given a talk? Then I should have listened, because there I was waiting to be squashed senseless. At last the uniform appeared. 'Come on ladies calm down, just calm down … what's happening here?!'

I could feel their anger on either side of me, but at least they'd stopped and were still. Reeta ignored the officer and didn't stop cursing everyone, especially Tango. Tango moved away towards the door all the time never letting go of Reeta's attention who watched her adversary with greater intensity. Past a couple of tables, onwards she advanced towards the exit. The officer diverted Reeta's intention with forceful arm movements as if channelling her down a side road whilst directing traffic. 'OK ladies calm down.'

Tango made one last accusation, one last criticism, one last remark, one last taunt over her shoulder. 'Reeta you're a racist and a fuckin' nutter … you need nutting-off you do … you need nutting-off … Miss let me out of here … I'm too big a woman now to get involved with all this shit.' To those unfortunate creatures shakily clinging on to sanity with their finger tips such prophetic advice held too much truth. That was the old Tango, her efforts to defeat Reeta's prejudice had failed so she'd regressed, found the dagger and twisted it. Reeta lunged past the traffic warden and pounced on Tango's hair before the rest of her escaped. Tango lurched sidewards, her head jerked down and around Reeta's clenched fist and she banged it on the door. The officer hauled herself across to separate them and tried to loosen the grasp on Tango's hair. I tried to pull Reeta away. Tango's head was being dragged towards the floor. We four continued in this rugby scrum outside the door and along the garden walkway. Reeta wouldn't loosen her grip and Tango's head was dangerously near to the concrete. The officer and myself were trying to free the two of them. I was being dragged backwards and the officer was sliding forwards. In the middle of us was Reeta, still pulling and hanging on to Tango's head.

'Press the panic button,' screeched the officer to whoever was around. 'Someone press the bell.' Teachers and students alike were all straining to witness the rumpus from their classrooms as we scrambled our way along the pathway in full view. We continued to slide across the concrete trying not to fall into the small Education Department garden. I sensed that we had passed the IT room because I could see pairs of shoes watching us slide slowly onwards from the open doorway. Then we drifted along further, past the cookery room until my back banged up against a metal recycling bin and plastic bags in the farthest corner away from my room and we all tumbled down amongst the debris. Our improvised theatricals took precedence over any classes in progress; stuck at each window our audience was thoroughly enjoying the show. Reeta wouldn't let go of the hair and started to beat Tango on the head with her other arm. Tango never once retaliated, just took the blows, took the hair pulling, and never landed one blow.

We were all trapped between two walls so I couldn't drag anyone away and the officer had no space left to pull the two bodies apart. There were repeated bangings of a swing door and an army of officers powered through. Within seconds the two women were split up. A vast clump of hair was left in Reeta's hand and she waved it triumphantly as she was forcibly escorted down to the Segregation Block between columns of officers. Tango requested to go back to the wing and left the department.

A committee of concerned students welcomed me back into the class; even Mary Ann in the craft shop right at the top of the building had left her post to make sure there were no casualties. Then when I asked if she'd left the door unlocked she raced back up the stairs ready to catch any intruder who she might find inside—although not before she had been given the low down about what had happened. Debriefing amongst the spectators brought such an incident to a satisfactory conclusion. They brought back all the excitement without any of the physical danger. My own reaction surprised me, since my thoughts about the incident moved me to worry about Tango and how she was. Without doubt it was a deeply disturbing event, mostly due to Reeta's violence and her expression as she fought and bashed and pulled. There was also the passivity as Tango's head twisted limply at the force of Reeta's anger. My sympathy surprised me.

'She's in the association room down there on your right.'

'What are you doing up here.' Tango looked up from the television in surprise.

'Just come to see how you are ... how's your head?'

'Fine, no problem.'

'Tango, I am so sorry that happened in my class, it was awful and I am so sorry you got hurt.'

'I'm fine Miss, really I am.'

I was getting quite upset and didn't realise just how badly the whole business had affected me. I kept apologising and telling Tango how rare that kind of incident was in my class, how maybe I could have handled it better, that I regretted that it had got out of hand and that I hope she wasn't too hurt. 'Listen Miss that's nothing to me, honest, nothing, piece of piss that for me … you know me Miss, you know what I'm like, trust me that was nothing, no big deal. I couldn't get stuck into her. I'm out of here tomorrow. I don't want extra days being added, I've got a nice pad, a family and all, what do I want this place for now? I'm too old for all that childish crap, but she was out of order Miss … right out of order … you can't say that kind of thing nowadays.' And that was that. Tango left the very next day and never returned. Reeta was transferred out to a special hospital and never came back to Holloway either.

Sometimes the Arts and Crafts Shop, which is still functioning and making annual contributions to Victim Support, provided the perfect restorative atmosphere. It was housed in a small room formerly used for toilets, but it had been redecorated and functioned well enough. It was close to the Art Room for ease of supervision. Mary Ann had increased the turnover and income. She'd learnt all about the wool business, could work out patterns, and had expanded the business. Meeting the needs of the institution, she'd decided to provide an outreach service for the women who couldn't collect their own purchases, in her own time without extra pay. She kept excellent records and the only ripple resulted from my wish that she would stay forever! I was lucky though because with only a couple of exceptions those chosen inmates taking on the job performed with dedication and loyalty. The other retail outlet in the Visits Centre also thrived. Both places stood out as positive achievements when everything else seemed to be going wrong.

It must have been wintertime because the days were short and workdays seemed to start and end in the middle of the night. It was so dark that I ignited the institutional strip lighting prematurely and all the students squinted and rubbed their eyes until they were used to the yellow glare. The prison gardens provided a wonderful view from the Art Room. Each year they looked more and more spectacular because they were cared for so well. That's why the seats nearer to the window were always the first to be occupied. It was restful to look out over the flower beds and the trees or just to stare outside. It gave a feeling of space and maybe it could even push the imagination over the walls and recall what was on the other side. As soon I put the lights on, that view disappeared to be replaced by a navy blue sky that closed in on all of us. We seemed isolated. Just a classroom, an island separated from the rest of the world. I could hardly see the dark stairwell outside my room because the bulb had broken and it hadn't been replaced, but I was aware of a presence standing there, looking in. That was another area of empty space that nobody owned so nobody tended it. Those forgotten nooks and crannies were usurped by inmates who left cigarette butts, old tissues and other debris, proof of temporary occupancy which indicated their otherwise covert meeting places.

Two quick getaway routes added to the attraction of that location. At the clink of keys from above or below trespassers could flit up the stairs and remain undiscovered, or they could flip through a door next to mine and escape directly into the garden. The ban on cigarettes in classrooms popularised the space leading to more and more flattened out cigarette ends which left a vile smell. Even at the end of classes when smoking was permitted, the stairwell space provided a suitable shelter in the cold or wet while numbers were counted in readiness for the return journey to the wings and home.

The prisoner stood just inches away from my door. Then a push and she slurred her heavy boots from the cold stone floor of the passageway onto the lino of the Art Room. She wanted to be in art that afternoon and she was determined to stay. Sandy always came closer to me than any other of the prisoners; too close. When we were in conversation there wasn't enough space left to feel comfortable. Some folk do that too, invade personal space, preventing gestures that decorate talk, leaving no scope to move naturally and in a relaxed way. I couldn't embellish the talk with head movements, illustrate my meanings with hand motions. I could only stand awkwardly with my hands at my sides and this made me feel exposed to whatever body language Sandy wanted to impose. It didn't seem natural and words came out like instructions, meanly and sparingly. The formality made me feel like I was in a courtroom or attending some court martial. On top of that Sandy expected superior treatment. She demanded preferential attention because she was 'better than anyone else' and most people caved in to her. Her arms hung straight down beside her and she reminded me of a puppet waiting to be animated, brought to life, seeming to hang on some invisible thread.

It could have been medication that affected her demeanour so strangely. Even when she walked, her arms remained in the same position as if they were magnetised by a metallic floor. Her head tipped down slightly like an inert marionette. Her boots seemed too heavy to lift off the ground so she dragged them along in slow strides. If any of those early deep sea divers had lost the leaded boots that secured them to the sea bed then they could have borrowed Sandy's. A lot of the time she spent down in the block because her anger was easily provoked. She couldn't tolerate anything that didn't match her immediate needs. She had no patience, couldn't negotiate. Sometimes she seemed to be like one raw nerve ending, frayed and at the end of her tether. The story went that she had applied to attend anger management classes but had been deemed too angry for admission. Low self-esteem, characteristic of so many students in Holloway, inverted itself with Sandy. She had the opposite: an unrealistic sense of her own capabilities and worth that surpassed us all.

'You're not on my register so you must be down for another class.' I apologised and asked her to leave. I talked to her somewhere between her chin and her bottom lip. Looking directly into her eyes could be perceived as confrontational because we were that close. I looked away hopefully terminating that conversation and started to check the other students. She came in closer and reinforced her demands, so I repeated myself with the same politeness. She moved in so close I could smell her leather jacket. A gold nose ring had been replaced by a dangling ring of cotton which blew the air to one side in its angry descent down one nostril. Either it had been lost or handed in for safety at Reception. Some inmates did that, they didn't like to keep their valuables with them so they put them in store until they were released. To prevent holes healing up they would thread pieces of cotton through them. There was more heavy breathing, too close to my face. I couldn't complete the work I was doing. Sandy stood in the way so I twisted around and tried to do something else. Collecting paints for one student I sensed the presence of Sandy close behind as a reminder that I wasn't going to get away with ignoring her demands so easily. The same shadow followed me to other students, her leather jacket creaking and her boots scuffing across the lino, always just a few inches behind me. My filling up a couple of water pots at the sink annoyed Sandy. It seemed to her that I had forgotten about what she was saying.

'I want my picture then and I'm off.' I felt her leather jacket slide over my shoulder as she skimmed past me and I swayed a bit from the draught. She was a ship forcing her way through the ice, breaking up everything as she advanced towards the store cupboard. Chairs got flung aside; wooden drawing boards were thrown out of the way, if she couldn't find the picture then she was going to mess things up. 'Where is it? I want it now, it better not be lost.' Other picture boards were smashed to the floor in the search.

The class filled to capacity. Three mothers with their babies took over the last free table. Lily walked in oblivious to anything but the seat in the corner. She had been around seven stone when she was convicted and now, just a few months into her prison sentence, she seemed to have put on nearly twice that amount. Yet she looked pale and pinched underneath, like the fat wasn't doing anything—as if it didn't belong to her because it had developed on weak foundations and just stuck to her for the sake of the weight scales. She looked frail and sick, her bloatedness delaying the inevitability of her terminal illness for a few months.

'Could you please sit somewhere else today Lily someone has already taken that place.'

'No I want to sit here.'

'Here's your picture, Sandy', I produced it from behind my desk. Inspired by Salvador Dali she'd painted dripping clocks and a crucifix.

'I want to take it off the board ... now, where's the Stanley knife?'

'Lily please don't sit there, that seat over near the window is free.'

'I'm not bloody moving.'

'Where's the Stanley knife ... give it to me.'

Sandy's boots banged into the store cupboard as she searched for the dangerous tool. All the old bits of furniture trembled as she stormed through my dilapidated domain. She could so easily have pulled the shelves over; they'd never been fixed to the wall properly. The classroom was already showing signs of disrepair. The lino on the floor was splitting and pocked with holes, and the domestic sink was forever getting blocked with powder paint and glue. None of the radiators worked because we were at the end of the line so far as the heating system was concerned. so that there was no heat left for us by then. Secondary electric heaters didn't work either, the only evidence that they were switched on was their thunderous sounds. No heat, just a loud rattling noise. Chests were insecure and their drawers needed a well-practised jiggling to open or close them. The shadow board, always kept locked, had thwarted Sandy's intention to claim her painting. I had the Stanley knife in my pocket and pushed it down deeper for safety with no intention of relinquishing it. 'I'll take it off the board ... Lily please don't sit there, go and sit by the window.'

'Why don't you give me the knife, I'll take it off the board.'

'I'm not fucking moving off this chair.'

'I'll take the painting off the board.'

'You just don't want me to have the knife do you? What's your problem? What do you think I'm going to do with it … Why don't you want me to have the knife? What do you think I'm going to do with it?' Then there was the abuse, as if I had done something bad and everything was my fault. Someone was calling me a thief because I wouldn't let her have the knife. I was accusing her of being untrustworthy because I wouldn't give her the knife. Lily was looking at the chair that couldn't be hers. The legitimate occupant was standing near the sink too terrified to move. It seemed that her decision about how to cope with this refusal and her response was formulating inside her head. There was indecision and a look of puzzlement as her backside was tempted to settle down in it. 'And you're a fucking Muppet,' Sandy yelled to Lily for trying to steal her thunder and compete in the attention stakes. That was the decider. Lily had made up her mind.

'You can have the bleedin' chair then;' Lily flung it across the room to Sandy, just missing a pram. Everything started to move and the room with its black blue windows seemed even more isolated. The lights were on, illuminating us against the darkness of the outside world, so that passers-by could have easily seen the situation and intervened—garden workers, officers, anyone outside could have looked in and come to my aid had they been around. Further away, if that high wall hadn't been ten yards away, any pedestrians on Parkhurst Road could have helped. But if no one was around, being illuminated was of no real benefit. We could have been a stadium waiting for an evening kick-off. We had two sides, a referee, an audience and floodlights. Only the spectators were missing.

'Push the bell.' I reinforced my words with a practical demonstration using my thumb. The bell seemed miles away in the far corner of the room. I had my back to the store cupboard so Sandy couldn't try to get another tool from the shadowboard. Over in the far corner a non-English speaking student tried to respond. 'Push!' I kept saying, pushing my thumb in the air to demonstrate the action that was required. With tentative, neat little arms the Chinese student walked besides the wall like a blind man feeling for a switch, searching for something to push. She pushed at everything that protruded, starting with a drawing pin. Right in front of me Sandy and Lily were taking their frustrations out on each other with wild threats and insults galore. I encouraged Miss Ho with another mime and pointed to the bell. She flicked something and a strip light was extinguished followed by pan-icky flashing as it reignited when she discovered her error. She tried to push a redundant phone connection, then the switch of a fan heater.

I got all the mothers to take their babies to the opposite side of the room and began to navigate the assault course of tables separating me from the panic button—just as Miss Ho found it and pushed and pressed and pushed again. At the sound of the resulting din she ran over to the mothers and babies and huddled up with them, covering her ears like all the rest of the class. Lily, with one hand on a chair and the other on a palette flung the lot high in the air. A sandstorm of multi-coloured powder fell on top of us. Sandy retaliated with another palette. It rained another mass of powder as the res-cue brigade burst, falling, into the room amidst the tickertape of swirling paper. The first officer screamed an order which was echoed by his disci-ple. No one wanted to hear it except me. He screamed again and advanced towards Lily who was high above us on a table, holding another chair ready to be crashed to the floored at any second and onto any poor soul blocking its fall. A gigantic male officer strode onto the table and grabbed both Lily and the chair in one swift action. Profiting by this impressive diversion, I quickly undid Sandy's painting using the Stanley knife and replaced the lat-ter in my pocket. I put the picture in a drawer.

Lily, squeezed between her captors, peered backwards through a muscular armpit and threatened to finish Sandy off down the gym. The taunt was cordially accepted by Sandy who couldn't wait for their next rendezvous. But she too was grabbed from behind and marched away in a different direc-tion before the exact date of the fight could be arranged. We were all now a muddied powder colour. The same mixture of colours marked the floor. There were handprints on the walls in a form of graffiti. We looked like paint wrestlers. Holloway Prison's version of a Jackson Pollock. I tried to summon up the will to restore the room as a viable work space.

A hand went up, 'You haven't given me any attention this lesson Miss, and now it's too late, the lesson's nearly over, and I've done it all myself, I've worked so hard and you never came over to see my work once ... Look Miss, I finished my woman, I did it all by myself, I did that woman like you asked.' She showed me a liquorice allsorts lady with a bunch of flowers and a hand-bag, all co-ordinated in the same sweet shop colours. The abstract shapes ran all over her long frilly dress and right across undersized, pointed slippers that popped out from under a ballgown. The same bubblegum effect, painted so precisely, extended to weenie lace gloves that covered undersized hands. She'd not forgotten a beauty spot of bright red high on the lady's cheek and her hair had been sprinkled with fancy fastenings all in the same delicious colours. You could have eaten her right off the page. But that neglected student left the class disappointed. Whether she had been aware of what had just happened and that it had forced me to abandon her I don't know. Perhaps she had and didn't care.

The rest of the class vacated the room, session over, everyone back to the wing. In front of me in the deserted classroom was the register that needed to be completed. I scribbled in what I thought I should say, what suited the education providers and those who paid our salaries. The chasm between our two bosses, the college and the prison, gaped wider. What should I really have written about Sandy? What were her plans? Another fight down the gym. When she had confronted Lily, should I have written that she had achieved her targets?! Both women were banned from the class indefinitely. Lily returned sooner than Sandy. She apologised with regret—she just seemed to get into those moods lately, she didn't seem to be able to stop herself— the anger just came out. But please, she didn't want to stay on the wing all day, she needed to get off it; she needed to take her mind off things that depressed her. So of course, yes she could come back.

Sandy was allowed back into the Education Department and into the cook-ery class after what was considered to be an appropriate length of time. She tried to keep away from my class, but liked art. After a few days she started to hover outside the door and peep in, or watch from under the stairwell, a reminder that she was still around and getting respectable enough to be allowed near the door. Then she came and stood outside my door after each class; just stood there and looked in as I cleared up or did some paper work. At the end of one of her cookery classes she was there again peering out of the darkness; a solemn gatekeeper biding her time and a bit spooky. Was she trying to scare me? Why was she there? Was she lying in wait? I thought over these possibilities in my refuge behind a wall. Straight ahead of me were the gardens and the fresh air and the path out. Just behind me on the other side of the door was Sandy, my road block. I could have patiently waited until she was automatically returned to the wing with all the rest of the prisoners. For what it was worth, the Art Room still represented some kind of sanctuary even if Sandy was just paying lip service to it. The stairwell just outside my room where she stood represented No Man's Land and she dominated that space. Enough procrastinating—I was beginning to feel stupid just standing against the wall knowing that Sandy was on the other side of it. It was too much like a comedy scene and besides the waiting weakened my resolve and my initiative. I was the one who was supposed to be in charge, not cowering in some corner. I stayed within my territory and pulled the door inwards towards me.

'Sandy … Can I help you?' Still inside my room I pulled the door closer towards me. 'I've been in cookery.' She didn't say any more for a while and neither did I. Her arm gradually raised itself from the straight position creaking the thick black leather of her jacket. That was it then, she was going to have a go now that we were on our own. I prepared to shut the door quickly before her punch landed. But in opening her hand she communicated a gesture of friendliness instead, in the same way a wave communicates a greeting. A packet of crisp greaseproof paper emerged from under her fingers and she shoved it over to me still adhering to her side of an invisible boundary line and me to mine. So we stretched out our arms and the exchange took place. 'You can have this Miss'

'Thanks.' I was going to say more, ask her about cookery now that her intentions were clearer, although I wasn't yet sure what I was thanking her for. I was so relieved that I hadn't suffered anything physical and was too enthusiastic to perpetuate our new agreeable form of contact. The greaseproof paper was warm in my hand. It was protecting something, keeping it hot. I unwrapped what looked like a dappled bun, soft and squidgy that let off a wisp of heat. 'Thanks Sandy, that's really kind of you.'

'It's a dumpling, Miss, I made it just now.'

'Thanks again Sandy, that's really kind of you … I'll have it for lunch.'

'When can I come back into art?'

Where else could she go? It was the end of the line this Holloway business, nowhere left to travel. Besides, giving up on someone always seemed to involve such a huge and negative statement about human nature. There was something inside me which I couldn't quite unravel and it symbolised competition or a pair of scales, something like that. I had to make art win. Art had to weigh more in the balance so that for me there could be no absolute bans. Besides that, Sandy had served her time and her ban was up. I had no alternative. On Monday she was on the doorstep again asking if she could she come in. 'Yes,' her name was on the register.

Everyone was working and it seemed to be going well. Not too many in that day, so the kitchen mural could be worked on. Always an influx of novices, that particular day they were enthusiastic, lively, cooperative and energetic. They'd been on the waiting list and were so pleased now that there was space for them. Arranging a workplace for one of these new students, I was in a good mood with high expectations. My eye caught Sandy's uncomfortable work area. She had her reference books piled high; her paints balancing on radiators and there was not much room left for the paper. So I called over to her that it would be easier if she sorted her work out so that she would be able to work more efficiently as one of the other students had done. It was an off the cuff remark uttered thoughtlessly, forgetful of Sandy's intense sensitivities. I had failed to make allowances. Instinctively she saw it as criticism. In comparing her with another student she had come off worst and she took this badly. Standing up to all of her six foot height she screamed, 'Don't shout at me like that!'

She turned around, fixed her eyes on the student, zoomed across the room and bopped her on the head. The student's crime, so Sandy said, was that she had smirked. She had smirked at Sandy—an 'I do it better see, thank you' kind of smirk. Fighting against that humiliation, that put down, that sneer, she had lost control. I rang for an officer who led the injured student along to the surgery whilst another officer escorted Sandy down to the block. Was this to be the final chapter in the odyssey of Sandy?

Raised gardens with lawns and flowers rose upwards into a gentle hillock from the main gate of Holloway. It served as the scenic route to the education block. Bordered with hedges the path rose upwards, passed flowers, benches and trees to where at the crest of the hill, wire netting encased the exercise yard for residents of the Segregation Block. In every sense it looked like a cage, with a small door at one end leading inside. This arrangement wasn't in place for long. It was too public and looked hideous, so that it was soon dismantled. Upwards rose four levels of residential dwellings which were attached to the rest of the prison and spread right around the grounds and joined up at both sides of the gate, as if they were protecting that beautiful landscaped garden. All the debris had gone. The food customarily ejected from the windows over many years had disappeared. Air conditioning had been installed and the windows wouldn't open now.

The small door opened. Out of the blackness, moon-walking and sliding backwards came a performer onto the stage of the exercise yard. Nothing was visibly recognisable as having human characteristics. The sleeves of the grey tracksuit were too long and hung over a pair of hands. A grey hood covered what was probably a head, though there was no sign of it, just a grey overhang that made a black shadow underneath. Tracksuit bottoms were tucked well around ankles. But I recognised the moon-walker sliding along the concrete right into the middle of the yard, into the fresh air. It was Sandy. Her boots, deprived of laces, seemed to have expanded and their tongues flopped out and nearly licked the floor. More like buckets they were, with no fastenings and holding a couple of ill-fitting feet. Like a wind turbine on a millpond everything hung downwards, until some wayward gust stirred up the blades and the arms of the figure slowly began to rotate. The hood lifted upwards and out popped a face celebrating the space and the woman's antics. The pace of motion intensified, her arms twisted and twirled and her legs hopped up and down, everything synchronised until she reached the wire and couldn't helicopter up and away into the sky. Several similar attempts jumping up and down and rotating her arms ended with Sandy in hysterics and exhausted in a heap on the floor. The helicopter had crashed. It was faulty. Some fundamental flaw now kept it grounded. A half-hearted push at the cage with folded arms demonstrated her frustration. With greater ambition she fixed her arms straight outwards and ran aimlessly around like a small child, upgrading her flying machine to a plane and careering around in circuits, but still she couldn't get airborne and instead she fell out of her leaden boots. Then the adult performance began. With straight arms she backed herself against one side of the yard and revved up like a Boeing 707, loudly, with a huge screech and she taxied down the runway to the opposite wire and crashed, aborting yet another take off. She fell backwards onto the concrete with her arms and legs in the points of a star, a big smile on her face. She looked up to the sky and the clouds for a temporary peace and caught sight of her audience of one. Well perhaps others had watched this tomfoolery, but I couldn't see anyone else. As far as I was concerned I was her only observer. Crunched up with one boot on and the other a couple of yards away she straightened herself, took off her hood, looked over and waved a big open-handed wave. I nodded a smile back.

She pointed to her forehead, then twisted her finger round and round and went cross-eyed. In an invisible drawing book she pretended to draw and then rub out her non-drawing with a imaginary eraser. On her knees she begged with her hands and repeated the mime. What she was saying is that she would go mad without drawing materials. 'Lunchtime. OK?', I mouthed. There were more pantomime capers to make sure I kept my promise and I nodded in reassurance. A door opened and an officer tapped her watch towards Sandy. Grinning and moon-walking backwards inside the block the performer waved goodbye to me with thumbs up and disappeared inside. Her short exercise period was over for the day.

Most of the times when I'd seen a lone occupant of that yard they'd just slithered outside along the wall a pace or two away from the door, wrapped around tightly with their coat and puffing on a roll up, and then they'd slipped back inside at the first opportunity. I'd never before seen someone enjoying the fresh air with Sandy's self-mocking spirit and 'Ode to Joy'.

'What was that all about then Sandy?' Eye-to-eye—and still too close up for comfort we talked through the hatch to her new digs down the block. 'Oh that … I was trying to fly over the wall.' 'No, before that in the art room, when you hit that student … why, what was it about?' 'Oh her, oh I don't know, I got a bit paranoid, I get like that a bit paran … must be the drugs. Have you got something to draw with?' I pushed the book and pencils through the hatch and, using the space at the bottom of the door, I slid Sandy's coveted painting to her, protected by a sheet of paper.

'What's that?'

'That painting you wanted.'

'Which … which painting is that?'

'Sandy, that painting you wanted so badly, don't you remember?'

'Oh that painting, I'd almost forgotten it. Let's have a look … Ah, now I remember. Not bad. Not bad at all, even if I say so myself … Thanks.'

Epilogue

What else should I have done to try and better the lot of the women in this book, or others from such backgrounds with similar problems. What else might I have wanted to do during my time at Holloway Prison?

Encouraging their creative side seemed to be far more understandable than many of the requirements and restrictions placed on us by the acronym that paid our wages. Ever since the Education Department was privatised it became 'a business' preoccupied with profit and loss. We became some kind of quick-fix, responding to each new buzz word. Every four years or so we worked for different providers. There were new terms and conditions, new job descriptions and new contracts. Before that people would be bussed into Holloway and shown around our department: the untouchables, looking up and down and deciding whether we were a sound financial investment. 'Untouchables' because we were forbidden to speak to them, couldn't know who they were and were never told when they would be visiting.

Sometimes terms that had been agreed previously were honoured, sometimes they lapsed, were forgotten or were simply ignored. Little research seemed to have validated what was being demanded of us and conditions seemed always to change for the worse. With little real support for us *as teachers*, morale tended to fall with each new contract.

Profits were the key and of paramount importance, so they said. How this can be reconciled with teaching as a profession, the special needs of prisoners and helping them to move on from criminality I never did quite understand. Constant changes meant that sensible, long-term planning became impossible. The providers would be satisfied if the women learnt how to fill in a curriculum vitae and a work-related application form. That would tick the right boxes, satisfy our paymasters.

We were told to make the women 'employable'—which we did on paper at least. For the arts to continue to exist at all in prisons, it meant fitting in with this kind of thinking. Along the way, the chasm between what we actually

273

did each day and what we were required to write down grew ever wider. We learned to tick the boxes, whilst the more worthwhile things we tried to do but which 'didn't count' went unrecognised, making a nonsense of our professional lives. We responded to new and trendy initiatives that often made us feel duplicitous (until bought, yet again, by the next entrepreneurs with yet further ideas about what to do and how and what to count). So the job became somehow fraudulent, a 'con', sterile and soulless.

Unlike staff in educational establishments on the outside, the prison teacher practises within an institution whose primary function is not educative. The students in Holloway Prison have to answer to a whole heap of obligations which necessitate their absence from the classroom and which take priority, such as legal and other professional visits, court appearances and medical appointments. Teachers are therefore limited in a way that is incomprehensible to practitioners working in mainstream education. Furthermore, Holloway has a rapid and varied turnover of population, over which the prison itself has no control.

Holloway's education staff must meet the needs of this unpredictable situation by providing a flexible and balanced timetable which attracts the greatest numbers of students. Education has been proved to be one of the main pathways to addressing offending behaviour. With the pressures dictated by the nature of the environment, it would be doubly 'criminal' if educators in prisons limited their teaching due to further artificial barriers or constraints thereby deterring students rather than encouraging them.

Index